D0268216

Howard Brenton

Plays: 1

Christie in Love, Magnificence, The Churchill Play, Weapons of Happiness, Epsom Downs, Sore Throats

Howard Brenton is one of Britain's best-known and most controversial dramatists. Selected from his work up to the end of the seventies, the plays in this volume all stem from the most innovative theatre companies of that decade. In them, Brenton wrestles with such issues as political imprisonment, practical communism, and private and public acts of terror.

Christie in Love: 'Like Genet, he feels for the outcast . . . But he's less sentimentally involved with his criminals, clearer about his ultimate strategy to show the unreality of straight lines in a curved universe, of the roles society forces on us.'   *Observer*

Magnificence: 'A wonderful piece of theatre; annexing whole new chunks of modern life and presenting them in a style at once fruitful and magnified.'
                                                                                              The Times

The Churchill Play: '[Brenton] finds a way of making us look again at the past which has shaped the future into which he sees us drifting . . . What is heartening is the way he uses the rich, theatrical language he and his colleagues have created to confront that bleak situation with intelligence and wit.'   *New Society*

Weapons of Happiness: 'He has a vision of revolution which is quite extraordinary in its creative ambiguity, its richness, its power to stimulate, to threaten, and to inspire . . . This is indeed a relevant play.'   *Sunday Times*

Epsom Downs: 'Echoes *Bartholomew Fair*: a great public festival, held on common land and pulling in punters of every degree . . . Half a dozen threads of plot are woven in and out of a teaming Brueghel-like composition . . . Altogether, a marvel of expressive economy.'   *The Times*

Sore Throats: 'Brenton, the man of political conviction, is examining issues of far greater scope and uses violence only in the service of larger social themes. At times the play almost becomes a stark, subtle poem, infused with concentric images, yet the sheer theatricality of the story alone keeps the play continually dramatic.'   *Theater*

Howard Brenton was born in Portsmouth in 1942 and educated in Chichester and at St Catherine's College, Cambridge. In 1968 he joined the Brighton Combination as an actor and writer, and in 1969 he joined David Hare and Tony Bicât in Portable Theatre. His first full-length play was *Revenge* (1969) which was performed at the Royal Court Upstairs; this was followed by *Hitler Dances* (1972); *Magnificence* (1973); *Brassneck* (with David Hare, 1973); *The Churchill Play* (1974); *Weapons of Happiness* (winner of the Evening Standard Award, 1976); *Epsom Downs* (1977); *Sore Throats* (1979); *The Life of Galileo* (from Bertolt Brecht, 1980); *The Romans in Britain* (1980); *Thirteenth Night* (1981); *Danton's Death* (from Büchner, 1982); *The Genius* (1983); *Bloody Poetry* (1984); *Desert of Lies* (1984); *Pravda* (with David Hare, 1985); *Greenland* (1988); *Iranian Nights* (with Tariq Ali, 1989); *H.I.D. (Hess is Dead)* (1989); *Moscow Gold* (with Tariq Ali, 1990); *Berlin Bertie* (1992); *Playing Away* (opera libretto, 1994), and *Faust* (from Goethe, 1995). His four-part thriller *Dead Head* was broadcast by BBC 2 in 1986. A novel, *Diving for Pearls*, was published in 1989 and *Hot Irons: Diaries, Essays, Journalism* in 1995.

HOWARD BRENTON

Plays: 1

Christie in Love
Magnificence
The Churchill Play
Weapons of Happiness
Epsom Downs
Sore Throats

Methuen Drama

METHUEN CONTEMPORARY DRAMATISTS

This collection first published in Great Britain in 1986
by Methuen London Ltd
This edition published in the United Kingdom in 1998 by
Metheun Publishing Limited, 215 Vauxhall Bridge Road, London SW1V 1EJ

8 10 9 7

Christie in Love first published in 1970 by Methuen & Co Ltd
Copyright © 1970 by Howard Brenton
Magnificence first published in 1973 by Eyre Methuen Ltd
Copyright © 1973, 1980, 1986 by Howard Brenton
The Churchill Play first published in 1974 by Eyre Methuen Ltd
Copyright © 1974, 1986 by Howard Brenton
Weapons of Happiness first published in 1976 by Eyre Methuen Ltd
Copyright © 1976, 1977, 1986 by Howard Brenton
Epsom Downs first published in 1977 by Eyre Methuen Ltd
Copyright © 1977, 1986 by Howard Brenton
Sore Throats first published in 1979 by Eyre Methuen Ltd
Copyright © 1979, 1986 by Howard Brenton
Introduction copyright © 1986 by Howard Brenton
This collection copyright © 1986 by Howard Brenton

The author has asserted his moral rights

Metheun Publishing Limited Reg. No. 3543167

A CIP catalogue record for this volume is available at the British Library.

ISBN 0-413-40430-7

Printed and bound in Great Britain by
Cox & Wyman Ltd, Reading, Berkshire

Contents

Howard Brenton
A chronology of first performances

PREFACE

Dear Reader . . .
Even theatre pros have difficulty reading plays. An excellent
American actress read my play *Bloody Poetry*, which is about
Byron and Shelley and set, therefore, in the nineteenth century,
assuming the whole thing was set in 1986 with the famous poets
lifting telephones, getting in and out of cars etc . . . This isn't
surprising. After all the text of a play has a similar relationship to
the real thing — a performance — as a musical score has to the
actual music and who in their right mind, but for a gifted musican,
will try to read a Beethoven symphony when they can play a
record or a tape?

It's All For Real
But, dear reader, I have to eat so I don't want to stop you buying
this book. Instead I offer these tips.

When you read a play, try not to see it performed in a theatre,
but imagine it really happening: the men sitting on oil drums in
strangely-coloured, worn uniforms in a delapidated aircraft
hangar that's part of the prison camp in *The Churchill Play*, in the
flat Lincolnshire landscape of endless cabbage fields; the
beauty of Moscow at night in the snow and the intense cold, the
two conspiratorial figures of Josef Frank and Clementis in
Weapons of Happiness huddled in black coats, their breath
plumes of condensation in the freezing air; the brilliant sunny
morning high on Epsom Downs, the grass fresh and not yet
trampled by a quarter of a million punters, and two horsemen out
for a ride, with a child's kite flying overhead.

Set Up Your Own Theatre
This way of reading, setting up a theatre in your head, in your
imagination straight out of the real world, may — I admit — come
unstuck in some of these scenes. I don't want to give you brain
damage, but the plays have some bizarre inventions. Winston
Churchill rises from the dead, sitting up in his coffin while lying
in state. Naked actors try to pretend to be horses running in the
Derby, talking in asides to the audience. The hallucinations of
Josef Frank, a man condemned to live simultaneously in the

present and in the past, call for some flashy staging and lighting. The 'streams of consciousness' of the characters in *Sore Throats* distort real time and action, their secret thoughts sticking out of the 'naturalistic' dialogue.

Nevertheless . . . imagine being in the parade ring at Epsom and a horse making a remark to you as he passes about the terrible day he is having, and you'll get the joke. Imagine being in the Great Hall at Westminster and seeing the great man coming out of his catafalque to the terror of the four servicemen on guard, and you'll get the force of the insult. Imagine Jack and Judy in *Sore Throats* with their minds splitting open, their innermost half-thoughts and feelings pulled out like ticker-tape, or ragged banners, from their heads, and you'll see what the author was seeing as he wrote.

Beautiful Words

The other tip to the reader is to bear in mind that the lines and speeches in a play are not written to be 'beautiful literature'. Any gracefulness they may have comes from the expression of a character, his or her language celebrated, and from speech pulled and pressed in the stress, or the joy, of a predicament. 'Set pieces' make for bad theatre. Drama is about men and women in action. Josef Frank's soliloquy in *Weapons of Happiness* — 'What do you expect me to see when I look in that mirror? . . .' — is triggered by the scene before, a meeting with Stalin, and is part of it. It is not a paragraph of 'fine writing' on its own. In human terms, there is nothing fine or beautiful about it. Another example: to get the meaning of Peter Reese's long account in *The Churchill Play* of his arrest, he should be seen speaking it to Captain Thompson, a man who does not want to hear the story and who is tormented by it, the more so because Peter is asking simply and innocently for help. The scene is as much about Thompson, who says nothing, as it is about the speaker.

An Argument

I had a strange conversation recently about words in a play with a well-known film actress. She loathed the comedy David Hare and I wrote together, *Pravda*. She fastened on a line spoken by Lambert Le Roux, our monstrous, tyrannical newspaper proprietor:-

'In my house in Weybridge I have a thousand books, but I don't need to read them, because my mind is made up.'

'What a terrible thing to say,' she said, angrily. 'How can a socialist say such a thing, that his mind is made up?' I protested that it was Le Roux speaking, not me and David, and that the line was actually a quotation from Adolf Hitler that fits Le Roux like a glove (slightly reworked, though the Führer may live on in Weybridge . . .). My protests were in vain. 'How can a socialist allow such things to said in a play?' she said. 'If you're going to dramatise evil, evil will be spoken on the stage . . .', I said. But it was no good. Even in 'show business' the — for a playwright — infuriating and fundamental misunderstanding that characters speak for the author is to be found.

Arrogant Artistes

It is true that some playwrights, in some plays that are great, parade themselves shamelessly across the stage, thinly disguised and lovingly written. I've not tried to do so (not yet, anyway). Not out of modesty. I am as arrogant as the next playwright — arrogance among playwrights is as common as obesity amongst barmen. Inevitably plays are riven with autobiographical bits and pieces, experiences of the writer disguised and chopped up. They may have a hidden and private subtext that is of no importance to the audience or even to the actors (*The Churchill Play* has one); you also write sometimes to resolve something at war within yourself, as *Magnificence* was written to try to resolve the author's confusions about the nature of revolutionary action. But I write about people who are strangers to me, not about myself, though more out of temperament than any theatrical theory. It's a challenge to try to reach and get inside, then dramatise an experience that is different from your own. It is possible. There is a common faculty, much misused and derided in these Gradgrindish, utilitarian times, called 'the Imagination'. To those who say good plays are only written directly out of a writer's life — I mean the purist supporters of naturalistic drama — the obvious question is 'Did Shakespeare have to be a mass murderer to write *Macbeth*?'

Love the Theatre?

Innovations in these plays are not done out of a 'love of theatre', they come out of a struggle to get the plays more real. To 'love the theatre' seems a most ill-directed passion. The theatre is basically an intractable load of old tat, cardboard, canvas, splintery wood, crude lighting and figures in garish colours in the middle distance gesticulating and hard to hear. It can be a load of tat behind the scenes too; managements easily become ghettoised, authoritarian, deluded that their 'product' is the cat's whiskers, content to stay behind the locked pass door to the front of house, discussing financial problems and not wanting to think of who the audience is out there, or even if it is having a good time. To get any fun and any sense of real life out of all that and to put it over to your audience is an uphill task. How to do so is, of course, a lifetime's preoccupation for theatre workers . . . but love the theatre? The point is to love life, lying on the grass in the park, children, jokes . . .

That Pudding Again

As in any art, 'innovations' in the theatre may at first seem bizarre, like the clashes of styles in these plays, with comedy and knock-about humour rammed into scenes that are serious and tragic. (I suppose they fit into Polonius's famous list in *Hamlet* as 'tragical-comical.') But these 'clashes' are merely attempts to get the theatre to be more real. The first scene of *Magnificence* is just about the closest I come to 'naturalism': that seemed the best and clearest way of dramatising the squatters moving into the derelict house. The setting is what used to be called 'kitchen sink'; it shows just how difficult and grotty a squat can be. This is followed by a scene that is almost a cartoon, between a bailiff and a young police constable, in front of a cloth flown in with a crude representation of the outside of the house painted on it, like a pantomime. The scene has to be like that because it is about the garish, frighteningly overheated mind of the bailiff, and the constable's home-spun ignorance. The two scenes display very different things. Writing them I just let them have their head and put them one against the other, ignoring the 'good playwrighting' maxims about 'unity of style'. At the time of its first production, I had to fight a bit of an artistic battle, but the audience won it for me — because the scenes clearly expressed something from 'out there' no one bothered or even seemed to notice. A good case of 'the proof of the pudding is in the eating'.

History and a Bar of Soap

I am much taken in these plays with this 'tragical-comical', or 'comical-tragical' clashing. Michael Bogdanov, who directed my later play, *The Romans in Britain*, once said, 'When you find yourself laughing away in front of one of Howard's plays, watch out — something horrible is going to happen. Someone will bring on a dead dog — or worse.'

My only defence is — dead dogs turn up in life all the time! The arbitrarily trivial and the comic go hand-in-hand with the profound. Hayden Griffin, the theatre designer, tells me that the actors' superstition never to wear green comes from the convention in the Jacobean theatre of unrolling a green carpet across the stage when a tragedy was to be performed. I called *Magnificence* a tragedy, because to me Jed's waste of his energy and his life is tragic. But the green carpet rolled out for that play would be covered with graffiti and with deliberately torn holes in it. The death scene, with the bomb going off by accident, is bitter high comedy. In *The Churchill Play* a scene about the Yalta conference is ridiculously also a scene about a bar of soap; and Judy in *Sore Throats* suffering a terrible beating and trying to confront the full force of sexual brutality, becomes fixated on the memory of an odd little bit of skin on her ex-husband's behind . . .

Anti-Theory Theories . . .
With *Magnificence*, and more fully with *Weapons of Happiness*, I was aware that I was trying to write a kind of Jacobean play for our time, a 'British epic theatre'.

In retrospect, these are the principles. The characters, like William Blake's poems, go from innocence to experience. The stories are journeys of discovery. The characters change radically. Their past is rarely referred to, what is of importance is their present. The writing has few 'secondary lines'. Julie Covington, who played Janice in *Weapons of Happiness*, said playing it was like opening a furnace door — your time comes, you open the door and blaze, then shut it. There is no 'edging up' to a relevation of a character as there is in, say, Ibsen. The scenes of the play are windows, opened at crucial points along the journeys of the characters, which show turning-points in their lives and struggles. Each scene is written and should be played as a little play, in its own right, with its own style — some have asides, some do not, some are internal and psychological, others are group scenes with naturalist settings. These differences should be emphasised, not smoothed over, therefore the stage should be wiped clear before each scene, a scheme of design that Hayden Griffin calls 'the magic box'. Disunity between the scenes will only help, not hinder. The end of the play is to be 'open', a gift for the audience — something for them to fall out over and keep warm with, while they're waiting for the bus home.

But, but . . . that is in retrospect. And, therefore, bullshit. I had no programme, only a drive to 'get more onto a stage' and to do it by ripping off the Jacobeans in some way. It was an instinctive approach that seemed to be right — it fitted the stories I wanted to tell. I have never come across any general theory that is of any practical use to those of us who actually make plays and shows. Of course, after you've made them you can invent theories two-a-penny.

Even Brecht's theories are really a series of running-battles he fought with casts or with the theatrical 'norms' of this day — or they are blatant puffs for the show he had on hand! — and can only be understood in the context of what he was actually doing in the theatre at the particular time he wrote. They were useful to him, but are useless to us — just as this essay is useful to me, thinking about what I'm trying to do in the theatre, and hopefully a help to the reader — but it will be meaningless to my contemporaries, David Hare, Caryl Churchill *et al.*, who will dismiss it as a shameless puff for the plays printed here (which, of course, it is).

The Rules of Aesthetics Set Down

There are two rules of aesthetics in the theatre. First rule: there are no rules. Second rule: because of the first rule, there cannot be a second.

You set the scaffolding up for the job under construction. Each time you have to reinvent the scaffolding. Again and again in a rehearsal-room, whether the play be by Brecht and the company left-wing, or the play be by Ayckbourn and the company Shaftesbury Avenue show-biz, you hear the question 'Does it work?', asked hundreds of times. The reply is always an instinctively agreed 'yes' or 'no', because to the performers it is obvious that a moment, a line, a move 'works' or not. Acting is a kind of singing. How can you theoretically describe a good tune?

A Swipe at Parasites . . .

Maybe I am over-reacting to the worst of academic criticism. There is a flourishing industry of well-heeled, humourless University people, on salaries and pension schemes most actors can only dream of, jetting around on freebies to conferences in Vienna, Paris, San Francisco, Prague etc. where they 'give papers' pulling our plays apart with nasty little surgical instruments called 'structuralism' or 'cultural materialism'. They write me letters and are a pain in the neck. Theatre workers are gypsies and vagabonds, anarchic in spirit — these people are like the DHSS coming down to the camp-site with meaningless questionnaires and plans to resettle you in their scheme of things . . . They are nearly all ignorant of what it is to stand up in front of an audience and seek to entertain.

Solve et Coagula

You often end up demanding the near impossible from what a stage can present and from what an actor can perform and, indeed, sometimes from what an audience can stand. But I'd rather be responsible for an overreaching, toppling tower of a show than one more easy-as-pie, 'ho-ho, clever-clever', 'well-made' play which the actors — in that damning green-room phrase — 'do on autopilot'.

You are always trying to work the old alchemist's formula 'solve et coagula' — 'dissolve and re-set'. The whole heap of the theatre — not only its artistic practices but how it is run, its administration, the way it sells tickets, its poster design — constantly congeals into 'traditions'. When a playwright takes a play into a theatre and they start talking about 'the traditions of this theatre', you know you are in trouble. A theatre becomes successful, with new work and a new artistic policy; but a few years on what made the success becomes a routine, then a habit, then rank decadence — the state of many of the classical productions by the Royal Shakespeare Company, for example, with stages raked so steeply because they always rake the stages . . . (decadence can be good box-office, it's a far safer bet commercially than regeneration). As Peter Brook put it 'the dead theatre is always with us', and it can be a corpse on the back of a new play.

Poli-lolli-tics

Because I have a Marxist view of the world, right-wing critics are forever labelling my plays 'political', which is, for them, a euphemism for 'preachy'. Conversely some critics on the left find the plays 'too ambiguous', which I take to be a euphemism for 'not preachy enough'. I do not win on the middle ground either, as it is social-democrats who really get riled by my plays, for some reason. Perhaps the plays remind them of the allegiances they have betrayed.

My political views are, I would have thought, naturally and

passionately expressed in these plays, as naturally and passionately as Tom Stoppard, say, expresses his rightist views in his plays. It is not a matter of 'pushing my ideology' at the audience. That is how the world appears to me. It is glaringly obvious to your author that the western world is in thrall to a system that respects nothing but money and power, that the Third World War began at the time of the Korean War and has been in progress, in slow motion, ever since, and that our liberation lies in democratic and socialist movements, and if we are to survive and have a common destiny it will be communist. It may not, I am very aware, be glaringly obvious to you, dear reader.

I believe we are living in the midst of a new Renaissance. It began with the Paris Commune in 1871. The Russian Revolution, whether you regard it with hope, hope betrayed, or with horror, has changed world history forever. There is no going back. The second Renaissance is historically young, though the cradle is full of blood. But the first Renaissance took several centuries, for mercantile capitalism to be established, for the Catholic Church to accept usury and for the Protestant ethic to become strong and father modern science and technology and, indeed, the United States of America. Between Copernicus and Galileo there were ninety years. You could have been born, become a mathematician at the University of Padua and died, without knowing you were living in the midst of the Renaissance, so heavy was the repression in Italy.

We too, in Britain, live on an historical ebb tide, in a mean time, when being a socialist is an exercise in damage limitation. *The Churchill Play*, though on something of an operatic scale and a densely-written play, is at its root a satire against the erosion of of civil liberties and union rights that began under Edward Heath's Government and spread apace under Margaret Thatcher's. But! A good red must keep the knives sharp in such times . . .

Big Little

What moves me as a playwright to anger and often to distraction is that the grand historical vision, the 'second Renaissance', the 'macro' overview does not help one jot in daily life. At the 'micro' level of waking every morning on a London housing estate without a job, or waking to join a queue for fruit at a Moscow store, it does not help to say 'here I am at a profound shift in history'. The Londoner wants work, the Muscovite wants an apple — now. The great socialist leaders wake in their cells in South Africa, in South America, as do the cadres in Soweto and

Nicaragua, confident that history is moving as surely as the planet moves. But millions do not have that vision, confidence and heroism, and some are traumatised by defeat. It is they whom I want to write about — the young, uneducated workers in *Weapons of Happiness*; Judy, the abused divorcee in *Sore Throats*; the young couple in *Epsom Downs* with their children, at their wits' end about making ends meet; the green police constable in *Christie in Love*, horrified by his job; the innocent prisoners in *The Churchill Play* caught in a national tragedy, the coming of a kind of fascism to Britain, which they don't even realise is happening until it hits them; Caroline Thompson the wife of an army officer in the same play, who in her own terms comes to see what the prison camp means; the good, middle-class children in *Magnificence* lost in ultra-leftist dreams of terrorism, what E.P. Thompson calls 'politics as psycho-drama'. For me, people like these characters are the salt of the earth. I try to dramatise them coming to life, gaining visions, confidence and courage in their own way. If the Left convinces and wins people like them, the British Revolution will be unstoppable.

Howard Brenton
London, 1986

CHRISTIE IN LOVE

Author's Production Note

CHRISTIE's first appearance is in the Dracula tradition. Happy horror, creeps and treats. He rises from the grave luridly, in a frightening mask. It looks as if a juicy evening's underway, all laughs, nice shivers, easy oohs and aahs.

But that's smashed up. The lights are slammed on, and the mask is seen as only a tatty bit of papier mâché. Off it comes, and what's left is a feeble, ordinary man blinking through his pebble glasses.

The Publishers asked for a production note, and I'm setting down the devices I tried to use in the show. That's the basic one. A kind of dislocation, tearing one style up for another, so the proceedings lurch and all interpretations are blocked, and the spectator hunting for an easy meaning wearies, and is left only with CHRISTIE and his act of love.

The play is a black sketch if played fast, and I suppose it would be quite funny if done at that pace. But I categorically forbid anyone to do so. I want it to last nearly an hour. It is written to be played very slowly.

Any director who's nervous about this slowness, please look at the first scene. David Hare, in the Portable Theatre production, got it right and it was taking at least twenty minutes to play. It's an old trick after all, to play the first scene of a slow play very slowly. Once the first scene is established, the actors make judgements about the pauses and little rushes needed for the interrogation scenes.

The 'Garden' is a pen, ten feet by six feet. Its sides are two and a half feet high, and made of chicken wire. It's brim full of torn and screwed up pages of a popular newspaper. The spectators sit all around, and very close — there's barely enough room for the actors to walk round the sides. The pen is a filthy sight. The chicken wire is rusty, the wood is stained, the paper is full of dust. It's used as CHRISTIE's garden, his front room, a room in a police station, an executioner's shed, a lime pit. But it's not a 'Setting' in a conventional sense. I don't want it to be *like* a garden, or a room. It's a theatrical machine, a thing you'd only see in a show. It's a trap, a flypaper for the attention of the spectators to stick on.

The doll is a little larger than life size. She must not be in any
way a pornographic object. She is dressed in a faded blue skirt
and dirty white blouse of the early fifties, her skin is grey, her
hair frizzy and short the way they wore it then. Her underwear
is massive, unfrilly, not sexy. The CONSTABLE has to undress
her – that scene's tricky and he must be able to strip her quickly.
Velcro can be used instead of buttons and eyes.

The CONSTABLE and the INSPECTOR are not 'characters',
apart from the facts of age and rank. (The INSPECTOR is in his
mid-thirties, the CONSTABLE in his late twenties.) They are
stage coppers. But they have 'sudden lights', unpredictable
speeches beyond the confines of pastiche. As if a cardboard
black and white cut-out suddenly reaches out a fully fleshed,
real hand. It's a bathos technique (the end of HEADS works by
it.) It is very cruel.

The artifice of the garden and the 'stage' nature of the policemen's parts are intended to throw the CHRISTIE part into
relief. With CHRISTIE I tried to write a fully fledged naturalistic
part.

I am greatly indebted to William Hoyland's playing of CHRISTIE.
That the part is in a style radically different from that of the
policemen is a fundamental dislocation in the play. Bill got it
right. Over fifty performances with the Portable Theatre, in all
kinds of conditions, he developed the part until it had an illusory
effect. An obscene insolence – in the middle of all that artificial
invention, all that tat, the garden, the doll, the role-playing
coppers, sat Bill's CHRISTIE, 'believable', 'real'.

H.B.
1970

Christie in Love was first performed by The Portable Theatre at Oval House, London, on 23 November 1969, with the following cast:

Christie	William Hoyland
Constable	Matthew Walters
Inspector	Andrew Carr

Directed by David Hare
Stage Management by Snoo Wilson
Set built by Tony Bicât

It was later performed at the Royal Court Theatre Upstairs, London, on 12 March 1970 with the following cast:

Christie	William Hoyland
Constable	Brian Croucher
Inspector	Stanley Lebor

Directed by David Hare
Stage Manager Betty Ritchie
Assistant Stage Managers Nick Hart, David Gotthard
Lighting by Gareth Jones

While the audience comes in, the CONSTABLE *actor digs in the garden, the* INSPECTOR *actor stands at the back, the* CHRISTIE *actor lies concealed beneath the newspaper. A tape broadcasts the facts again and again.*

TAPE. John Reginald Halliday Christie was born in Halifax, April of 1898.
He hated his mother, his father and his sisters.
His childhood was normal.
December of 1938, Christie moved with his wife to London.
His marriage was normal.
In March of 1953, Police arrested Christie for murder.
In Christie's London house, the Police found the following corpses.
Buried in the garden, a Miss Eady.
Buried in the garden, a Miss Fuerst.
Hanging in the concealed kitchen alcove, a Miss MacLennan.
Hanging in the concealed kitchen alcove, a Miss Maloney.
Hanging in the concealed kitchen alcove, a Miss Nelson.
Laid beneath the boards of the living-room floor, Mrs Ethel Christie.
Questioned, an old school mate said of Christie 'He kept himself to himself.'
Christie wrote 'As I gazed down at the still form of my first victim, I experienced a strange, peaceful thrill.'
Christie was hanged July of 1953.

When all the audience is in, the tape fades.

Scene One

The CONSTABLE *digs in the garden. Paper falls from the spade. He continues, very slowly, until everyone present is looking at the paper, as it falls from the spade. The* CONSTABLE *stops. He stares at the paper. He looks up, and around at the audience. He recites the first limerick. His recitation is uncomic, deadly.*

CONSTABLE. In the Garden of Eden lay Adam.

A pause.

In the Garden of Eden lay Adam
Complacently stroking his madam.
Very loud was his mirth,
For on all of the Earth,
There were only two balls, and he had 'em.

A pause. The CONSTABLE *reflects.*

There were only two balls, and he had 'em.

The CONSTABLE *nods to himself. He digs again. Paper falls from the spade. He stops digging, and looks up.*

There was a young girl named Heather.

A pause.

There was a young girl named Heather
Whose cunt was made out of leather.
She made an odd noise,
For attracting the boys,
By flapping the edges together.

A pause. The CONSTABLE *reflects.*

By flapping the edges together.

The CONSTABLE *nods to himself. He digs again. Paper falls from the spade. He stops digging, and looks up.*

A bawdy young rake from Tashkent.

A pause.

A bawdy young rake from Tashkent
Had a cock that was horribly bent.
To get over the trouble,
He pushed it in double,
And instead of his coming he went.

At once the INSPECTOR *shouts from the back. The* CONSTABLE *jerks to attention.*

INSPECTOR. Constable!

CONSTABLE. Sir!

INSPECTOR. What you doing!

CONSTABLE. Digging Sir!

INSPECTOR. Digging for what Constable!

CONSTABLE. Bones Sir!

INSPECTOR. Right! Bones!

CONSTABLE. Digging for bones Sir!

INSPECTOR. Right again! You keep bones on your mind!

CONSTABLE. I've got bones on my mind Sir!

INSPECTOR. Good man! You keep them there and you won't
go far wrong!

A pause.

INSPECTOR. Get on with it then!

CONSTABLE. Sir!

The CONSTABLE *digs vigorously. After a while, he wearies,
slows down and stops. He looks up.*

CONSTABLE. There was an odd fellow named West.

A pause.

There was an odd fellow named West
Whose cock came up to his chest.
He said 'I declare',
'I've got no pubic hair',
So he covered his balls with his vest.

INSPECTOR. Constable!

CONSTABLE. Sir!

INSPECTOR. Kind of bones!

A pause.

CONSTABLE. Sir?

INSPECTOR. What kind of bones you looking for? Bones of
what animal? Of what genus or species?

CONSTABLE. Women's bones, in't it Sir? The bones of . . .

The CONSTABLE *searches for the word.*

Ladies?

INSPECTOR. Right. How very right you are. The bones of
English Ladies. That's what he's been burying down there,
somewhere. Burying English Ladies in his garden! We're going
to do him for that!

CONSTABLE. We're going to do him for that Sir!

INSPECTOR. I've heard of some nasty things in my life. But burying English Ladies in your own backyard just about takes the candle. Dig 'em up!

CONSTABLE. Right!

The CONSTABLE *starts digging again, vigorously.*

Right!

INSPECTOR. First sign of a bone, give me the word.

CONSTABLE. Right!

INSPECTOR. The mothers of England depend on you.

The CONSTABLE *digs on. After a while, he wearies, slows down and stops. He looks up.*

CONSTABLE. There was a young man from Coombe.

A pause.

There was a young man from Coombe
Who was born six months too soon.
He hadn't the luck,
To be got from a fuck,
But a toss off shoved in with a spoon.

A pause. The CONSTABLE *reflects.*

A toss off. Shoved.

The CONSTABLE *shakes his head, appalled. He wipes his brow. The* INSPECTOR *comes from the back. Looks the garden over. Looks right and left to see if they are private. Takes out a flask, and offers the* CONSTABLE *a drink. The* CONSTABLE *hesitates, wary of rank, but accepts and sits on the side of the garden. The* INSPECTOR *actor tells the following joke in this way — he works out the pace of a bad joke teller, the abominable and humourless timing, and then exaggerates the pauses. He stretches it to breaking point.*

INSPECTOR. Know the one about the faith healer?

CONSTABLE. Actually, no Sir.

The INSPECTOR *looks around.*

INSPECTOR. Keep this to yourself.

CONSTABLE. Eh, yes Sir.

INSPECTOR. There was this faith healer you see.

A pause.

CONSTABLE. Sir?

INSPECTOR, Wait for it.

CONSTABLE. Yes Sir.

A pause.

INSPECTOR. There was this faith healer. The most famous in the land. Anything he touched, he . . .

A pause.

CONSTABLE. I see Sir.

INSPECTOR. Cured. He had what you'd call a wonderful touch.

A pause.

CONSTABLE. Cured, Sir.

INSPECTOR. Anyway, this faith healer, he got married. And the first time in bed with his wife he ran his hands all over her, and sealed her up.

A long pause.

INSPECTOR. Just a little joke between ourselves.

CONSTABLE. Yes Sir. Very funny Sir.

INSPECTOR. Get on with it.

The INSPECTOR *turns away.*

CONSTABLE. Bleeding hell.

The CONSTABLE *puts the spade in once. He stops dead still, staring down. Simultaneously the* INSPECTOR, *who was walking away, stops dead still. A pause. The* CONSTABLE *speaks quietly.*

Oh my God.

The INSPECTOR *turns. A pause. This passage very loudly.*

CONSTABLE. Bone Sir!

INSPECTOR. Bone!

CONSTABLE. Bone here Sir!

INSPECTOR. Bone there!

CONSTABLE. Got a bone here Sir!

INSPECTOR. What dug up a bone!

CONSTABLE. Bone here!

A pause. The CONSTABLE *speaks quietly.*

More than a bone.

The INSPECTOR *goes to see, climbs into the garden. This passage spoken ordinarily.*

What were she? Tart?

INSPECTOR. Who knows?

CONSTABLE. What he do to her?

The INSPECTOR *shrugs.*

INSPECTOR. What he wanted. No more, no less.

The CONSTABLE *gestures at the grave.*

CONSTABLE. It's beyond me. All that.

INSPECTOR. Takes all kinds. The General Public is a dirty animal.

CONSTABLE. It's beyond me.

INSPECTOR. Don't brood on it Lad. There're many ways of pleasure, most of 'em filth.

CONSTABLE. Still beyond me.

A pause.

Look at that fucking great slug.

At once the INSPECTOR *and the* CONSTABLE *stand back to back. They turn round on the audience in unison with each line, shouting out the limerick. They end facing each other, shaking with rage.*

INSPECTOR AND CONSTABLE. THERE WAS A YOUNG MAN FROM BENGAL
WHO WENT TO A FANCY DRESS BALL.
JUST FOR A STUNT,
HE WENT AS A CUNT,
AND WAS HAD BY A DOG IN THE HALL.

A pause.

INSPECTOR. Right. Let's pack up and get out of here.

The INSPECTOR *and the* CONSTABLE *climb out of the garden, and go to the back. They collect a stretcher and a tarpaulin sheet. They come back, open the stretcher beside the grave. They lay the tarpaulin over the corpse. From here, the lights begin a long fade to the end of the scene.*

CONSTABLE. Sir, what you reckon he did?

INSPECTOR. Did?

CONSTABLE. He whip 'em? Make 'em . . . Adopt poses? Stick feathers on 'em?

INSPECTOR. Lad, I'll give you a word of warning. I been on these pervy cases before. And the word of warning is, don't brood. You brood, and it'll get you down.

CONSTABLE. It could get you down.

INSPECTOR. It could.

CONSTABLE. It is already.

The CONSTABLE *feels his stomach.*

INSPECTOR. Now copper. Have a bash at controlling yourself.

CONSTABLE. I'll have a bash Sir.

INSPECTOR. Get her up.

They stand, the CONSTABLE *at the front of the stretcher, the* INSPECTOR *at the back.*

Come on my little darling.

They step out of the garden. They carry the corpse out to the back during this passage, with a funeral step. The light is nearly gone.

INSPECTOR. Pleasures of the General Public. You see them all, all the fads. How some like it hot, and some like it cold. How some like it live and some like it dead. And sometimes, why, your own fancy is tickled.

They stop.

INSPECTOR. We are human.

CONSTABLE. We are human.

They go on.

INSPECTOR. So don't brood. Just clear up the mess.

CONSTABLE. I'll do that Sir.

In near darkness.

INSPECTOR. Just clear up the mess.

It's a blackout.

Scene Two

The lights are snapped up. Very bright. The INSPECTOR *and the* CONSTABLE *are businesslike.*

INSPECTOR. Ladies and Gents, John Reginald Christie did six women in.

CONSTABLE. The manner in which they were done was not nice.

INSPECTOR. So if anyone feels sick, go ahead. Throw up. We won't mind.

CONSTABLE. If you want to spew, spew.

INSPECTOR. Right. Let's have a look at him shall we.

The INSPECTOR *nods to the stage management. Blackout.*

Scene Three

In the blackout.

INSPECTOR. Out you come Reg.

CONSTABLE. Come on out Reggie.

INSPECTOR. John Reginald Christie!

CONSTABLE. Mr Christie Sir, out you come like a good Sir.

INSPECTOR. Come on Reggie. Let's have a look at you.

The INSPECTOR *and the* CONSTABLE *switch hand lamps on. They let the beams flick over the garden. The tape begins. The* CHRISTIE *actor raises his hand out of the paper. A beam catches it, then whisks away. The lamps go out. Then come on and off, at the discretion of the actors. The* CHRISTI *actor rises from the paper.*

He wears a grotesque mask, a papier mâché head that distorts his features. He undoes his fly, and takes out a length of rubber tubing. He lets down his trousers. He blows into the tube, the effect should be that CHRISTIE's *activities are obscured, the beams of the hand lamps do not allow the audience a good look. The taped speech is spoken by the* CHRISTIE *actor.*

TAPE. Love. Love. Reggie knows his mind 'bout love. And Reggie's never been a one for it. S'all bunk. S'all got up by women. Not that I can't handle them. Women. The bloody female. I'm a dab hand with the ways of love and women, when I want. Much of the time I don't want, that's all. Bah. They give me the pip. Women. With little women's things. Brushes. Tweezers. Sanitary towels. Hairclips. Nasty little instruments to cut you. Coming at you with teeth to give you bites. They're violent, women are. The bitches! Coming up to you, getting violent. Start to paw you about. Get you doing things to them. And they doing things to you. My mother cut my hair. Very, very short. Came at me with scissors, the bitch. Gouging. Cutting off my length. I am a private man and I know my rights. I am, also, a dark horse. Women women women . . . The streets are full of them. In their nasty skirts. You can hear their skirts, rustle rustle. And their shoes like little metal rats, clip clip upon the pavement. All over. And their beady eyes sweeping the area like birds of prey. And their nails folded ready. They're on the look out! Women out at night for men. Scissors in their handbags to cut you off. Slice you where you're private. Each tit a nail to make you bleed. Each mouth a mousetrap. Cheese nearly in your chops when click! Back's broke. And each cunt a bacon slicer whittling manhood away. A woman's body that's a machine for death.

Panting breaths, the CHRISTIE *actor at climax in the garden. Then he throws himself full length. The handlamps go out. Silence. Then the tape continues.*

I am not worried. I know what I like. It is no trouble. It is lovely. It is . . .

A pause.

Cooling.

Scene Four

The lights snap on. CHRISTIE with his trousers down. He takes off the head, and blinks. Then buries it. The INSPECTOR is standing by the garden, looking on.

INSPECTOR. Presentable yet, Reg?

A pause.

I don't want to bother you if you're not . . .

A pause.

Presentable.

CHRISTIE blinks at him. Hurriedly pulls up his trousers, does up the fly.

CHRISTIE. I'm all right. Thank you very much.

INSPECTOR. Oh! You're all right.

A pause.

CHRISTIE. I am.

A pause.

INSPECTOR. Let's get on with it then.

The INSPECTOR quickly goes to the back, and comes forward with a battered card table and a battered wooden chair. He sets them in the garden.

INSPECTOR. Take a chair.

CHRISTIE. Oh. Right.

CHRISTIE sits on the chair.

INSPECTOR. Right!

A pause.

Good. There we are then. That's it.

A pause.

Then. Good.

A pause.

Then.

A pause.

Ten Rillington Place.

A pause.

Your property?

CHRISTIE. My property.

INSPECTOR. Oh, it's *your* property.

CHRISTIE. That's my home.

INSPECTOR. But I thought you rented.

A pause.

I thought you were a rent-paying tenant. OF the property.

CHRISTIE. The house is my home.

INSPECTOR. Your rented home.

CHRISTIE. I said. The house is my home.

INSPECTOR. But the freehold. That's not yours. Reggie I can't see, I mean I cannot understand, why you are reluctant to admit that you pay rent. I'm speaking frankly now.

CHRISTIE. Oh ay.

INSPECTOR. Are you saying, you fancy yourself as the landlord?

A pause.

You fancy you are a property developer?

The INSPECTOR *smiles, chuckles at the absurdity.* CHRISTIE *attempts an imitative chuckle, but fails. He covers up with a slight cough.*

I mean, that's ridiculous, isn't it? You're not, are you?

CHRISTIE. Oh ay.

INSPECTOR. You're just a grubby rent payer.

CHRISTIE. Oh ay.

The INSPECTOR *holds out three fingers.*

INSPECTOR. Three weeks behind.

A pause.

In fact, after you left Ten Rillington Place, and before Constable Thomas picked you up on the embankment at two o'clock in the morning, the landlord came round and found, not only that you owe two weeks, but you had sublet the flat for the sum of seven pounds ten shillings in advance.

Sublet illegally. I'm not criticising you Reg. Not for that anyway. But you're no bigtime owner of property.

A pause.

CHRISTIE. Oh ay.

INSPECTOR. Still, be that as it may. Tiny isn't it?

A pause.

A tiny place.

CHRISTIE. It's a small house.

INSPECTOR. Cramped.

CHRISTIE. It's on the small side.

INSPECTOR. So you'd agree. It's cramped.

CHRISTIE. I said, it's a small house.

Suddenly the INSPECTOR shouts.

INSPECTOR. Oh ay. It's . . .

A pause.

Cramped all right.

INSPECTOR. You could say crammed.

CHRISTIE. You could say that.

INSPECTOR. Crammed with, eh, people?

CHRISTIE. There are a lot.

INSPECTOR. Why there's your Mrs, but then she's moved away hasn't she? Gone off? Still it's tiny and there's you downstairs. Poor old Mr Kitchener on the first floor. And on the top there's that young couple, the Evans's.

CHRISTIE. Browns.

INSPECTOR. Oh. Silly of me. Of course. The Browns were involved in that affair weren't they? Timothy Brown. Did his wife and little baby in.

CHRISTIE. No. Evans.

INSPECTOR. What?

CHRISTIE. Timothy Evans. Did his wife and little baby in.

The INSPECTOR slaps his thigh.

INSPECTOR. I am a stupid clot! Evans was the bloke not Brown.
Course you helped us a lot there, didn't you Reggie. Timothy
Evans did his wife and kid in, and stuck 'em in the washhouse
out the back of your property. You helped us a lot.

CHRISTIE. I did my bit.

INSPECTOR. You did.

CHRISTIE. I did my bit for public good.

INSPECTOR. And you're going to do your bit again Reginald.
Aren't you?

A pause.

CHRISTIE. I'll give what help's within my power.

The INSPECTOR *is delighted.*

INSPECTOR. You mean that?

CHRISTIE. Oh ay.

The INSPECTOR *is suddenly brisk.*

INSPECTOR. Good. First point. The house you rent is crammed
full not only of living, rent-paying tenants like yourself, but
crammed full of dead women.

A pause.

I say women loosely. Most of 'em far as the pathologists can
tell were tarts. The real dregs, and hardly a loss to humanity.
But women, tarts, ladies or bleeding duchesses, your small
house is stuffed to the roof with their remains.

A pause.

Now I don't want to get emotional. And I know that you are
not an emotional man. So there is no reason to get het up.
But I got to ask you this Reg. Can you help us with our
enquiries?

CHRISTIE *sits stock still on his chair for a second, then
shifts slightly.*

For example. The 22nd of June last year, a very hot day,
you were observed by a tenant to be sprinkling Jeyes' Fluid
in the passage. Between ourselves, man to man, couldn't
you stand the smell?

At once, CHRISTIE *half rises from his chair.*

CHRISTIE. I'm not going to sit here . . .

INSPECTOR. Oh you are. You are going to sit there.

CHRISTIE *sits. The* INSPECTOR *smiles.*

INSPECTOR. Remember, you are not an emotional man.

CHRISTIE. No. I don't like to let my feelings show.

INSPECTOR. Stiff upper lip!

The INSPECTOR *laughs.*

Everyone in the street says that of you, all your neighbours. Mr Christie keeps a stiff upper lip. Keeps himself to himself. Keeps . . . Neat.

A pause.

All right we'll forget about the Jeyes for the time being. Why shouldn't a householder that is a rent-paying tenant keep his place sanitary? Jeyes is just the thing in hot weather. Clean and pungent, overriding any other odour. I'm not unreasonable Reg. I'm not going off on an emotional tack. Like accusing you of doing your Mrs in and burying her under the floorboards in the front room. From where, by the way, we dug her up the other day. I mean I'm not going off at a tangent. I just don't know where to begin. But I wondered if you could help.

A pause.

With a few details.

A pause.

Like why you killed those tarts.

A pause.

And did you fuck them before or after?

Blackout.

Scene Five

Lit by a camera flash bulb, CHRISTIE *rises, leans over the table and masturbates. On the tape women's voices call out, overlapping and laughing.*

TAPE. . . . Reggie.
   . . . Reggie Weggie.
   . . . Reggie No Dick.
   . . . Where is you Reggie?
   . . . What you doing Reggie?
   . . . It dirty Reggie?
   . . . It nasty?
   . . . Nasty little boy we going to get you.
   . . . Reginald! Stop that at once!
   . . . Going to get Reggie No Dick.
   . . . Reggie! Stop that nasty thing!
   . . . Going to cut off Reggie Weggie's Dicky Wick.

The lights are snapped up. CHRISTIE *whirls round, looking at the audience section by section, terrified. He sits down. By a series of gestures, he attempts to recover — he hitches his trousers, straightenes his tie, smoothes his lapels.*

Scene Six

The INSPECTOR *approaches* CHRISTIE, *holding out a glass phial.*

INSPECTOR. Know what this is? It intimately concerns you.

CHRISTIE. Oh ay.

INSPECTOR. It is your semen Reginald.

   A pause.

   The Christie family jewels. Hot stuff, eh Reg? You reckon that's hot stuff?

The INSPECTOR *steps into the garden, and shoves the phial under* CHRISTIE's *nose.*

   Eh? Go on have a whiff. Don't mind me.

CHRISTIE *leans back, to avoid the phial. The* INSPECTOR *puts the phial on the table.*

Medical Science tells us there are millions of potential little Reginalds in that tube.

The INSPECTOR *shakes his head.*

What a waste. But you did not encourage them to come to fruition did you. The use you put your spunk to did not encourage birth.

CHRISTIE *mumbles, indistinctly.*

CHRISTIE. You're being bloody personal.

INSPECTOR. What you say Reg? Speak up.

CHRISTIE. You're being bloody personal.

INSPECTOR. Enunciate with clarity you fucking pervert.

CHRISTIE. Bloody personal!

CHRISTIE *puts his hand to his chest.*

Gas. Got load in First War.

INSPECTOR. What? What?

CHRISTIE. Got load of gas. 1918. Three years, couldn't speak.

INSPECTOR. Ah! Your war disability.

CHRISTIE. Honourably disabled.

CHRISTIE *breathes heavily.*

INSPECTOR. You sniveller. I dunno, it's disappointing. Why can't a mass murderer be just a bit diabolical? Why can't a pervert like you, already in the annals of nastiness, have fangs or something? Roll your eyes around. Sprout horns.

The INSPECTOR *kicks up the paper in a fury.*

Go on Reg, let's have a real bit of horror!

A pause. CHRISTIE *speaks weakly.*

CHRISTIE. I've overlooked my inhaler. Could you send round for it? Do you think? For my catarrh?

The INSPECTOR *shakes his head, saddened.*

INSPECTOR. And Madam Tussauds has been onto us all day for a plaster cast of your head.

CHRISTIE. My inhaler.

INSPECTOR. No you can't have your bloody inhaler!

CHRISTIE. I got my rights.

INSPECTOR. That inhaler is the property of the Crown. We don't know what you been up to with it, do we.

CHRISTIE. I don't know what you're inferring.

INSPECTOR. Lots Reg. The whole filthy bundle I'm inferring.

CHRISTIE. If I don't have my inhaler, I'll come over with an attack.

The INSPECTOR *speaks confidentially.*

INSPECTOR. Don't threaten me.

A pause. The INSPECTOR *points at the phial.*

Forensics, Reg. It is all a matter of traces. The chalky soil from the flowerbed on the cat thief's boot. The tell-tale powder burn on the bank robber's sleeve. To the forensic scientist the criminal is always leaving his signature. It may be his finger prints. His dandruff. His spit, or his urine. Or, as in your case, his sperm.

A pause.

The dead tarts, Reg. They're full of your stuff. Science knows you fucked them all.

Scene Seven

CHRISTIE *and the* INSPECTOR *freeze. The* CONSTABLE *has been drinking at the back.*

CONSTABLE. Bloody hell!

The CONSTABLE *stumbles to the centre.*

Oh bloody hell. I'm bloody overwhelmed. Went home to my Mrs. You smell she said. Course I smelled, all day digging in his graveyard. Had three baths in a row. Disinfected me all over. Scrubbed me nails. Pumiced me palms. No good! Me Mrs could smell 'em. The dead women on me. I could not stand the look my very own and loved and cherished gave me. Went round the pub. Started to knock it back. And it all went round in my head. Him. In his kitchen he had a tin. Old Holborn 'baccy tin, of two ounce size. Know what he had in that tin? Pubic hairs, cut off the women he had. Bloody hell.

He cut off their pubic hairs and kept them in a tin. I tell you it's all too . . .

The CONSTABLE *searches for the word.*

Deep for me.

The CONSTABLE *stumbles to the back, and kneels down by the* DOLL *on the stretcher.*

Scene Eight

INSPECTOR. Our pathologists conclude, the women were getting cold. You had 'em dead, didn't you.

CHRISTIE *stands violently, and knocks over the table and chair.*

INSPECTOR. Finally got to your bent have we? Touch of the necrophiliacs, eh?

At the same time the CONSTABLE *picks up the* DOLL *in his arms, and talks to her.*

CONSTABLE. Eh my love? What? What? I dunno.

INSPECTOR. Like your women drained of blood? Like your women cooled off? Don't work any other way for you, eh? Got to get 'em ready, hang 'em up stuck like a pig? If you weren't a well known anti-semite I'd say you were after a good kosher fuck.

CHRISTIE *faints, full length. He crawls feebly in the paper. The lights begin to fade.*

Tell me how you really like it. Love. I will not be shocked. I am a policeman of the realm. I am conversant with it all. The sinks and sewers of the minds of men and women. I spend my professional life in the General Public's shithouse. I am a father to your kind, Reg. Tell your father.

The light is almost gone.

Scene Nine

Red light. The INSPECTOR *goes to the back. The* CONSTABLE *comes forward with the* DOLL *in his arms, circles the garden, showing her to the audience.*

CONSTABLE. Just a scrubber. Twenty-six. Tits a bit worn. The rest of her, a bit worn. A very ordinary bint. I wouldn't have minded a go. I mean, if she weren't a rotting corpse I'd have, perhaps, chanced my arm.

CHRISTIE *stands.*

CHRISTIE. NO ONE PLAYS THE FOOL WI' ME. SEE? NO MAN NO WOMAN. PLAYS THE FOOL WI' ME.

CHRISTIE *lifts a foot.*

See my plims?

CHRISTIE *steps out of the garden.*

No woman ever knows if I'm near or not. I pass like a ghost through Society. The petty criminal in his den, the tart in her red room. I come and go, a military looking gent. A good citizen, in plims.

CONSTABLE. She were only a common day fuck. That's all. Used, yeh, but a common . . .

He searches for the word.

Woman.

To CHRISTIE.

So what you have to go and do perversions for? She offer first? Or did you have to force your foul desire? And what she say when she first approached? She say . . .

The CONSTABLE *actor holds the* DOLL *before him, and works the arms and head for occasional gestures. He speaks the woman's part, in a falsetto voice, over the* DOLL's *shoulder.*

DOLL. Want a touch love?

A pause.

Want a touch love?

A pause.

Want a touch love?

CHRISTIE. No one touches me!

DOLL. Sorry I'm sure.

She turns away.

CHRISTIE. Eh up there.

She turns back.

DOLL. What?

CHRISTIE. Want to touch me do you?

DOLL. All the same to me love. Touch or not touch, if the price is right.

CHRISTIE. Bloody tarts! Coming up, touching you!

DOLL. All right, all right.

CHRISTIE. Want to get your hands on me don't you. Get your fingers. On. Want to poke me.

DOLL. I don't have to stand here and talk to you. There're too many queer fishes about nowadays. A girl's not safe. The Government should do something.

She turns away.

CHRISTIE. Eh up there.

She stops, and turns back.

DOLL. Do you don't you? Make up your bleeding mind.

CHRISTIE. See my plims?

DOLL. Very nice.

CHRISTIE. I creep about in them.

DOLL. I don't doubt it.

CHRISTIE. I come up unawares in them.

DOLL. Do you.

CHRISTIE. Then I pounce.

DOLL. That's not very nice, is it.

CHRISTIE. It ain't nice come to think of it. Come to think of it, it's . . . Nasty.

DOLL. It's very nasty.

CHRISTIE. Women bring out the nastiness in me.

DOLL. Do they.

CHRISTIE. They bring it out. And they love it, the stupid bitches. That's all they want. To be kicked about a bit. Be scared to shits. You scared to shits, girly?

DOLL. Cost you money to scare me.

CHRISTIE. How much?

DOLL. Two quid.

CHRISTIE. One pound ten.

DOLL. Thirty-five bob.

CHRISTIE. Thirty-five bob.

DOLL. I'm scared.

CHRISTIE. Ha!

> CHRISTIE *backs away, pointing at her.*

> Ha!

> *He holds out his police identification. She peers at it.*

DOLL. Constable John Reginald Christie. You're a fucking dick.

CHRISTIE. Just a Special.

DOLL. Still a fucking dick.

CHRISTIE. Still very much a fucking dick.

DOLL. What a come on. You deliberately encouraged my soliciting, pretending you were a queer fish just to get a girl arrested.

CHRISTIE. I'm a respectable citizen girly. I was gassed in the First World War. Couldn't speak for three year. I served my country.

DOLL. An amateur policeman. Just my luck.

CHRISTIE. Watch your lip yer whore.

> *A pause.*

DOLL. Well come on. Take my name. Take my address. Take me down the station for a good laugh with your friends.

> *A pause.*

> What you waiting for?

> *A pause.*

Ruth Fuerst, 27, Ladbroke Grove. Twenty-six years old. I'm not wholly on the game. I would describe myself as an experienced amateur. I have prostitutes among my friends. I work as a nurse. I get bored a lot.

CHRISTIE. Do it for free.

A pause.

You don't want to be charged for soliciting.

DOLL. You making a proposition?

CHRISTIE. Little arrangement.

DOLL. Stone me. If I take my knickers down to you, you let me go?

CHRISTIE. Don't be coarse.

DOLL. I'll believe anything of the police force now.

CHRISTIE. You keep respectful.

DOLL. I do it, you let me go. I don't do it, I get charged for prostitution. That really takes the pip.

A pause.

Haven't got much choice, have I?

CHRISTIE. None.

DOLL. I think that I'm in your power.

The CHRISTIE *actor embraces the* DOLL. *He takes her arm, they walk round two sides of the garden.* CHRISTIE *steps into the garden, the* CONSTABLE *actor follows, with the* DOLL. CHRISTIE *goes to a corner and fiddles with a cup and saucer and a teapot.*

DOLL. What a filthy house.

CHRISTIE. It's clean enough.

DOLL. What's all this stuff?

CHRISTIE. It's clean I said! Spotless.

DOLL. All right.

CHRISTIE. There's no dirt here!

DOLL. All right, all right!

She speaks aside.

He is a queer fish. THOUGH I've had queer fish in my time, AND left 'em to swim away. If you get my meaning. Here we go.

The CONSTABLE *actor strips off the* DOLL's *clothes.*

'Ere. What you doing out there?

CHRISTIE. Making cup of tea.

DOLL. Highly romantic. Two lumps please.

CHRISTIE, *to himself.*

CHRISTIE. Two lumps eh? Two lumps eh?

DOLL. Could do with a cup of tea.

CHRISTIE, *cup and saucer in one hand teapot in the other, whirls on her.*

CHRISTIE. Who said you were getting a cup?

DOLL. Ooh la la. Sorry I spoke I'm sure.

CHRISTIE. Tea's for after. That's how I like it, after.

DOLL. Come on then. Let's get it over with.

Scene Ten

The INSPECTOR *comes forward.* CHRISTIE *puts his hands on the* DOLL. *He speaks to the* INSPECTOR.

CHRISTIE. I have something on my mind. It comes back to me in flashes. If it does come back, I will tell you, I truly will.

CHRISTIE *puts his hand between the* DOLL's *legs.*

CONSTABLE. Hello! I think he's off.

CHRISTIE. I don't remember what happened. But I must have gone haywire.

The INSPECTOR *hands* CHRISTIE *a short length of rope.* CHRISTIE *whips it round the* DOLL's *neck, and strangles her.*

CONSTABLE. Sir! He's off! He's well away!

And CHRISTIE *has gone down, still pulling the rope tight. The* CONSTABLE *ends up in the paper, under the* DOLL, CHRISTIE *on top of them both.* CHRISTIE *lets go the rope.*

CHRISTIE. The next thing I remember she was lying down, a rope about her neck. I left her there and went into the front room. I had a cup of tea, and I went to bed. I got up in the morning, and washed and shaved. She still lay there. I had a cup of tea. I pulled away a cupboard and gained access to a small alcove. I knew it was there because a pipe burst in the frosty weather and a plumber opened it up to mend the pipe.

CONSTABLE. This is getting out of hand. Right out.

CHRISTIE. I was in love with her.

Scene Eleven

The lights change from red to bright white. The CONSTABLE *throws the* DOLL *and* CHRISTIE *off of him, and rises to make his protest.*

CONSTABLE. That's not love.

INSPECTOR. Is to him.

CONSTABLE. Dead bodies?

CHRISTIE *takes up the* DOLL, *and carries her on his knees to the other side of the garden, and buries her as best he can in the newspaper.*

CHRISTIE. Took her out the back. Wrapped her up in old newspaper. Buried her.

CONSTABLE. Love's the bleeding moon. And bleeding doves cooing. And bleeding Frank Sinatra crooning. And holding hands. And a lovely bunch of roses from the one whom you admire. And a nice church ceremony, and the Mrs tearful eyed at the photograph. We went to Clacton for our honeymoon, my wife and me. The sea was gentle as a baby. The moon was smoochy yellow. That were love. Not a corpse, in a dirty garden.

During his speech, the INSPECTOR *sets the chair in the centre of the garden, stands on it, and rigs a noose up through the rafters.*

INSPECTOR. One bloke we nicked, had a thing about handbags. Couldn't keep himself out of them. 'Nother bloke we nicked, had a thing about pussycats. The handbag man we got for shop lifting. The pussycat man we got for cruelty to animals. See Reg, you got to keep love in bounds. Else it gets criminal. And we can't have that, can we.

Standing on the chair, the INSPECTOR *bellows to all the audience.*

Society cannot allow the fucking of handbags. Pussycats. Dead women. What would happen if we all went right ahead, according to desire, fucking all? Bleeding anarchy Reg. Larceny, mutilation of animals, murder.

The police shout angrily at CHRISTIE, *who is still kneeling over the* DOLL's *grave.*

CONSTABLE. You filthy beast! You utter cad!

INSPECTOR. Bloody pervert!

CONSTABLE. Bloody pervert!

INSPECTOR. Go one better than us would you, eh? Eh? Defile English Womanhood?

CONSTABLE. Cast aspersions on my mother!

INSPECTOR. Cast aspersions would you!

The CONSTABLE, *all self control gone, grabs* CHRISTIE, *who's limp and barely whispers, and drags him up to the noose. The Police bang* CHRISTIE. CHRISTIE *falls into the paper, the noose still about his neck. A pause. The* INSPECTOR *steps down from the chair, straightens his uniform. Both policemen are shaken, shamefaced.*

INSPECTOR. That's that then.

CONSTABLE. Yes Sir.

INSPECTOR. Another crime solved.

CONSTABLE. A blow struck for married life.

INSPECTOR. Yes.

CONSTABLE. Yes.

The INSPECTOR *puts the chair upside down on the table, picks the table up, about to carry it off. He stops.*

INSPECTOR. Just . . . Clean up a bit. Someone else's garden now.

CONSTABLE. Sir.

INSPECTOR. Get on with it then.

CONSTABLE. Sir.

The CONSTABLE *covers the body of* CHRISTIE *with the spade, slowly, smoothes the surface of the paper down, then looks around the audience, shamefaced, and slips away. End play.*

MAGNIFICENCE

To Max

Sink into the mire
Embrace the butcher
But change the world.

Brecht: *Die Massnahme*

MAGNIFICENCE was first performed at the Royal Court Theatre, London, on 28 June 1973 with the following cast:

Will	Michael Kitchen
Jed	Kenneth Cranham
Mary	Carole Hayman
Veronica	Dinah Stabb
Cliff	Peter Postlethwaite
Constable	James Aubrey
Slaughter	Leonard Fenton
Alice	Geoffrey Chater
Babs	Robert Eddison
Old Man/Lenin	Nikolaj Ryjtkov

Directed by Max Stafford-Clark
Designed by William Dudley
Lighting by Andy Phillips

Scene One

A dirty room empty but for a mound of old newspapers in the corner. Silence. Then a bang on the door. Voices off.

WILL. Bust in. Just like that.

MARY. What a smell.

JED. Let's get the stuff.

MARY. That on the stair, that a dead . . . Something?

    A pause.

JED. Just a bit o' rag, love.

CLIFF. Let's get the gear in.

WILL. I want a peep upstairs.

CLIFF. Give me a hand, girls.

VERONICA. Right.

    WILL's *footsteps coming up the stairs.*

JED. Dump the stuff in the hall.

    The door tried. It won't open. The door tried more violently.

WILL. Jed?

JED. What?

WILL. Door's stuck.

    The door banged. JED's *footsteps coming up the stairs.*

JED. Can't be.

WILL. Is.

    The door banged.

JED. But we looked the place over twenty-four hours ago.

WILL. The door is stuck.

    The door banged, hard.

JED. Don't do that!

WILL. Gotta bash it down, Jed.

JED. Can't you fiddle it? Like the front door?

WILL. Dead lock, in't it. Such locks are simple. Many an old key will flip 'em. Got an old key on you?

JED. No.

WILL. No. So.

The door banged.

JED. Don't do that!

CLIFF. What's up?

JED. Door's stuck.

CLIFF. But we looked the place over twenty-four hours ago.

WILL. Don't think the landlord's been round? Barred it up inside?

JED. Why should he?

WILL. Could have got wind. Of us.

JED. What barred a door, first floor, on the inside?

The door banged.

WILL. That's barred.

JED. Don't do that.

WILL. Barred. Vast iron impediments. Bet the landlord's in there crouched in the middle o' the room with a shot gun.

VERONICA. What's up?

CLIFF. Door's stuck.

VERONICA. Wonderful.

The door banged.

JED. No unnecessary damage.

WILL. Theft Act 1968. Breaking and entering no offence if no larcency intended. Therefore . . .

The door banged. A pause.

Oh, look the doorknob's fallen off.

JED. I love you, you silly little man but I wish you wouldn't piss about . . . Don't poke it through!

The doorknob falls onto the stage. A pause.

You poked it through.

WILL. Well. That's the revolution. No doorknob to get in and start it.

JED. We'll go up through the window.

MARY. What you doin'?

JED. We're going up through the window.

VERONICA. What about the gear?

JED. Up through the window.

WILL. There won't be a ladder. Too much to ask of the world for there to be a ladder.

Footsteps going down the stairs. Silence. Then their voices off, from the back.

Well, what d'you know, a ladder. Bet its rungs are rotten!

The end of a ladder appears, waving around outside the window. It crashes through the window. Real glass. A pause.

I broke the window pane.

CLIFF. Malicious damage, Jed.

JED. I know. I know.

A pause. Then WILL's head appears outside the window.

MARY. How's it look?

WILL. Like a dirty room. Yeh a dirty room. But to me, the promised land. All manner o' birds and beasts at play in the revolutionary pastures.

JED. Hurry up, Will. There's two old ladies over the street, staring at us.

WILL. Hand the old dears a few pamphlets.

JED. Christ, Will, what's the matter?

WILL. Glass! (*He works.*) 'Ang on.

He clears the frame and climbs in. The others follow. VERONICA, MARY who's pregnant, CLIFF and JED. As long as this takes, in silence. They're in. JED puts his arm round MARY. VERONICA stands close to CLIFF. They stand there, embarrassed.

JED. Well. (*A pause.*) Here we are.

MARY. Yeh.

WILL. Yeh. Yes.

> MARY *and* WILL *giggle. A pause.*

VERONICA. And what happens now?

WILL. We occupy the place.

> *A pause.*

CLIFF. Funny feeling.

> WILL *takes out a paint spray. He writes ANARCHY FARM on the wall.*

WILL. That about sums it up.

MARY. Let's put our names on.

> WILL *hands MARY the paint spray. They write their Christian names on the wall, all except VERONICA.*

VERONICA. What about the old ladies?

WILL. Didn't you give 'em the pamphlets?

> *During* VERONICA's *speech*, CLIFF *looks at the door.*

JED. Where's the list, love?

MARY. In the bag.

> JED *takes a clipboard out of one of the bags. He goes down the list carefully.*

VERONICA. The first old lady took the second old lady's pamphlet. The first old lady then tore up her pamphlet and the second old lady's pamphlet, and threw the pieces to the pavement. The second old lady then looked distressed, tut tutted, and bent with difficulty to pick up the pieces of paper. All the pieces picked up, she walked briskly down the street to put them in a litter bin by a postbox. The first old lady followed, talking. And they'll be back.

> WILL *offers* VERONICA *the paint spray. She half turns away.*

WILL. Come on. A celebratory gesture?

> VERONICA *shrugs, takes the paint spray and writes her name. MARY has taken a flash-light polaroid from her bag. WILL strikes a pose. She takes a flash picture of the wall, and WILL and VERONICA before it.*

Base camp. The journey to the Pole begins.

CLIFF has given up the door. It's still closed. He looks out the window.

CLIFF. Our ladies are back.

JED. Barricade the front door, eh Cliff?

CLIFF. Right.

CLIFF climbs out the window. WILL goes through the lavatory door.

JED. I'll move the stuff into the front garden. Will?

WILL (*off*). In the john.

JED. I'll hand the stuff into you.

WILL. 'Wonderful'.

The sound of CLIFF barricading the front door, heard off. VERONICA takes out a cigarette and lights it. MARY takes a rolled-up banner out of her bag.

MARY. Take 'old, V.

VERONICA. What's that?

MARY. Banner.

VERONICA. Didn't know anything about a banner.

MARY. Take 'old, then.

They begin to unfurl the banner, face down on the floor. Don't let the audience see the slogan yet.

VERONICA. You make this thing, Mary?

MARY. Yeh.

VERONICA. What are we going to do with it?

MARY. 'Ang it out the window.

VERONICA. 'For all the World to see'?

MARY. That's the idea.

VERONICA. Why?

MARY. Why? (*Uncertain.*) To let 'em all know we're 'ere.

VERONICA. Fond of banners are you? (*A gesture at the walls.*) Graffiti?

MARY. We did a project at Art College on loo scribblers.

VERONICA. On what?

MARY. In public lavatories.

VERONICA. Good God.

MARY. Euston Station Ladies was the best.

VERONICA. I know the visual arts are in deep trouble, but that's ridiculous.

MARY. Not really. You find all kind a' agonies, scrawled out on walls.

The banner is now unfurled.

Oh, dear it's crinkly. Should 'ave ironed it 'fore we left. (*She moves along, tugging it top to bottom.*) Help then, V.

VERONICA *shrugs, kneels and helps to stretch the banner. CLIFF can be still heard off, nailing up the front door. VERONICA and MARY finish stretching the banner, then go to either end and lift it. The audience see the slogan for the first time. It reads: WE ARE THE WRITING ON YOUR WALL. WILL comes out of the lavatory.*

WILL. A very uplifting message.

VERONICA. Bit childish.

WILL. Why?

VERONICA. For one thing, it's not *on* a wall.

WILL. A bourgeois quibble, ducks.

VERONICA. How are you going to hang it up?

MARY. Outside.(*She shrugs.*) Out the window.

VERONICA. But it's huge. It'll sag.

VERONICA *droops the banner.*

WILL. It won't. It'll . . . (*A vague gesture.*) Blow about.

VERONICA. No one will read it. Just a rag, hanging there in the street. It's utterly pathetic.

JED *appears at the window, one arm round a cardboard box.*

WILL. Doing our 'umble best, Ma'am, to wreck Society.

JED. Would the wrecker of Society take hold of a box of baked beans?

WILL *goes at once to the window and takes the box.*
Throughout the following passage JED *is continually*
appearing at the window with supplies and handing them to
WILL. *They spread out over the floor.*

MARY. V, tight again.

They hold the banner tight.

Yeh, the W's wonky. (*She thinks. A pause.*) Down, please.

VERONICA *and* MARY *lower the banner onto the floor.*
MARY *kneels, takes out sewing things from her bag and sews*
the 'W'. VERONICA *lights a cigarette, annoyed. A pause.*

Made the letters out o' old material my Mum 'ad. Blackout,
she said. But my Mum says any bit o' old material in the 'ouse
was blackout.

'That was blackout,' she says, and nods. As if saying . . .
'That'll teach you.'

I hope the black won't run. Do you think it'll run?

VERONICA. Probably. Almost certainly. (*She turns away.*) One
more botched good intention, drooping in the rain.

MARY. A searchlight would be great.

VERONICA. A what?

MARY. Searchlight.

WILL. With slides?

MARY. Yeh, messages. On the 'ouses. We'd shine 'em out the
window, at night.

WILL. Great.

VERONICA. Are you serious?

MARY. And on the clouds. They used to do that in the thirties.
Flash up an advert at night. Suddenly all over the sky . . .
Wright's Coal Tar Soap, or something.

VERONICA. What messages?

MARY. You what?

VERONICA. What messages shall we . . . Flash upon the night
sky?

WILL. Something simple. (*Grandly.*) 'Seize The Weapons of
Happiness.' (*Change.*) 'Ere that's not bad. Where's the aerosol?

WILL *takes the paint spray from* VERONICA *and writes WEAPONS OF HAPPINESS on the wall.*

VERONICA. All right. All right. What are they?

A pause. WILL *writing.*

'The Weapons Of Happiness.' What are they?

WILL. 'Alf a brick through a window?

VERONICA. Is that all we have to offer?

WILL. If that is all there is to 'and, yeh . . . Bit of blackout . . . Tin of baked beans . . . Just what's to hand, and simple.

VERONICA. There is nothing simple in this brutal world, only the simple-minded.

WILL (*to* MARY). She mean me?

MARY. Yeh.

WILL *and* MARY *laugh.*

VERONICA. Will, I know I've come late to the group. And I wasn't with you when you argued out what to do. But don't let's write messages and slogans. If we've got to scrawl over everything, let's at least scrawl how it is. Like . . . (*She thinks.*) Like . . . After all the official figures, sums, percentages and lies there are . . . (*Writing 1,000,000 on the wall.*)

MARY and WILL. Ohh . . . Ohh . . . Ohh . . .

VERONICA. Homeless in the city. And where are they? Why aren't there tents all over Hyde Park? Human foxholes in Kensington Gardens? But the people are there, poked in somewhere. Like trying to hide litter, ramming it into the cracks in the walls. Ramming people, into cracks in the walls.

WILL. I know that. We know that. That is what we are here for. So what's the big bone of contention, lady?

VERONICA. That we've got to be clear. Not simple-minded. Clear about how it is.

WILL. Doing the best we can. Saying . . . Look at this place. Empty. And how many other places, good houses, all over the city . . . Empty.

VERONICA. But we've got to be . . . (*A short pause.*) I don't know.

Real! Real to the old ladies outside. So we can say . . . Look, it's real. The decay. The vicious city. The brutal squandering. It's real, here . . . (*She stamps.*) Down your street. Dear God it matters.

WILL. I know it matters.

VERONICA. Then don't festoon it with half-baked idiocies. (*She jerks the banner with her foot, viciously.*)

MARY. Careful! You lost my needle.

WILL. Now you gone and lost this little girl's needle.

JED at the window. The banging off, stops.

JED. What's going on?

MARY. I lost my needle.

VERONICA. Jed. They'll look at this, ordinary people will look at this and say 'How stupid'.

WILL. It makes me feel good.

JED. It makes him feel good.

VERONICA. It'll make them feel sick.

WILL. If they're gonna spew, they're gonna spew.

VERONICA. I don't think we should put it up. We've got to be . . . Responsible.

WILL. They're gonna spew.

MARY finds the needle.

MARY. *There* it is.

VERONICA. Jed?

A pause. He shrugs.

JED. Put it up?

He goes back down the ladder, out of sight.

VERONICA. You want ordinary people to look at us in here and put it all down to a dose of clap and the Welfare State?

CLIFF climbs in through the window. He is carrying pieces of wood, a bag of nails and a hammer.

WILL. I don't mind being called a clapped-out milksop. There are worse things in this big, beautiful world to be called.

CLIFF. I've nailed up the front door.

He kneels before the door, carefully measuring the bit of wood. JED appears at the window.

JED. Mary, love, make some tea. The Calor gaz-stove is in the black box.

MARY. I know I packed it.

JED. Don't forget to measure out the water in cups.

MARY. I won't. (*She's cross.*)

JED. You all right?

MARY. Yeh.

JED stares at her then goes down the ladder again. A pause. VERONICA lights another cigarette. MARY sewing the 'W'. CLIFF sizing up the door. WILL takes two loads from JED, and begins to move them around. By now there are boxes and equipment out over the floor. MARY finishes sewing.

Done.

A pause. MARY gets the stove working, puts on a kettle.

WILL. Can tell you work for the BBC, 'cos of the way you go on about ordinary people.

CLIFF. Give over, Will.

WILL. No I'm genuinely interested. We're going to see a lot of each other's knickers in the next few days. (*He smiles at VERONICA.*)

CLIFF. Just let's have a little . . . (*A gesture, calming down.*)

WILL. Why not? (*Imitates the gesture. A pause. Then WILL pipes up nonetheless.*) You TV skulls! Like a plague of locusts upon every hopeless good cause in sight. You only got to begin a hopeless good cause, and there you are, a dark cloud upon the horizon and soon on the poor hopeless do-gooder. Chomp chomp. Adventure playgrounds, free contraceptive clinics, schoolroom abortion service, chomp chomp. Hells Angels last week, geriatric wards next. And in between, why, the English Revolution, ta-rum-ta-ta. I've had you lot, I've had you sick. Marxist are you? Are you? Eh? Eh? Lot o' Marxists in the BBC I'm told. Turning out fascist crap. Argue it's the dialectic lets 'em. That dialectically straight up, it is a very good thing, straight up year in year out to turn out fascist crap. I don't think, on the whole, they are very sincere people. You can tell, the way they go on about pollution. Running through the electric corridors, pulling their hair out with worry 'bout pollution. I am probably the only man in England who is in favour of pollution. I think it's a very good idea indeed. All that lovely filth. (*He grins.*) Am I riling you? What's the thing you worked on last?

VERONICA. I worked on a documentary, about lead content, in the blood of Lancashire children.

WILL. Having heavy babies up there, are they?

CLIFF *begins to batten up the door.*

VERONICA. For Godsake.

WILL. I am riling you.

VERONICA. No, but I think I'm going to kill you. You know your trouble?

WILL. No.

VERONICA. Never mind.

WILL. Come on.

VERONICA. No.

WILL. Don't be shy. I've been abused by all kinds of people in my time. Policemen. Little children. Trotskyists. All have heaped abuse on me.

VERONICA. No.

WILL. I am so frightened of hard ladies.

VERONICA. I'm frightened of soft men.

WILL. How much do you make a year?

VERONICA. Piss off. (*She looks at* CLIFF.)

WILL. That much eh? Had an argument with Cliff 'bout you coming along. Media bitch I said. Mess us up. Get us all on the box, dirty squatters, 'ow we ate off the floorboards. Had group sex 'anging from the light fixtures.

JED *appears at the window, not carrying anything. He climbs in.*

Eh, Jed, we checked there's no electric?

JED. Switch a light on and see.

WILL. No bulb.

CLIFF. Bound to be off, in't it? (*Finishes battening the door.*)

WILL (*to* (VERONICA). Got time off have you? You come an-occupyin' with us?

VERONICA. Two weeks' holiday.

WILL. What if we're stuck in here longer than that?

> JED *stops listening to* WILL *and* VERONICA, *and begins to sort out the supplies. A pause.*

VERONICA. I'll resign.

WILL. Ah.

VERONICA. What does that mean?

WILL. Just 'ah'.

CLIFF. Two doors they'll bash in.

WILL. Great. If you're goin' to be done by due process, may as well get well and truly done.

> VERONICA *stares at* CLIFF. *He smiles.*

Funny. Plonkin' yourself down in London Town. Wanting all the big boots to come running. (WILL *suddenly goes down on all fours, lays an ear to the ground.*) On there, please, Mr Bailiff. Make the blood flow please, Mr Bigboot. (*He comes out of that. And starts to help* JED.)

VERONICA. Can't we make the door harder to 'Bash in'?

CLIFF. They'll have trouble with that.

WILL. Yeh, splinter nicely.

VERONICA. But thicker wood. And screws. We could stop them.

CLIFF. Why . . . ?

WILL. . . . Why?

CLIFF. Why should we?

> *A pause.* VERONICA *about to say something fierce, but she shrugs.*

VERONICA. For the hell of it?

WILL. Ah now that's more like it. Pricks and kicks I can understand.

From here CLIFF *and* VERONICA *join* WILL *and* JED *in sorting the supplies out. An effect: the supplies have come through the window, and are all about the floor.* JED *begins to sort them out.* WILL *joins them. Then suddenly they are all sorting the things out. The room becomes transformed into an orderly, indoor camp. Space out the following exchanges while this is being done.*

JED. V, tin of baked beans. (*He throws the tin to* VERONICA *who catches it.*)

WILL. With little Frankfurters I hope. They are my favourite.

A pause.

VERONICA. One packet of crisps.

WILL. With or without added protein?

VERONICA. With.

In the following passage JED *is taking baked bean tins from a box tossing them to* CLIFF *who tosses them to* MARY. *Suddenly tins are flying through the air and they're all laughing.*

Condensed milk.

JED. Baked beans.

·VERONICA. Corned beef.

JED. Baked beans.

VERONICA. Irish stew.

ALL. Baked beans.

VERONICA. Sardines.

ALL. Baked beans.

VERONICA. Tuna fish.

ALL. Baked beans.

VERONICA. Garden peas.

ALL. Baked beans.

VERONICA. Mixed veg.

ALL. Baked beans.

VERONICA. Spaghetti rings.

ALL. Baked beans.

VERONICA. New potatoes.

ALL. Baked beans.

VERONICA. Why so many baked beans?

WILL. Me. I love 'em.

Handfuls of tins . . .

MARY. What I thought was, food should be cold. Or just heated on the stove without water. Keep water for fresh drinking, you see.

VERONICA. Soup. (*She looks at a label.*) Asparagus.

A pause. MARY with a big polythene bag. It chinks.

MARY. Knives and forks in here.

WILL. The booze in here.

Five cartons, with bottles in. WILL quickly taking all the bottles out, arranging them in a square on the floor.

MARY. Don't do that, Will.

WILL. What?

MARY. Keep the bottles in the boxes.

WILL. But it's nice to see what we've got. Spread out. 'Fore we cross the Gobi Desert.

MARY shrugs. A pause.

VERONICA. Marmite. Strawberry jam. Apricot jam. What's this?

MARY. Rags. My Mum's got a thing about rags. If you've got to lock yourself up for weeks on end she said, you've got to have lots of rags.

VERONICA. Wise lady.

MARY. She's a silly cow.

CLIFF. Only got the three lilos. We thought the girls'll have two, and we'll argue it out.

WILL. Fair enough.

MARY. 'Ere, Will, Jed, it's like when we were in France, with the tent.

WILL. The Gypsy Life. Stars, cold water, taken short in the Camargue.

MARY. Better clear up now.

But she doesn't move, looking at the supplies now arranged.
They all look except for CLIFF, who keeps pumping a lilo.
CLIFF pumps a few more times, then stops, realizing they're
all looking at the supplies. A long pause.

Got to live off that for the next . . . (*She shrugs.*) Don't look
much, does it. (*A pause. Then, simply:*) Like when I was a kid.
We hid in a tree house. You know, few old planks, nailed up
together, up in a tree. On the Common. Got smashed up, o'
course. Doll's house. And tough kids came running from all
over, to smash it up. But we hid up there for a while. And
dogs came up, at the foot o' the tree, an' barked at us.
We planned to live up there forever.

Who's gonna chuck the ladder away?

They look at each other. Suddenly festive.

CLIFF. Christ!

JED. Forgot that.

He puts his arm round MARY.

WILL. Who's going to do the honours?

They look at JED.

JED. V?

VERONICA *shrugs, and goes and throws the ladder down.*

VERONICA. Isolation.

A rumbling sound. An OLD MAN rises from the pile of papers
in the corner. He is dressed in the heavy, dirty clothes of a
street dweller. He limps to the door, disregarding them. He
takes out a key but is at a loss to find the door nailed up. He
gestures hopelessly. Hangs his head and thinks. Rubs his hands
on his coat. Then he turns and shambles across the stage,
going through the door to the lavatory. All looking after him.
A short silence. The light down fast.

Scene Two

The street outside the house is painted on a drop cloth. The chanting is heard from behind the cloth. A young CONSTABLE and MR SLAUGHTER, a heavy man in his late forties, step onto the stage. They look up. For all his aggression MR SLAUGHTER shows a nervousness chewing little mints.

JED. At the sign of the Third World War.

ALL. At the sign of the Third World War, the whole structure of imperialism will collapse.

MARY. The future is bright.

ALL. The world is progressing, the future is bright.

MARY. In the end.

ALL. In the end, it is the people who are really powerful.

JED. The people.

ALL. And the people alone.

MARY. A force so swift and violent.

ALL. The people, a force so swift and violent. Will smash all the trammels that bind them.

JED. The reactionaries.

ALL. Warlords, corrupt officials, local tyrants, evil gentry. They are blind and all is dark before them.

CONSTABLE. They're still up there, Mr Slaughter. Hymn singing.

SLAUGHTER. That what you call it?

CONSTABLE. Like a churchload of old women, singing 'All Things Bright and Beautiful'. May scare you rotten, but it don't mean anything.

SLAUGHTER. I don't see what's so scary in a church congregation.

CONSTABLE. All fanaticism, in't it.

SLAUGHTER. Is it indeed.

CONSTABLE. The beast in man.

SLAUGHTER. I beg your pardon?

CONSTABLE. The beast.

SLAUGHTER. Ah yes.

A pause.

CONSTABLE. You see, man's intelligence has grown so . . . Very big that he can no longer contain his animal nature. Which he retains. And that accounts for wars, criminal acts, and all other irrational behaviour.

Though there is another theory.

SLAUGHTER. Oh dear.

A pause.

Sleepy-bys. (*Beats his gloved hands together, blows in them.*)

CONSTABLE. They on the mains up there? Got power for heating?

SLAUGHTER. Nope.

CONSTABLE. Must be very cold for them.

SLAUGHTER. I hope so. Water's cut off too. The loo must be stinking something terrible by now.

I hope.

The CONSTABLE, *embarrassed.*

CONSTABLE. Yes?

A pause.

Yes, we're all Martians.

SLAUGHTER. ?

A pause.

I'm sorry I thought you said we are all Martians.

CONSTABLE. That's the theory.

SLAUGHTER. Ah.

A pause.

CONSTABLE. A Russian scientist believes in it.

SLAUGHTER. Oh.

CONSTABLE. Millions of years ago, Martians landed on earth. And found apes. They doctored the apes, and made 'em think.

SLAUGHTER. Why?

CONSTABLE. What?

SLAUGHTER. Why?

CONSTABLE. Well . . . As an experiment.

SLAUGHTER. Pretty cruel.

CONSTABLE. Martians have got a higher sense of morality than us.

SLAUGHTER. They must have.

CONSTABLE. Stuck bits of their own minds in the poor apes' heads. And those apes, they're us.

A pause. SLAUGHTER *frowns.*

From time to time. Martians come down to see how we're getting on. Like Jesus.

SLAUGHTER. Jesus was . . . One of 'em, then?

CONSTABLE. Stands to reason. How else did he ascend into Heaven?

SLAUGHTER. You tell me.

CONSTABLE. Anti-gravity drive.

SLAUGHTER. That would explain it.

CONSTABLE. They have to come down every so often, 'cos the experiment's gone wrong you see. We've run amock. Laboratory animals run amock, that's us.

SLAUGHTER. What a load of cock.

CONSTABLE. Yeh. A Russian scientist believes in it though.

SLAUGHTER. The Force has become highly philosophical since my day.

CONSTABLE. It's our Chief Constable. He's got a degree from Cambridge.

SLAUGHTER. When I was a copper, they were all leftovers from the British Raj. Wonderful men.

CONSTABLE. He's keen on us getting O Levels. I got Art. Failed English Language, though.

SLAUGHTER. Thought of leaving?

CONSTABLE. The Force?

SLAUGHTER. Made a packet since I did.

CONSTABLE. Did think of being a Security Guard. But I didn't like the uniform.

SLAUGHTER. How about my line?

CONSTABLE. I don't think I'd like being a freelance Bailiff.

SLAUGHTER. Why not? It's a healthy life. Booked a room in the Athens Hilton for our holidays this year.

CONSTABLE. That is healthy. I suppose.

SLAUGHTER. Better than piles from riding wet bicycles. That'll be your lot, my son.

CONSTABLE. We got motorbikes now. Scotts. Lovely little jobs. Watercooled, horizontally opposed cylinders, four stroke, shaft driven . . .

SLAUGHTER. Presumably rain still falls upon the saddle leather?

CONSTABLE. Trouble is, no offence, Mr Slaughter . . .

SLAUGHTER. None will be taken.

CONSTABLE. What you do is barely legal.

A pause.

Mr Slaughter?

A pause.

You all right?

SLAUGHTER. Sorry, lad. It's just that I'm getting paranoid these days.

CONSTABLE. Ah.

SLAUGHTER. What do you mean by 'ah'? What do you mean by 'ah'?

CONSTABLE. Nothing, Mr Slaughter.

SLAUGHTER. 'Scuse me just one minute. Let me swallow three times.

CONSTABLE. Sure. G . . . Go ahead.

A pause.

SLAUGHTER. That's better. I've not been the same since that telly crew came round.

CONSTABLE. World In Action.

SLAUGHTER. You saw 'em crucify me, did you?

CONSTABLE. I thought it was a very fair programme.

SLAUGHTER. *Fair?*

CONSTABLE. Camera work was a bit arty.

SLAUGHTER. One.

> *A pause.*
>
> Two.
>
> *A pause.*
>
> Three.
>
> *A pause.*
>
> Learnt that trick in Kenya. Keep down your fear o' Mau Mau.

CONSTABLE. Got a bit lost with the statistics.

SLAUGHTER. It was all a grotesque distortion. For a start, I'd been up all night and hadn't shaved. No wonder I looked a villain. Also, it was totally untrue.

CONSTABLE. What, all of it?

SLAUGHTER. Every close up, hazy zoom in lens whatnot.

CONSTABLE. You never put shit through that old lady's letter box, then?

SLAUGHTER. Never.

CONSTABLE. Abduct her pussycat? Present her with an invalid eviction notice?

SLAUGHTER. You been reading the Sunday Times, haven't you?

CONSTABLE. The Chief Constable likes us to keep abreast intellectually.

SLAUGHTER. That old lady. See, she had five hundred quid from the landlord to move. It was a straightforward deal. She was the only one left in the property. Well, he wanted her out, to redevelop. All was above-board. He paid her to move, found her another place. True she lived in Chalk Farm and the new place was a ropey basement in Brixton . . . But she agreed. Come the day vacancy was due to fall. Fall upon, if you get my meaning . . .

CONSTABLE. Quite. Judgement Day.

SLAUGHTER. Yeh, time to chuck the old bag out. And what she do? Protest innocence. Deny the payment was made. Telephone Sunday papers and television news desks. I would not have thought a seventy-five-year-old spinster had it in her.

CONSTABLE. Pity she died.

A pause.

SLAUGHTER. One.

A pause.

Two.

A pause.

Three.

I dunno.

O.K. O.K. I was leaning upon a poor old girl, oh yes, and my mother's hair too is shining white.

But I dunno. That affray with the old lady and the pussycat cost me dear. Thirty families I had leaned on before her. At two thousand pounds a go.

CONSTABLE. Two thousand?

SLAUGHTER. Plus perks.

CONSTABLE. Dear me.

SLAUGHTER. What's the matter?

CONSTABLE. Nothing.

SLAUGHTER. I know you think I am corrupt.

CONSTABLE. No I don't . . .

SLAUGHTER. Developers buy some clapped-out two-storey pile. Ten thousand, two years back. Chuck out whoever may be living on the rat-infested floors. And today, auction in a flash West End Hotel . . .

CONSTABLE. A lot o' money?

SLAUGHTER. Thirty thousand. Maybe in a year's time, forty thousand. Well, they can spread a few quid my way.

CONSTABLE. I feel . . .

SLAUGHTER. Heady at the raz-ma-taz of it? The money pouring down the bomb-damaged walls? The gold-plated slates gleaming on the leaky roofs?

CONSTABLE. Something like that.

SLAUGHTER. Still I did make a boo-boo with the old lady
and the pussy what's it. I can't say 'pussycat' again or I'll have
to swallow.

CONSTABLE. What exactly . . . Did go wrong there?

SLAUGHTER. Sentiment. Female, white-haired white-skinned
and a lover of . . . Furry animals. (*He swallows.*)

CONSTABLE. What were the other thirty families you evicted?

SLAUGHTER. Pakis, that kind of thing.

The CONSTABLE *sniffs.*

You sniff at me?

CONSTABLE. No, no, Mr Slaughter.

A pause. They're looking up.

SLAUGHTER. I dunno.

A pause.

I just do not know.

A pause.

I'm getting old. Can't see the world in black and white no
more.

A pause.

According to my old Dad, the great enemy was Bertrand
Russell. He'd rage on for hours, 'bout how Bertrand Russell
was putting round ideas of free love on the order of Moscow.

When was that. Before the War? First or Second? The world
was simple then. Clear who you had to hate and bash.
Bertrand Russell and the commies.

A pause.

My Dad was a copper. Visions open before me, that my life
has been ruined by that old man, my father. Still got a photo
at home, of me on my fifth birthday. Dressed up in his helmet
down to my chin, truncheon in my puny hand. (*Shades his
eyes with one hand, mimes holding a truncheon in the other.*)
Don't shuffle, Constable.

CONSTABLE. Sorry, Sir. I mean, Mr Slaughter.

SLAUGHTER. Am I becoming maudlin?

CONSTABLE. Oh . . . No, not really.

SLAUGHTER. Sorry, Lad. Don't blame you. Who wants to love an ageing Bailiff on the slide?

CONSTABLE. See it from my point of view, Mr Slaughter. We are both the law, and must act in concert. But you are a private sector, I am a public sector. Er . . . (*Looks about. Touches his nose, meaning 'savvy'.*)

SLAUGHTER. Oh, I am embarrassing you.

CONSTABLE. I'm very . . . Flattered to talk to you.

SLAUGHTER. You're nervous I'm going to make another boo-boo.

CONSTABLE. No, Mr Slaughter, please I don't want to offend.

SLAUGHTER. No offence.

CONSTABLE. I just don't want you to get out of hand. *Things* to get out of hand.

SLAUGHTER. Ah.

CONSTABLE. Have you been drinking?

A pause.

SLAUGHTER. Does it show?

CONSTABLE. Smell it from here. Sir.

SLAUGHTER. I've been sucking mints for the last half hour. (*A violent change.*) Buffoon. Sucking mints. I am a heavy man, why should I lick arses? They even have a laugh at me down at Shelter. 'Billy Boy's going in again,' they cry. And laugh. A bogey for do-gooders, that's me.

Well.

A pause.

Well.

A pause.

I tell you.

CONSTABLE (*scared*). What?

SLAUGHTER. I tell you, there is not a man alive I'd vote for.

CONSTABLE. No?

SLAUGHTER. Not a man alive. Fit to have my ballot slip.

CONSTABLE. Oh.

SLAUGHTER. They see me coming. A comedy routine. 'Here comes the Bailiff big and tall, to do us all no good at all.'

Alright! Alright!

But I tell you, I've got murder in my heart.

CONSTABLE. I believe you have, Mr Slaughter.

SLAUGHTER (*nods to himself*). Yes. That's a way of putting it. Murder. (*A pause. Suddenly he produces a court paper.*) Order issued for the eviction of that lot. Under the High Court Rule number one one three.

CONSTABLE. The old one one three, eh.

SLAUGHTER. The Bailiff's charter, mate. (*Fiercely.*) I am going to pull this off. One last stroke. Ousting our fervent friends up there. I am going to bust that lot, cleanly, utterly. A matter of wounded pride.

CONSTABLE. Like Achilles in his tent.

SLAUGHTER. What you bloody well say?

CONSTABLE. Nothing.

A pause.

Listen, dawn chorus.

SLAUGHTER *looks at the* CONSTABLE *with disgust. A pause. The* CONSTABLE, *nervously.*

Sending your boys in then?

SLAUGHTER. First light. 'Fore the shoppers are out. Providing the mood is right. And something tells me it's going to be.

CONSTABLE (*nervously*). I have been detailed, Mr Slaughter. No breach of the peace.

SLAUGHTER. Don't worry. I'm a professional. A good dustman. Just pick the bin up, and *bang*.

CONSTABLE. Oh. (*Frowns.*) Good.

Scene Three

The room. It is now in chaos. On the walls rows of polaroid photographs. Dawn light growing through the window, VERONICA is awake smoking. The OLD MAN, huddled in a blanket, crouches watching her cigarette. A pause.
    MARY *wakes up.*

MARY. Been awake long?

VERONICA. Yes.

MARY. We still got those codeine?

VERONICA. No. You all right?

MARY. Got a bit of a headache.

    A pause.

VERONICA. We had another visitor.

MARY. What?

    VERONICA *points to a turd lying on the stage.*

    Oh no. Not another turd.

VERONICA. It arrived at first light.

MARY. The paper boy again?

VERONICA. I heard him laugh as he ran away.

MARY. Little bleeder, I'd love to thump him.

VERONICA. He's getting sophisticated. Can't be easy to catapult dogshit through a broken window, and this is the third time he hasn't missed.

    How are you?

MARY. O.K. You?

VERONICA. It's the grot. The . . . Granular nastiness of it all. Got under my eyelids.

    She stubs her cigarette out. The OLD MAN scuttles forward, picks up the stub and scuttles back. VERONICA ignores him.

    Look at it. Liberation City.

MARY. Yeh. I dunno 'ow it gets so . . . Tumbled up. Spend most of the day cleanin'.

VERONICA. I've got so many blackheads my skin's beginning to creak.

MARY. Want me to pop 'em for you?

VERONICA. That would be kind.

MARY. Lie over then.

She lies over in MARY's *lap.*

VERONICA. In between thee shoulder blades.

OLD MAN. Fuggin'? Fuggin'? (*He makes a gesture of striking a light.*)

MARY. What's he want?

VERONICA. Ignore him.

OLD MAN. Fuggin'?

VERONICA. He just wants a light. We have this relationship. I sit there smoking through the small, mean hours. He glares from his mouldy blanket, not at my tits in the moonlight, but at the fag butts I stub on the floorboards. I'm glad we gave up trying to explain to him just what the fuck we're doing. We 'social activists' . . . We're just a passing phenomena, which leaves fag butts on the floor.

OLD MAN, *his match lighting gesture.*

OLD MAN. Fuggin'?

VERONICA. Free the land Mr! The social spaces Mr!

OLD MAN. Fuggin'?

VERONICA *throws a box of matches at the* OLD MAN. *He touches his forehead.*

VERONICA. Ow!

MARY. Sorry. Big one. Want a look?

MARY *shows* VERONICA *her thumbnail.*

VERONICA. Gosh.

MARY. Left a bit of a pit I'm afraid. (*Pause.*) You know what V?

VERONICA. What?

MARY. I like you.

VERONICA. How do you mean?

MARY (*laughs.*) That make your flesh crawl?

VERONICA. Yes. Sorry.

MARY. Big one coming up now.

VERONICA. Oh God . . .

MARY. Hold your breath . . . Pop.

A pause.

VERONICA. Didn't feel a thing.

A pause.

Mary, have you thought . . . You may have it here?

MARY. What?

VERONICA. The baby. Have you thought that it may . . . Come on while we're in this place?

MARY. I'm only six months. It's not even viable yet.

VERONICA. Viable?

MARY. Doctor's word. You're not viable 'til you're seven months. And if you lose your baby after six months, they call that an abortion. And if you lose it after seven months, they call that a miscarriage.

You ever thought of 'aving a baby, V?

VERONICA. I'm on the pill.

MARY. I went on the pill, but I got fat. And fed up. So Jed and I thought.

A pause.

VERONICA. It's just . . . Not the right time for it.

MARY. How d'you mean?

VERONICA. It seems more . . . (*Bitterly.*) Apt.

MARY. What, to be barren?

VERONICA. 'To be barren.'

MARY. Oh V.

VERONICA. Have I shocked you?

MARY. No . . .

A pause.

What, you mean 'cos of ecology?

VERONICA. God no.

MARY. I dunno. The Sahara Desert's gettin' bigger every year, you know. Then there's the bomb.

They laugh.

VERONICA. For Godsake.

A pause.

No. I can't express myself.

A pause.

I feel a daughter at my skirts would be . . . Obscene. It would be her happiness. I couldn't stand that. I can't bear the happiness of kids. Three years old, and everything new . . . And language just come . . . Voracious little animals, gobbling the World down. *This* world. It's obscene.

MARY. Crikey, V. You do think yourself into funny corners.

VERONICA. Yes I do. Don't I.

A pause.

I envy you Mary. The point is . . . It's easy for you. You just arrive at things naturally. Like when we came through that window ten days ago . . . You just came through that glass . . . Blithely.

And I envy you.

MARY (*annoyed*). Ta very much.

VERONICA. What's the matter?

MARY. You . . . Twist things up.

VERONICA *turns, and holds* MARY's *arms.*

VERONICA. I'm sorry, Mary . . .

MARY. I don't hate you. I just . . . Hate to hear you. Not what you say, but the sound of what you say. (*She tries a little laugh.*) I hate it.

VERONICA. Yes.

A pause.

Yes. 'The voice of my accursed, human education.'

JED *wakes up and sits up.* MARY *nods at the turd.*

JED. Oh no. Will!

A pause.

Will! Wake up.

WILL. Help! (*He wakes up.*) What? What?

JED. Turd. And it's your turn.

WILL *springs out of his sleeping bag.*

WILL. The world come to us again, 'as it?

MARY. I'd better put the kettle on.

MARY *gets up and puts the kettle on the camping stove.*
VERONICA *turns to* CLIFF.

VERONICA. Hey you.

CLIFF *turns over.*

They've formed a Committee of Public Safety and they're
shooting Members of Parliament in Trafalgar Square.

CLIFF *turns over.*

Oy Mister. Trotsky lives.

CLIFF *grunts. And suddenly wakes up.*

CLIFF. 'Morning.

VERONICA. Good morning.

CLIFF *wipes his eyes and sees the turd.*

CLIFF. Another . . .

VERONICA. Indeed.

CLIFF. His turn.

CLIFF *points at* WILL *and gets up.* VERONICA *gets up, and
scratches.*

VERONICA. Sure that was the last of the Calamine two days
ago?

MARY. Yeh. Sorry.

They brush their teeth around a saucepan. MARY *finishes,
then* VERONICA. JED *and* CLIFF *begin to shave.* WILL *hunts
for the dustpan and brush.*

VERONICA. Baby jerks?

MARY. O.K.

VERONICA. Got the book?

MARY *tosses a book to* VERONICA. *It's* The New Childbirth *by Erna Wright.* WILL *comes forward with a dustpan and brush and a scrap of newspaper.*

Ugh, the photos in this thing.

(*She reads.*) 'As the baby is born she turns slightly and is quite difficult to grasp because she is slippery.'

MARY. Lesson five. Page fifty-one.

VERONICA. Fifty-one. 'Sit on the floor tailor fashion.'

MARY *does.*

They say a cushion.

VERONICA *quickly gets a blanket and folds it for* MARY *who sits on it.*

'The exercise you are about to learn will help to increase the suppleness of the pelvic floor.'

MARY. Yeh.

VERONICA. 'It is really an exercise taught and practised by dancers. For our purpose though, it is done in reverse.'

MARY *less certain.*

MARY. Yeh.

WILL. The turd of their malcontent.

WILL *goes to the window with the turd in the dustpan. He's about to throw it out, but stops.*

They're there.

A pause.

They're all there.

At once JED, CLIFF *and* VERONICA *go to the window and look down into the street.* MARY *stays sitting tailor-fashion, staring at the* OLD MAN.

At last he lights the cigarette butt, and takes a drag. He stares at MARY. *Suddenly he offers her a drag.* MARY *shakes her head, shyly.*

A pause.

Then WILL *throws the turd out of the window, throws the dustpan down and smacks his hands.*

Turn the bugs over? Bug hunt eh? Come on, come on, let's stir up the little bleeders . . . (*He turns over the bedding violently.*) If it's the last thing I'm gonna do it's see one of 'em . . . There! There! No. (*He stops momentarily, waves his hand before his eyes.*) Flecks on the old cornea.

JED *and* CLIFF *go back to shaving.* MARY *pulls the book toward her.* WILL *turns over the bedding.*

MARY. Put the soles of yer feet together . . . (*She does so. Grasps her feet together with one hand and puts the other hand under her knee. She pushes her hand towards the floor with her leg and then brings the leg to its previous position with her hand. She reads aloud, carefully:*) 'The muscles on the outer side of the thigh are pulling against the muscles on the inner side, which are called the *abductors.*'

VERONICA. Stop it, stop it. Stop stop stop.

A pause. They look at her.

Oh God I want a bath.

A pause.

They're getting ready to bust their way in. Bust us. They're going to come through that door . . . And what are we doing? Nothing. What have we done? Nothing. Zero . . . Sat it out in a grubby room the grubby end of London, for what? Fag butts for him?

The OLD MAN *touches his forehead.*

OLD MAN. Fuggin'.

VERONICA (*near tears*). Liberation City? (*She draws back the tears.*) I loathe us. I loathe all the talks we had. That we'd really do it. Come down to the people whom it really hits . . . And do it for them. I loathe us, I loathe our stupid, puerile view of the World . . . That *we* have only to do it, that *we* have only to go puff, and the monster buildings will go splat . . . I loathe us, I loathe what we've descended to here . . . Our domesticity . . . Ten days with the fleas and the tin opener lost, never for once questioning . . . That we are in any way changing the bloody, bleeding ugly world . . . Direct action? For us it's come down to sitting on a stinking lavatory for

ten days . . . Why didn't we get the local people on our side?
Oh we bawled a few slogans at passers-by. Got the odd turd
back from the street, and philosophized there upon. But
'Mobilize the people?' We can't mobilize a tin opener . . .

WILL. Still lost, is it?

VERONICA (*at* WILL, *fiercely*). Not a tin opener, let alone real
people . . . Out there. (*Quietly*.) I think we're done for. I think
we're dead.

JED. What did you expect?

MARY. 'To make the muscles covering the *back* of the pelvis
more supple, push your buttocks out backwards — like a duck
lifting its tail.'

VERONICA. For Godsake Mary!

MARY. I don't know about you, but I'm pregnant. So piss off.
(MARY, *intent, on the book, sits back on her heels*.)

JED. I dunno. Maybe we should have come down here like a
carnival . . . Bonfires for the kids, landlords burning . . . I
dunno.

*At once there is a fearsome crackle of a loudspeaker from
outside, which doesn't work too well.*

SLAUGHTER'*s voice through it. The group move and sit
close together, during his speech.*

MICROPHONE. This . . . This is a Court Bailiff, authorized . . .
What? . . . Constable, this machine . . . What? Crackles don't
it, listen to it crackle . . .

A roar, he's blowing on the mike.

What? . . . I did blow on it . . . I'll blow on it again . . .

A roar. Silence. And the microphone comes on again.

Right you boys and girls in there . . . In that building . . . This
is a Court Bailiff, Bailiff of the Court . . . What the bloody hell
is the matter with this thing . . . Knob? What knob? . . .

The microphone gets louder . . . more frightening.

Right you boys and girls . . . Right! You are in unlawful
occupancy of private property . . . I am authorized to eject
you . . . Constable this instrument is right out of hand,
ramshackle electrical equipment getting in the way of a

job . . . It's going to go badly, I can feel it's going to go
badly . . .

The roar twice.

Now I am sending my boys up to you . . . Please co-operate
with them . . . Don't let's have any trouble, boys and girls,
eh? You have made your point . . . Whatever it may be . . .
But you have made your.

*A loud click. Silence. The group in the room have begun to
smile, then laugh together. The* OLD MAN *huddles, hiding his
face. A great blow, off . . . It's the Bailiff's men, coming
through the front door.*

VERONICA *chants from the* Thoughts of Mao. *Leafing back
and forth through the book. Each line increases their
hysterical laughter.*

VERONICA. We will be ruthless to our enemies!

A blow.

We must have power, and annihilate them!

A blow.

Not to have a correct political point of view is like having
no soul!

A blow.

The crimson path!

A blow.

Thousands upon thousands!

A blow.

Heroically laid down their lives for the people!

A blow.

March along the path, crimson with the blood!

A blow.

Do not be deluded!

A blow.

Do not be deluded!

A blow.

Do not be deluded by the outward strength of·the aggressors!

A blow. Laughter and tears. Tears.

Go to the masses!

A blow.

From the masses to the masses!

A blow.

Go to them! Help them!

A blow. A splintering. People blundering up the stair.

Help them to achieve liberation and happiness!

A blow on the door in the room. It flies open. SLAUGHTER walks in.

SLAUGHTER. Don't let's all get carried away.

JED points at SLAUGHTER, soundless with laughter. The CONSTABLE comes in. That's too much for JED.

Can I share . . . The joke?

A silence. At once the laughter leaves the actors. They wait until the theatre is silent. Then the CONSTABLE sees the Calor gaz-stove, with the soup cooking on it.

CONSTABLE. Better have that out. Fire hazard.

He kneels and turns the Calor gaz-stove off. From this action there springs the incident in which MARY loses her child. The CONSTABLE stands, and steps back into WILL. The CONSTABLE falters, and goes down on one knee. WILL kicks him once, and backs away with a curiously apologetic gesture. The CONSTABLE grabs WILL, and pulls him. WILL falls over MARY. SLAUGHTER kicks MARY not WILL. SLAUGHTER immediately realizes what he's done.

SLAUGHTER. No. No. No.

The actors freeze in a tableau. The lights change. Dark shadows from bright lights low across the tableau. An effect of a sudden negativing, and X-ray. The blows throughout JED's speech are made by the actors stamping and a drum offstage. JED speaks aside to the audience.

JED. And they came through.

A blow.

Oh did they all come through.

A blow.

Slaughter and his boys.

A blow.

The Bailiff and his boys, with their great big boots.

A blow.

With spite and relish, beyond the call of duty.

A blow.

They came through.

A blow.

And came through us.

A blow.

And bust us.

A blow.

Oh they broke us, broke us good.

A blow.

Our little Wendy House.

A blow.

Our little Wendy House of good intent.

A blow.

Trod on our toys.

A blow.

Trampled all over our model farm.

A blow.

All the toy animals, killed them. Smashed their tiny delicate bones.

A blow.

True story.

We took over an empty house. Talked of liberating it for the poor. We were innocents.

Bailiffs broke in, beat us up. My wife was with child. They booted her, my wife's beautiful baby bulging tummy, booted. She lost the child.

MARY *cries quietly then is silent.*

Lights going down. A spot on JED.

True story from London Town. I got nine months in prison, got hooked. Hooked up, strung up, all up, *right up there*. Speed. On speed. A dangerous and proscribed drug, Sir and Madam. To the scandal and enlightenment of lost souls, freely circulating in Her Majesty's prisons. The speedy brain rotter, activator of the dark, the mighty mover, the killer action.

A pause.

And nine a.m., one clear day . . . Came out the little prison door in the big prison door.

Released.

Honed down.

Pure.

Angry.

Blackout.

Interval.

Scene Four

A bare, bright stage. Dappled sunlight to one side. ALICE *there.*
He speaks aside.

ALICE. Early morning garden. Cambridge College. A lovely day.

*BABS comes on. He's an older man, in an academic gown. A
dark suit. He walks with a stick.*

BABS. Alice!

ALICE. Babs!

Shaking hands.

BABS. Nice of you to come up, Alice.

ALICE. Nice of you to have me come up, Babs. (*Aside.*)
Thinking, I wonder what the old man wants?

BABS (*aside*). Thinking, I piddle and he comes running. (*To*
ALICE.) Shall we walk?

They walk.

And what news from the throbbing heart of the national
groin, to torpedo my own metaphor?

ALICE. I'm sorry?

BABS. What's happening in the Cabinet these days?

ALICE. Oh tedium. No one talking to anyone else.

BABS. And our National Saviour?

ALICE. Full of beans for the job. His words.

BABS. Mmm . . .

A pause.

Effortless dignity, in a flurry.

ALICE. I'm sorry?

BABS. That's what the local papers said, when I lost my
constituency. 'He bowed out of public life with effortless
dignity, in a flurry of optimism for new horizons.'

ALICE. Babs, why did you want to see me?

BABS. All in good time all in good time, dear. Don't get fidgety.

(*Aside.*) Thinking, he's all shiny and bright! Either the aura of high office, or a sunlamp.

ALICE (*aside*). Thinking, he's playing the Elder Statesman out to grass disgracefully.

BABS (*aside*). Thinking, sunlamp, because his pores are standing out. Just like him to turn up, blazing away by artificial means.

ALICE (*aside*). Thinking, I hope the old man's not gone gaga. There's something bad with his eye, there, it's wandering. My mother's eye wandered, when she lost her mind. Oh God, what am I going to do if he's gone gaga?

BABS (*aside*). Thinking, and he was young and golden in the heyday of his youth. And once he deeply moved me. And now? Bloody breakfast cereal. Sunshine wrapper. Threepence off. Worthless gift inside. Still as the saying goes 'I did love her once.' And now must make some crass, appalling gesture. Last kiss, wave a hanky. In my cirumstances. (*To* ALICE.) Effortless dignity.

Actually I cried. I raged and screamed. Threw a terrible scene at the third recount. No, I did not go gentle into the House of Lords.

ALICE. The seat's back with us now.

BABS. And my nephew sitting on it. Utter nincompoop. In the eighteenth century, our family was prone to syphilis. Its effects appear to have popped up again in that poor boy.

ALICE. He's doing well on Ways and Means.

BABS. The firmament gasps.

A pause. ALICE *glances at his watch.*

ALICE. How do you like it at Corpus?

BABS. Like a rick in the rectum.

ALICE. I thought the academic life appealed.

BABS. As piles in the passage. (*He points.*) *That* is the new College building.

ALICE. Ah.

BABS. What do you make of it?

ALICE. Sub Le-Corbusier.

BABS. What?

ALICE. Ugly.

BABS. It's got a damn good laundry.

ALICE. Ah.

BABS. What?

ALICE. Nothing, nothing.

BABS. We had a survey of college laundry.

ALICE. That's . . . Intriguing.

BABS. Turned out ninety percent of undergraduates foul their sheets. The other ten percent don't sleep in sheets at all. Thought the least I could do was argue for a laundry. Free washing machine, free bleach. My legacy to Res Academia! A plentiful supply of chemicals, to eradicate young men's semen stains.

I hate the young men of the University. No grace. All contempt. Jargon spewers, or silent vacuous eyes. One, a jargon spewer, put me through an intelligence test. Do you know my mental age?

Eight and a half.

He showed me the calculations, at my mild protest. I couldn't understand them. Having a mental age of eight and a half . . .

Rest.

ALICE. Sorry?

BABS. Rest a moment.

BABS *leans on* ALICE's *arm*.

ALICE. I'm sorry to find you . . . Bitter.

BABS. I am bitter.

ALICE. You know, a great many look back to what you did.

BABS. Did?

ALICE. For the country.

BABS. That came out with a thunderous clap of insincerity.

ALICE. True though. You're . . . Sorely missed.

BABS. You trying to be sarky?

ALICE. We miss your steadying influence.

BABS. Oh do shut up! My flesh is crawling. I know the depths to which I have fallen.

BABS *walks on a little. Stops.*

I'm dying.

ALICE (*behind him*). I'm sorry?

BABS. Didn't you hear?

ALICE. Didn't quite catch . . . What you said.

BABS. Oh sod. Been looking forward to this moment for weeks. And I ballsed it up. Sod.

ALICE. I really didn't catch . . . Your remark.

BABS. I'm dying.

A pause.

ALICE. What . . .

BABS. What have I got?

ALICE. No, I mean . . .

A pause.

Oh God.

BABS. Absurdly gauche of me. Both the deed and the telling.

Had in the back of my mind, some great, dignified gesture.

Spend a pleasant day with you. Sunny morning on the backs. Lunch. Come evening, some gentle sunset scene. Some . . . Falling cadence.

Then I go and blurt it out in a fit of pique. Bet you didn't even realize I was piqued, just then. Well I was. And I blurted it out.

ALICE. Is . . . This definite?

BABS. I'm pregnant all right. For your peace of mind, the disease is disgusting.

ALICE. Is there anything I can do?

BABS. Spend the day with me.

ALICE. Yes.

BABS. Good.

ALICE *embarrassed, a slight cough.*

That's a nasty cough.

ALICE. Summer cold. Caught a chill at Maudy's last weekend . . .

BABS. You should wrap up well.

ALICE. Yes.

A pause.

BABS. Delicious!

ALICE. What?

BABS. The embarrassment. Ever since it got round the College that I was falling apart . . . Actually I put my condition round, left photocopies of my doctor's report in a few key places . . . Ever since, cavernous pauses have followed me. It's reached gigantic proportions in the Senior Common Room. Every remark, you can see the minds panicking — oh God, have I punned on his disease?

ALICE. You . . . Seem to be enjoying yourself.

BABS. On the contrary. I am full of fear, and loathing. (*Change.*) Right! River!

ALICE. What?

BABS. Punt!

ALICE. Ought you?

BABS. Don't be such an old woman. Come on!

He goes off, sprightly. For a moment ALICE hangs behind. Frowns, hand to the bridge of his nose. Then follows. A pause. They glide back onto the stage in a punt. ALICE poling. They have been drinking.

ALICE. Don't wobble!

BABS. Not me wobbling!

ALICE. You are wobbling!

BABS. *I am not wobbling!*

ALICE. Don't, just don't!

BABS. It's a question of balance, you fool!

ALICE. I know it's a question of balance!

BABS. Let me pole!

ALICE. Don't move!

BABS. Can't stand up. Hope my inner ear's not gone. Remember in the war, shell-shocked lads, falling, and lurching, endless retching. (*Points, suddenly.*) That a corpse in the river?

ALICE. Just an old tyre. (*Manipulating the punt at the front of the stage.*) I'll pull into the bank. (*He does so. Sits in the punt. A pause.*)

BABS. Alice.

A pause.

Are we drunk?

ALICE. Very.

BABS. That would explain it.

ALICE. What?

BABS. I suddenly had an overwhelming urge to join the Roman Catholic Church. One moment. I'll breathe regularly and the feeling will go.

A pause.

That's better. Avoid that, at all cost. Taken a terrible toll amongst my contemporaries, Catholicism. Many bright young things of the right have ended up old men, wetting themselves with the joy of redemption. Ex-communist poets go that way too, so I'm told. (*He hiccups.*) Oh dear. I'm in a terrible state. (*He takes out a handkerchief.*) Look I've dribbled. Hope to God there are no Maoist Undergraduates, lurking in the bushes. They're the worst you know, the Maoist Undergraduates. (*Stretches his eyes to slits.*) Jaundiced eye-balls. (*A pause. Sly.*) Get your phone call in?

ALICE. Phone call?

BABS. Put off your meeting this afternoon.

ALICE. Ah. Yes.

BABS. Ha!

ALICE. What's funny?

BABS. I do think you're almost there.

ALICE. And 'where' would that be?

BABS. Wishing that I would . . . (*A gesture.*) Plop.

ALICE. You're disgracefully drunk.

BABS. I'm dying.

ALICE. Cheers.

BABS. They will you know. Our monstrous observers hidden upon these banks. Steaming with indignation, watching their enemies at play. They will . . . (*A gesture.*) Inherit the earth.

ALICE. Improbable.

BABS. I wonder if it's really there.

ALICE. What?

BABS. China.

ALICE. I doubt it.

BABS. It is not the perfection of the idea I fear, but its imperfection.

A pause.

My all-purpose quotation on Marxism-Leninism.

ALICE. Rather fatuous.

BABS. Do you think so? Do you really think so?

ALICE. Yes.

BABS. Oh dear.

ALICE. I'm sorry.

BABS. No no.

A pause.

Key sentence of a speech I made to the United Nations in nineteen fifty-two actually. Rather thought it was what got me the job here. Not as rotund as Winnie's 'An iron curtain has rung down . . .' More abstract, wouldn't you say? Moral?

'Iron . . .' 'Rung'. 'Yron, rrung.' Where did the old bag get her lovely words from?

ALICE. Natural talent?

BABS. That, perhaps. And a profound contempt for the rest of us. The rhetorican's contempt for his listeners. A warping of meaning, even elementary gist, anything for that quiver, the rattle of a million tiny bones in a million inner ears . . . Got trouble in my inner ear, by the way. Keel over sometimes . . . described the sensation to a student of mine. 'Like' he said, 'a natural high'. Get the same effect if you hold your nose, tight, and blow . . .

A pause.

Go on.

A pause.

ALICE. What? (*He's not been listening.*)

BABS. Have a go.

ALICE. ?

BABS. With your nose.

ALICE. Oh?

BABS. Pinch both nostrils.

He does so. ALICE *follows.*

Now blow.

They blow.

Hard! Really hard! Pop your ears.

A long pause. Both blowing. ALICE *lets go,* BABS *lets go. A pause. They both suddenly lie back. A pause. From offstage, a languid musical scale on a xylophone. An area of the stage darkens a little. Pause.*

Corrupter of youth. In the latter days of his Cabinet career, he farted a great deal. It was the first shadow of the disease which killed him. The Cabinet Room was flooded with an odour of death, adjourning many a discussion in unseemly haste. With this eccentricity, he contributed a minor but consistent influence for the bad upon the many blunders made by the Government, of which he was a distinguished member.

A pause.

I'm speculating upon my Obituary in the Times.

Don't seem to be getting it quite right.

A pause.

Corrupter of youth.

A pause.

Um.

A pause.

Outrageous old queen, happily no longer with us.

A pause.

Um.

A pause.

What do they do with Ex-Cabinet Ministers, who are queer and
dead? There should be some . . . Splendid event, should there
not? Some massive ceremonial. A number of masturbatory
images rise up. Ten thousand working men, jeering sweetly . . .
The mind wanders . . . But the Ministry of Works would
foul it up. Terribly butch lot. Commit some grave error of
taste. Nude Guardsmen riding bareback . . . The mind wanders,
appalled.

*The xylophone scale. Another area of the stage darkens a
little. A pause.*

Alice?

He raises himself a little, looks at ALICE.

How did you get that absurd nickname? I remember. Some
bad joke about Wonderlands.

He lies back.

Ah Alice, fair Alice. Is that Elder Statesman hair real?

Peers forward.

Ha! Due for tinting the roots I see. No no, mustn't go on like
that. These may be my last moments, don't want to spend
them bitching. But I have, all day. Bitched. And I invited him
up, some . . . Wild notion of delivering my political testament,
and all I've done is bitch.

He lies back, looking at ALICE. *Airily, but with care.*

You came from the Army and Oxford. Credentials shining
like an angel. To London Clubs and your nineteen fifty-one
constituency, somewhere indeterminately the wrong side
of Leicester. A dull area, which you didn't see much. But
you were bright! The old Tory Guard looked at you, all
bright and in your early thirties. You caught their glance,
and greyed your eyebrows to make you older . . . No no,

mustn't bitch. Must get this right . . . With your eyes browed
grey, and your firm young neck, you were one-up for minor
ministerial rank. All the Cabinet of that time had rolling
double chins. 'Cept for myself . . .

Pats his chin, then cross with himself . . .

No no! Last day alive, must achieve some reasonably elevated
level . . . Get up there, somehow . . .

Composes himself.

And so to Junior Ministry. Angelic whizz kid of your age, you
spoke smoothly and with concern, of Tory utopias of
efficiency. At garden fêtes, the silky calved wives of aldermen,
told you you were so right about . . . Fishing limits? England's
role in the world? And oh, the sun rose over the wrong side of
Leicester, to touch your shoulders as you stood, atop your
campaign van in the General Election of nineteen fifty-nine. A
little quiff in the breeze of hair already artificially mature, a
phrase about Britain Going Forward, and an increase of your
majority by six thousand or so. And so . . . To inner councils.
Matters of moment. In and out of famous doors, to flashlight
bulbs and puny hurrahs of tourist crowds. Ah silky, you are
silky. It's all in the throat. On television your honeyed words
have a silicone effect. Coating the tube with a silvery slime.
You are a politician.

You have never had a political thought in your life.

Raises himself. An effort here, for the first time.

And, Alice my dear, you are a fascist. Oh, I don't mean
jackboots and Gotterdammerungs. You are a peculiarly
modern, peculiarly English kind of fascist. Without regalia.
Blithe, simple-minded and vicious. I hate you. You scare me
sick. Mao had better come quick, for I think there's a danger,
a very real and terrible danger, that *you* may inherit the earth.

A swallow, a deep breath, he kicks ALICE.

Wake up!

ALICE. What?

BABS. You fell asleep, you thoughtless bugger.

ALICE. I feel dreadful.

BABS. Could have had the decency to stay awake.

ALICE. I'm sorry. (*Feels his head.*) Is there an Alka Seltzer?

BABS. No there is not an Alka Seltzer. I'm very upset.

ALICE. Why?

BABS. No there is not an Alka Seltzer!

ALICE. All right, it doesn't matter.

BABS. Fascist!

ALICE. I beg your pardon?

BABS. Nothing.

ALICE. We'd better go back. Are you cold?

BABS. Yes I'm cold.

ALICE. We'll go back.

BABS. No we will not.

ALICE. We ought to.

BABS. No we will not! We'll stay up all night. Disport ourselves in the meadows. In the villages.

Come my beloved.

Let us go forth into the field;
Let us lodge in the villages.
Let us go up early to the vineyards;
Let us see whether the vine hath budded, and its blossom be open
And the pomegranates be in flower.

The Song of Songs.

ALICE. Just stay where you are, I'll punt from this end.

BABS. I beg of you, I beg of you. No.

Grabs ALICE's *hands.* ALICE *sits reluctantly.*

ALICE. All right, Babs.

From here a long fade of the light. Imperceptible at first, to the end of the scene. A pause.

BABS. I can't feel anything.

A pause.

Yes I can. There's a nail in this boat, sticking into my behind.

ALICE. Let me move you . . .

BABS. Oh no. I appear to have some . . . Equilibrium like this. Do not disturb it, or I may really, finally, fall apart.

A pause.

ALICE. Are you . . . Comfortable?

BABS. You mean 'In pain?'

ALICE. Yes.

BABS. 'Yes' is the answer.

ALICE. Babs we ought to go back . . .

BABS. Embarrassed?

ALICE. Let's be sensible.

BABS. Got a better idea. Tip me in the river.

ALICE. Don't be ridiculous.

BABS. Go on.

ALICE. You're being ridiculous.

BABS. Do it myself, if I had the strength.

ALICE *holds the bridge of his nose. In a worried temper.*

ALICE. No.

BABS. Don't think I've not tried it, the last six months. A terrible series of farcical attempts. Thwarted at every turn. Pyjama cords snapping in the middle of the night, that kind of thing.

The news that I wanted to bump myself off, got round the undergraduate body. Boat club night, the darling boys hanged me in effigy outside the lodge. Sweet of them.

Am I living every moment of this?

ALICE (*bitterly*). To the hilt.

BABS. Oh good. Do you still shave your legs?

ALICE. How did you know I . . . clean my legs?

BABS. Saw you in the bog at the House once. With a lady's razor. Not got that razor on you, have you?

ALICE. I'm afraid not.

BABS. Pity. Are all your family ginger on the body?

ALICE. Yes, actually.

BABS. Cold.

> ALICE *moves close and cradles him. A pause.* BABS *dead still, a long time. Then suddenly he's lively.*

> Are you wearing a corset?

ALICE. I don't think you should bother yourself . . .

BABS. Funny.

> The last information you take in. The last . . . Image to flit . . . (*Taps his head.*) Final insight. You are a corseted, ginger-haired, English fascist.

ALICE. And what are you?

BABS. Oh . . . (*A gesture, completed.*) I'm . . .

> *He's dead. A pause. And the lights down.*

Scene Five

Bare stage. MARY *there.*

MARY. Day Jed came out, couldn't bear to go an' meet him.

> Though, in a way, full of love for him.

> But then, I've always had funny ways, like when I was a kid . . . Oh, picking up birds with bust legs. Nursing sick mice. Soppy, daft, funny ways. Asking for it. You know, your heart to break. Mouse dying, bird breakin' his other leg. (*A little laugh.*) That kind of thing. Soppy, daft, oh mushy things that you can't stand. And make you go cold inside. (*Quickly.*) Not that Jed's a bird with a bust . . . Jed's Jed. Just Jed. On his own way. (*Shrugs.*) Jed.

> *A pause.*

> But I told myself, I couldn't go. When they let him out. All night I was awake, tossing and turning, thinking of it, and I'd got the morning off work, and agreed with Cliff and V, when we would meet. Early, get the tube at eight. 'Cos they let them go, out through the little door in the gate. (*A little laugh.*) Million times I seen that, films, telly. Letting 'em go at nine, out the little door in the big door.

> The bastards.

A pause.

I told myself I couldn't go, 'cos I was afraid. And I told myself I couldn't stand it, and would go cold inside.

She goes off. A pause. CLIFF *and* V *come on. He has a bottle of champagne.*

A pause. CLIFF *glances at his watch. A pause.* JED *comes on. His head is shaved.* CLIFF *at once, cheerful.*

CLIFF. Christ Jed, what they done to your head?

Nothing from JED. *Silence.* MARY *comes on fast.*

MARY. Jed, told myself I couldn't come, then I couldn't . . . Not come. And I rushed!

They've cut your hair off.

A pause.

But you look nice.

A pause.

Jed.

A pause. Uncertain.

Jed?

And the stage floods with red, awash with banners and songs.

JED. Vlad?

The effects growing.

Vlad?

LENIN *appears at the back of the stage. He moves through his heroic gestures. A wind machine blows a gale across the stage.* MARY, CLIFF, *and* V *stand stock still through this passage.*

What do you make of it, Vladimir Ilyich?

LENIN. A noble, proletarian hatred for the bourgeois 'class politician' is the beginning of all wisdom.

JED. Right Vlad!

LENIN. Only a violent collision, which indeed may be forced upon the people, will wipe out the servility which has permeated the national consciousness.

JED. Yeh but, Vlad, yeh but . . .

LENIN *sweeping down the stage through many gestures.*

LENIN. Force! Force is the midwife of every old society which is pregnant with a new.

JED (*shouting over the gale*). Yeh but Vlad! Not got much here for you, Vlad! Little bit of hate. Dangerous intent. In my pocket somewhere, here, screwed up bit o' paper. Morsel of contempt. What I do with it Vlad? Help you out, little bit, little bit o' spite?

LENIN *sweeps past behind him.*

LENIN. Granite! Work!

Diagonally back upstage.

Work upon a granite theoretical foundation, legal and illegal, peaceful and stormy, open and underground, small circles and mass movements, parliamentary and terrorist.

Right at the back now. The effects deepening.

Left-wing communism is an infantile disorder. Politics is an art and a science that does not drop from the skies.

He goes. The banners and songs, the gale cease. Still red light.

JED. Yeh but, Vlad. (*Spreads his arms, mockingly.*) What can a poor boy do?

Drops his arms and at once lights back to what they were before LENIN *appeared. Pause.* JED, *angrily.*

Where's Will?

CLIFF. Couldn't get off work.

JED. You're lying through your teeth.

CLIFF. Will's . . .

JED. What?

CLIFF (*shrugs*). As ever.

JED. Tell him I want to see him. Tonight. Round our place.

A pause.

MARY. We got some champagne. 'Ere Cliff, what about the champagne?

A pause.

Celebration?

Blackout.

Scene Six

Lights up at once. Bare stage. WILL *there.* JED *walks on.*

WILL. Hello, old son.

>*A pause.*

>Jug bring on many changes?

JED. Some.

WILL. Little bird whispered to me, you been abusing your mind and your body. Speedy Gonzales?

>*He giggles. No response from* JED.

>What were you trying to do? Elevate the whole of Brixton Gaol? Turn it upside down? Shake all the nasty creepy crawlies out? Every night I looked out my bedroom window, expecting to see . . . Whoosh! Brixton Gaol go by, spaceship to the stars, my old mate Jed for Captain. (*Suddenly embracing* JED.) Me old China. God, Jed, missed ya. 'Cor you're lovely, Jed. Sandpapered your nut down a bit, han't they? Still it's my old Jed's nut.

JED. For fucksake.

>JED *shrugs him away.*

WILL. Sorry.

JED. What's the matter with you?

WILL. Dunno. I felt moved.

JED. You felt what?

WILL. At seeing you again.

JED. Well fuck you.

WILL. Jesus, Jed, I was only tickled to see you. Tickled pink, to see you.

JED. You gone soft in the head?

>*A pause.*

WILL. Christ, oh Jesus. Jed? I'm getting all kinds of bad things from you. Jed?

>*A pause.*

>Oh Jesus.

>*A pause.*

You were . . . I blush to say it, but you know, me and you, like . . . (*Fingers entwined*.) I mean you were beautiful.

JED *scoffs*.

Finicky. Bit tetchy. Bit of paranoia in there. But that was your way o' getting it together. (*Laughs*.) Jesus, I remember you spending all day, when we were setting up the occupation . . . All one Sunday, pouring out cups of water to reckon what we'd need. An' how you went on like an old woman, remember? 'Bout sleeping bags. And us all getting warm. Happy days, eh? Christ we were mad then, eh? Insane. It was great then, I mean we really . . . Didn't we?

A pause.

Eh?

A pause.

Wow.

A pause.

Jed?

JED *stares*.

Picking up a lot of static here, Jed . . .

JED. What's all this freaky talk, Will?

WILL. Freaky?

JED. Been to America, while I've been 'rotting in my cell'?

WILL. Hounslow actually. Moved in with a little chick, ta-tum ta ta. Substances and dream machines under the floorboards, in the food. Can't have a slice of bread an' marmite, without losing your mind. She's taken to injecting acid in the eggs for breakfast now. We lead a very peaceful, domestic life.

JED. Do you know you're full of crap?

WILL *shrugs, tries to jolly things a little more* . . .

WILL. Yeh. Well . . .

Fails. A pause.

Jed, old son, changes, old son. Many changes . . . brought on. Y'know?

JED. Look at you.

WILL *looks about, perked up*.

WILL. Why, where am I?

JED. There, on the floor.

WILL. Oh yeh.-Hello, Will.

JED. Hello, Will.

WILL. I think he's smashed out of his mind. (*Looks over 'himself' lying on the floor.*) Yeh, he's in a bad way. But he's smiling to 'imself. Maybe he's seeing things. Think he's seeing things? (*He sniffs.*) He's not washed much. There's a distinctly under-pantish whiff about this dreamer. (*To* JED.) Yeh, he's far gone. Far away. Lotus eater.

But don't you think unkindly of him. Don't abuse 'im. If you come upon 'im, lying on the pavement, Piccadilly piccadilly, don't you kick 'im. Please eh, Master? Pass 'im by, tiptoe.

'Cos his dreams are very fragile, Jed. Delicate. Precious. And his brain wall's thin, and liable to rupture, as a result of all the changes . . .

Jed?

JED. I remember a sharp little man.

WILL. Please don't, Jed.

JED. Childish. A talker. Got on your nerves.

WILL. Please don't, Jed.

JED. But loyal. Hard. Diamond at the core. Fearless.

WILL. Please don't, Jed.

JED. A sharp little man, who for all of his being a fool, did . . . I really do believe he did . . . love the people. And had the guts to do a little about his love. And I'm standing here, looking down at what's left of him.

You got a daisy sewed on your arse?

WILL. Little bit o' colour.

JED. Bend over.

WILL. What?

JED. Bend over your fucking groovy arse, you fucking stinking little child of God.

WILL. Eh . . . Don't let's get heavy, Jed.

JED *grabs him by the neck.*

It's only a daisy. What you got against daisies? Unfair to daisies!

JED *rips the daisy off.*

JED. And the shirt.

WILL. What?

JED. Get that shirt off.

WILL. Not me Che shirt.

JED. And that.

He tears a badge off WILL's *jacket. Several tugs.*

WILL. No! No! No!

Not me Ho Chi Minh Memorial Badge!

JED. Shirt.

WILL. Worse than down at West End Central . . .

JED. Get that trash off.

WILL *jerks away from him.*

WILL. Whatsa matter with you?

JED. That obscene tat. Get it off. Get it off.

WILL. All right all right!

JED. Get/it/all/off.

WILL. All right!

He takes off his jacket, then his Che shirt. He crouches shivering, arms across himself. JED *picks up the Che shirt, and crouches too. He stares morosely at the shirt.*

Speedy freak.

A pause.

That you?

A pause.

Eh?

A pause.

Rot your brain, that, Jed. Sored up yet, eh?

Speed freaks sore up fast.

'Course, Revolutionary drug, in't it. As recommended by the Weathermen. You are putting yourself in the big league. Speedy heavies. Like the Panthers, come down on their Harleys, to the beach . . . Dead of night . . . To meet Jean Genet, smuggle him into America. And away they go into the dark . . . Eh?

I suppose I get the appeal.

Oh to be black, in black leather, on a black motor-bike, in the blackest night, Jean Genet on my pillion and my brain rotting away . . .

A pause.

Can I put my jacket on?

JED *with a sharp movement turns the image of Guevara to* WILL.

JED. What's Mr Guevara to you?

WILL. Tee shirt. (*Shrugs.*) I mean, it's just a tee shirt.

JED. There's a face on it.

WILL. Oh come on.

JED. Years ago, you'd have pissed on the very idea o' going about in this.

WILL. 'S just a shirt.

JED. *What happened* to you?

WILL. 'S just a shirt! Could be Marilyn Monroe on there, or Benny Hill.

A pause.

Mickey Mouse. Steve McQueen. Apollo moon landing. Stars an' stripes. Hammer an' Sickle.

A pause.

'S just a shirt.

JED. Got the poster of him dead?

WILL. What?

JED. This great man. This stupid, great man. Got the poster of him dead?

WILL. No, don't think so.

Short pause.

Hanging in our loo.

Sorry.

He shrugs. JED *throws the shirt, screwed up, at* WILL. *Who unravels it as he speaks.*

But you're coming on strong, Jed. Oh are you. Like some Sunday School teacher. Rapping me over the knuckles. Caught me pencilling a moustache on a picture o' Jesus. Rap rap. Naughty. O.K. O.K. you got busted.

O.K. that give you a halo? Come an' bash your old mates with? God given right?

I know you suffered. And all. Really though, I do.

Know.

Just maybe it's easier, sittin' in a cell. Having visions, Armageddons two a penny. Chalk 'em up on your ball an' chain, eh? Lurid scenarios.

But it's very hard, for us down in Hounslow . . . No not hard, that's insulting to you. Dreary. Dreary, day in day out. The jungles of Bolivia seem rather far away. Keeping a correct political point of view is something of a chore. Your mind begins to wander. I mean . . . I know when the milkman calls, you should grab him by the throat, and politicize him on the spot. But it's difficult. Specially if you owe him six weeks. An' you want your cornflakes soggy.

He puts the shirt and the jacket back on. A pause. He's slumped, round shouldered.

What happened to me?

A pause.

Nothing to it. Everyday life. All fervour gone.

One day, find yourself ranting on with the old, steamy enthusiasm 'bout something . . . Spectre of International Capitalism . . . And suddenly, urrgh. Sluch.

And you get smashed a bit, then most of the time. Millions are one way or the other. Smashed.

Urrgh. Sluch.

A pause.

JED. Come here.

WILL *stands and goes over to* JED.

Down here.

WILL *crouches down.* JED *slaps him in the face. Fairly hard, ad repeatedly, but carefully — like someone bringing someone round, who's unconscious.*

You and I.

Slap.

Are going on a little journey.

Slap.

WILL. Oh yeh.

He flinches. A slap.

JED. Wake up.

Slap.

WILL. I am awake.

Slap.

JED. Wake up.

Slap.

WILL. Stop it.

Slap.

What you doing?

JED. You and I.

Slap.

Are going to the West Country.

WILL. That's nice.

Slap.

Where? Bristol, Bath?

Slap.

JED. Never mind where.

Slap.

You got bread?

Slap.

WILL. Yeh.

Slap.

For the fare?

JED. Right.

WILL. Yeh.

Slap.

JED. And fifty quid.

Slap.

WILL. What you want fifty quid for?

Slap.

Stop hitting me in my face.

JED. Can you get the fifty quid?

Slap.

WILL. Don't hit me in my face.

JED grabs him by the shoulders.

JED. Can you get fifty pounds?

WILL. Yeh. Maybe I'll deal or something . . .

JED. By the weekend.

WILL. Dicy. I'll try. But what for?

Slap.

Don't do that!

He hits JED back. JED grabs WILL's hand by the wrist, tight.

JED. Why, old son. Can't you guess?

WILL. Surprise me.

JED. You and I are going to change the world.

WILL. Really? That will be a nice . . . Surprise.

A pause.

Can I have my wrist back, please?

And at once lights down fast. JED still holding his wrist.

Scene Seven

Lights up at once. At the front. Bare stage. MARY, VERONICA and CLIFF.

MARY. Don't wanna talk about it.

VERONICA. You're being a silly little cow.

MARY. Don't wanna. Won't.

VERONICA. Mary . . .

MARY. Want some tea?

VERONICA. No.

MARY. Want some tea, Cliff?

　CLIFF *shakes his head. A pause.*

VERONICA. Anyway, when will they be back?

MARY. Said they'd be back yesterday.

VERONICA. Have you heard from them?

MARY. Why should I?

　A door slams. JED *and* WILL *come out of the dark. Pause.*

　We been arguing about you. They think . . . Well they think.

JED. Do they.

VERONICA. Go far?

　JED *stares at her. Then turns to* WILL. *Who takes off his haversack carefully, helped by* JED. *They take a biscuit tin out of the haversack.* JED *takes off the lid, carefully. Then sits back on his haunches looking at* VERONICA. WILL *gives a short giggle.*

　Wow. Shazzaam. Kerpow.

　A pause.

　That what you want me to say?

　A pause.

MARY. What is it? What they got there?

VERONICA (*straight at* JED). Gelignite, sticks of gelignite that's all, nothing but sticks of gelignite. Silky fireworks. Make a big bang, that's all. One big bang, and after all that, silence. Nothing really to concern yourself with. Just big bangers.

MARY. Gelignite?

A pause.

WILL. Don't think that lady's gonna come on our picnic, Jed. 'Fraid o' creepy crawlies in the cucumber sandwiches.

He giggles uneasily. A pause. JED *looks at* CLIFF.

CLIFF. No.

A pause.

Oh no. Not that. There's only one way, time was you knew it, Jed. Work, corny work, with and for the people. Politicizing them and learning from them, everyone of them. Millions. O.K., O.K., come a time you'll have to go out there. (*Sharp gesture, his fingers as a gun.*) But only with the people, as a people's army, borne along by them. You know all this, Jed, we've worked together . . . You know you are, right now, there . . . A nothing. Zero. A crank with a tin box of bangs. I dunno, I dunno . . . That you've degenerated, oh come down to this, Jed. Some fucking stupid gesture . . . (*He scoffs.*) An explosion! And they'll call you a 'Revolutionary' of some kind, but a 'Revolutionary.' You know what a mockery that will be.

A pause as JED *carefully packs the gelignite and tin away in the haversack, and helps it onto* WILL's *back. They're going, upstage into the dark. But at the last moment* JED *turns, and speaks to* CLIFF.

JED. Went to see a terrible film once. Carpet-baggers. With Carole Baker. Right load of old tat, going on up there on the big silver screen. Boring, glossy tat, untouchable being on the silver screen.

And there was this drunk in the front row. With a bottle of ruby wine. And did he take exception to the film, he roared and screamed. Miss Baker above all came in for abuse. Something about her got right up his nose.

So far up, that he was moved to chuck his bottle of ruby wine right through Miss Baker's left tit.

The left tit moved on in an instant, of course. But for the rest of the film, there was that bottle shaped hole. (*With a jab of his finger.*) Clung. One blemish on the screen. But somehow you couldn't watch the film from then.

And so thinks . . . (*With a bow.*) The poor bomber. Bomb 'em.
Again and again. Right through their silver screen. Disrupt
the spectacle. The obscene parade, bring it to a halt! Scatter
the dolly girls, let advertisements bleed . . . Bomb 'em, again
and again! Murderous display. An entertainment for the
oppressed, so they may dance a little, take a little warmth
from the sight, eh? (*He laughs.*) Go down into the mire eh?
Embrace the butcher, eh?

A silence.

Think on't.

He goes.

MARY. Jed?

A pause.

Yeh, I'll make some tea. Anyone want me make some tea?

CLIFF. Yes.

VERONICA *puts her arm round* MARY. *The lights go down
fast.*

Scene Eight

Bare stage. WILL *at the back, the lights narrowed upon him. He
speaks aside.*

WILL. All night. Walked about London. Hours and hours of talk.
And so tired. And Jed going on and on. Re-lentless. Burning it
all up.

And mid-morning, train from Euston Station. Lovely day. Into
Hertfordshire. Got off at a little station. And 'ouses, and
gardens . . . In the Indian Summer lovely weather. And we
walked for miles, over the fields, in the lanes. Jed like he was
on a laser beam. Through the English Countryside. Burning on
and on.

To here.

At once lights up all over the stage. JED *comes on.*

JED. The man's garden!

WILL. I'm so hot. A bathe in me own exhaust fumes. Fuckin' 'ell!
Aren't the trees high.

JED. All we've got to do is relax. Sun ourselves. And he'll be out, doing his garden.

WILL. Yeh.

A pause.

Jed, Jed . . . With that . . . load, do you think the grass'll burn? And there'll be a gale won't there. Shake all the petals off the rhododendrons. The birds'll rise for miles around.

A pause.

I wonder if the air, y'know the oxygen in the air, that'll burn too . . . God Jed I wish I was smashed out of my mind, I could do with it, I could do with it right now . . . In the English Countryside. In the Indian Summer weather. Yer English lanes. Burning, burning, burning on and on . . . (*Suddenly.*) Jed I'm sick scared!

JED. Sun . . . Ourselves.

WILL. Yeh. Right.

A pause.

Funny.

JED. What?

WILL. My old Dad was a gardener. Dead sure this isn't the time of year rhododendrons are meant to . . . Y'know, flower.

A pause.

Oh I'm so tired. (*Change.*) 'Ere! Maybe 'e forces the rhododendrons out by torture. Yeh.

A pause.

Look at the . . . Lawn. Look at the . . . Trees. Look at the . . . Flowers. Look at the . . . Chimneys o' the 'ouse . . . Look at the . . . Fucking English Garden 'e's got.

Off stage a motor starts. ALICE glides the length of the stage on a lawn-mower with an attached seat. A watering can hangs on the handlebars. He's slumped rather badly. He's off. The motor stops. A pause.

Far out.

A pause.

Utterly amazing.

A pause.

Eh, Jed.

JED. Shut up. And watch him.

WILL. Cat and mouse? Meow we are the black cat gang with red claws.

JED. Just SHUT UP.

The lawn-mower's motor heard off stage again. ALICE drives the lawn-mower on and down stage. JED and WILL crouch down at the side of the stage. ALICE stops the lawn-mower. A pause. He speaks aside.

ALICE. The old fool, died in my arms. I think he'd sent for me, that day, not necessarily to do that . . . Though he was prone to what he called scenarios. Rigged niceties of behaviour. Genteel excesses.

Punted his dead body back along the river in the dusk. Lost half the deposit for being out late. The boatman haggled, 'til he realized. Taking Babs out of the punt one leg of his corpse . . . got wet. There was a smell. His viciousness and cunning knew no end.

And going over the events of that day . . . I think he set out to destroy my peace of mind. And going over the events of that day, I feel . . . Perhaps he succeeded only too well. Set off a chain of thoughts. Self-realization?

And now? (*A helpless gesture.*) At a loss. With a kind of self loathing. That old man! His last day alive. He treated me like an old lover. I felt . . . curiously dirtied.

I knew he bitterly opposed me in the party, and my friends. Set me up, but in the later days, did all he could against me. Bitterly . . . That last day could have been one long, last political act . . . The old High Tory's last throw at me. That viciousness and cunning.

Something catches his eye on the ground before him.

Oh bloody weeds.

He gets off the mower with the watering can and waters the weeds. JED and WILL rise with kids' Indian yodels . . . Very fast this . . . And overpower ALICE. JED handcuffs him, hands behind his back.

JED. Mask get the mask!

WILL. Right the mask!

JED. With the funny grin!

WILL. Right right!

WILL *goes over and gets the haversack.*

ALICE. What do you . . . What do you hope to achieve . . .

JED. Shut up!

ALICE. What possible end!

JED. *The* end, mate! (*To* WILL.) Right!

WILL *takes out a string of gelignite from the haversack, with a short ignitable fuse. It's arranged round a sack.* JED *and* WILL *hold it up carefully.* ALICE *flinches away.*

Peace!

ALICE. What?

JED. In peace! Understand?

ALICE. I'm sorry?

JED *lets* ALICE *see he has a knife.* ALICE *nods. They put the mask over* ALICE's *head. A pause. Then* JED *and* WILL *look at each other.* WILL *gives a little giggle. Stops.* JED *lights the fuse.* ALICE *gives little jerks of his head in panic, side to side, but mute. The moment* JED *lights the fuse* WILL *grabs the haversack and runs upstage.* JED *takes a few steps away upstage but suddenly stops, stares at* ALICE, *then crouches down again.* WILL *realizes* JED *is not following and skids to a stop.*

WILL. Jed.

JED. Get away.

WILL. Jed, it's burning!

JED. Get off.

WILL. Jed, thirty seconds there'll be a meat haze.

JED. I said . . . Get!

WILL. Molecules. Just a smell of the breeze . . .

A pause.

Oh.

(*Backing away.*) Oh, Jed. (*Backing away.*) Oh no, oh, Jed. (*Backing away.*) You were, oh Jed.

He stops. A pause. Then he turns and runs. Let the fuse burn right out. A long pause. Nothing happens.

ALICE. Could you . . .

A pause.

Could you tell me what's happening out there?

JED (*quietly.*) Oh Mr Public Man here we are.

ALICE. I'm sorry?

JED. It's all right. The fuse failed.

ALICE. What did you say?

JED. Fuse failed.

ALICE. What?

JED (*shouts*). I said . . . The fuse failed.

ALICE. Ah. (*Little twitches of his head, which he brings under control.*) Is it going off or isn't it?

JED. I don't know.

ALICE. What did you say?

JED. I don't know.

ALICE. What?

JED (*shouts*). I said . . . I don't know if it's going off or not.

ALICE. Ah. (*Little twitches of his head, which he brings under control.*) Perhaps you should try another fuse.

JED. Not got one.

ALICE. What?

A long pause.

Look I do think it's your move.

JED. Do you? (*Shouts:*) Do you?

A pause. Then JED *goes and takes the gelignite mask off.* ALICE's *face twitches badly. He turns his head aside, closes his eyes, controls it.*

ALICE. And now? A knifing? 'The boot'?

A pause.

Perhaps a strangulation?

JED *shrugs.*

Please let me know. Sooner or later.

JED. I don't know.

ALICE. I am a rather nervous man. Perhaps you could make your mind up.

JED. I'm doing my best.

ALICE. I'm sure you are.

JED. Oh Christ.

ALICE. Indeed.

JED. What . . .

A pause.

What did you do to the rhododendrons?

ALICE. Do you mean why should they be in flower this time of year? Forced feeding. Chemicals. A second flowering.

JED. Why not?

ALICE. Will you . . .

JED. *I don't know!*

ALICE. I have fibrositis, you see. Under the right shoulder blade . . . (*He falters.*) Bubbles on the muscle.

JED. All right all right!

ALICE (*with open panic*). Don't, don't, don't harm me . . .

He controls himself. A pause. He moves his shoulder. Then indicates the mask with his foot.

What is this?

JED. Industrial gelignite.

ALICE. With a burning fuse?

JED. Any objections?

ALICE. No no . . . I just seem to remember from the war one is much better advised to use an electrical charge, from a battery. Where did you get this?

JED. Off a man.

ALICE. Quarry man?

> JED *shrugs.*

> Looks like he sold you a pig in a poke.

JED. Looks like that.

ALICE. You don't seem to mind.

JED. No?

ALICE. You're a very sullen young man.

JED. I 'have my troubles'.

ALICE. Don't we all. I mean I'm very glad you were fobbed off with . . . Dud goods. I seem to owe my life to a dishonest trader of the criminal classes. Though what comfort there is in that, I'm not quite sure. But you seem quite unconcerned at the . . . Failure of your escapade. Perhaps it's the thought that counts?

JED. Why not?

ALICE. The politics of gesture. I know all about that. The Special Branch ran a Summer School Course on Revolutionary Theory the other summer. Let me see what you are . . . (*He falters.*) 'Into,' as they say. Situationist theory?

JED. Really?

ALICE. A violent intervention. A disruption. A spectacle against the spectacle. A firework in the face of the Ruling Class.

JED. Sounds fun.

ALICE. How did you come to choose me to be a . . . Roman candle in the Revolutionary Struggle?

JED. Housing. Once upon a time I . . . Had a concern for housing. And you're in the Ministry of the Environment.

ALICE. I am not.

> *A pause.*

JED. Oh come on.

ALICE. I am in the Office of the Paymaster General.

JED. Don't piss about.

ALICE. There was a Cabinet Reshuffle. I was moved downstairs. How incredibly inefficient of you not to know.

JED. Oh I wish I'd blown your head off, you bloody and you arrogant man.

ALICE. You do me an injustice. Apart from the obvious injustice of trying to blow my head off. I am not a bloody and an arrogant man.

JED. What do you see yourself as, then? Queer, failed and fifty?

ALICE. Perceptive little bitch. (*Suddenly angry.*) You young thug. I'm trying to be brave.

JED. So am I!

ALICE. Some dignity . . . You must allow.

JED. Me too.

ALICE. Yes, yes of course . . . Though I don't see why.

JED. I could beat you, I could beat you now!

ALICE. C . . . Come on then!

JED. Oh Christ!

ALICE. Kick me. Where are you? Come up behind me. Kick my spine. Go for the nervous system, boy. Total pain. Or be witty, go for the hair, get me by the hair . . . Get your fingers in my eyes, oh Dear God . . . Take me apart with your hands you hoodlum. You young, brutal, would-be change the worlder.

JED. Christ, Christ!

ALICE. You've got me in your hands. Isn't that what you want? What you hate in your hands. To tear. A butchering job on the World. That it, that it, young man?

JED. Oh Christ!

ALICE (*suddenly quietly*). Jed? . . . Your friend who ran away, called you Jed? Jed, we seem to have reached a state of . . . balance. Either you butcher me, or we stay out here all night. The evenings are drawing in. Chilly. Heavy . . . (*He falters.*) Dew.

JED. Sun'll still be hot for a bit.

JED *lies back, his hands under his head. A pause.*

ALICE. A friend of mine died.

A pause.

I know you . . . Hold me, in some way personally responsible. For what I don't know. The world's ills? Some particular event? Or just, perhaps, for being in public life? Having dirty hands? No . . . Purity of intent. Is that what you see yourself as having? Purity of intent? No doubt you do. How dreadfully unfair.

A pause.

For being myself? For being me? The terrorist's vendetta, there's no answer to it, then. It may come from anywhere. Perhaps you've had a bad life. Have you had a bad life? I would like to know. Because you may yet decide to assault me, and it is very easy to injure . . . It would be a mild comfort Jed, if the balance is going to tip . . . And you are going to come at me and kick me . . . (*He swallows.*) Why?

JED. Oh, Mr Public Man.

JED *stands up.* ALICE *flinches. But* JED *releases* ALICE *from the handcuffs.*

ALICE. Thank you. You couldn't . . . Give my shoulder blade a rub could you?

JED *ignores that and picks up the gelignite mask.*

JED. Dunno. I dunno. Can't get rid. Can't shake it off. Magnificence, that it would be magnificent to have you bleeding on the lawn.

ALICE. I can't understand that. Dear God. How can any human being understand that?

JED. No. I do. Late, late summer, musky smell from the FUCKING RHODODENDRONS. An English garden with its Englishman. Done at last. DONE. Oh Mr I am deeply in contempt of you. All of you. Bubbles is it, in the muscle? Your nails, hair, little bits. And your mind. I am deeply in contempt of your English mind. There is BLAME THERE. That wrinkled stuff with the picture of English Life in its pink, rotten meat. In your head. And the nasty tubes to your eyes that drip Englishness over everything you see. The cool, glycerine humanity of your tears that smarms our ANGER. I am deeply in contempt of your FUCKING HUMANITY. The goo, the sticky mess of your English humanity that gums up our ears to your lies, our eyes to your crimes . . . I dunno, I

dunno, what can a . . . What can a . . . Do? To get it real. And
get it real to you. And get at you, Mr English Public Man, with
oh yeh the spectacle, the splendour of you magnificently
ablaze for the delight and encouragement of all your
enemies . . . I dunno I dunno . . . So I thought . . . (*He raises
the mask.*) A little danger. Into our sad.

JED *lowers the mask. Hangs his head. A pause.* ALICE *stands.*

ALICE. Drink?

Nothing from JED.

Would you like a drink?

JED. What?

ALICE. I'll go into the house, and bring a drink out. Be a
lovely . . . Early evening on the lawn.

JED. You'll phone the police.

ALICE. Perhaps. But then . . . We could both do with a drink.
Scotch? Long, with ice? I'll bring a tray out. (*Uneasily.*) End
up sloshed together.

A pause.

Once I was eager to . . . How shall I say, 'Claw at the World'?

JED (*softly*). Christ.

ALICE. There is no reason why we should not attempt some kind
of . . . Humane resolution . . . Between us.

JED. There is every reason.

ALICE. I'm sorry, didn't quite catch . . .

JED *shakes his head.*

Drink anyway.

JED *raises the mask.*

JED. The gelly. Oh why, why couldn't, just once . . . Couldn't it
be real?

JED *throws the mask to the floor.*
At once an explosion and blackout.
Three seconds silence.
Lights up.
Upstage the JED *and* ALICE *actors lie faces down. There's
something strange about the position of* JED's *arm. Smoke*

drifts over them. CLIFF *is standing downstage at the edge of the stage. He speaks aside.*

CLIFF. Jed. The waste. I can't forgive you that.

A pause.

The waste of your anger. Not the murder, murder is common enough. Not the violence, violence is everyday. What I can't forgive you Jed, my dear, dead friend, is the waste.

Blackout.

THE CHURCHILL PLAY

As it will be performed by the
internees of Churchill Camp
somewhere in England

In memory of G.J.

The Churchill Play

The Churchill Play was first presented at The Nottingham
Playhouse in 1974. It was revived by the RSC in 1978 at The
Other Place theatre, Stratford-upon-Avon, and then at the
Warehouse Theatre, London. For the RSC production I took the
opportunity to rewrite the text, particularly in Act Four. This
was a 'plumbing and re-wiring job', not to change the play's drift
or meaning, but hopefully to get it better. The Nottingham
version had been written at desperate speed, the last twenty pages
while the play was already in rehearsal (its director, Richard Eyre
had great patience and iron nerves, more so than the author). In
rewriting I did not update the play, or change the year of its
setting. (1984, ten years in the future when it first went on), but
altered only the minor things. Though it may not be a minor
matter to a Leeds supporter, there was a reference to Leeds
United in 1984 being at the bottom of the fourth division, since
in 1974 they were invincible at the top of the first; but by 1978
they were at the bottom of the second division, so the line
became bewilderingly pointless . . .

I wish the whole play was pointless now. But too much of it
has begun to happen, though inevitably in a different way and
tone and degree to how the play describes it. It is a satire which
says, 'Don't let the future be like this . . .'.

H.B

The Churchill Play was first performed by The Nottingham Playhouse Company on 8 May 1974 with the following cast:

Prisoners

Joby Peake	Paul Dawkins
Ted Barker	Roger Sloman
Mike McCulloch	Jonathan Pryce
Jack Williams	Colin McCormack
Furry Keegan	Bill Dean
George Lamacraft	Bob Hescott
Peter Reese	James Warrior
Jimmy Umpleby	Tom Wilkinson

Guards and Wives

Sergeant Baxter	Dave Hill
Corporal Taylor	Eric Richard
Colonel Ball	Ralph Nossek
Mrs Glenda Ball	Mary Sheen
Captain Thompson	Julian Curry
Caroline Thompson	Jane Wymark
Private	Buz Williams
Private	Stephen Chapman
Roger	Brer

The Committee

Rt. Hon. Jonathan St. John M.P.	John Joyce
Rt. Hon. Gerald Morn M.P.	Richard Simpson
Mrs Julia Richmond (A Parliamentary Private Secretary)	Louise Breslin

In The Play

Winston Churchill	Paul Dawkins
A Private	Roger Sloman
A Marine	Colin McCormack
An Airman	Tom Wilkinson
A Seaman	Jonathan Pryce
A Black Dog	James Warrior
A Dervish	Bob Hescott
Uncle Ernie	Bill Dean
Auntie Annie	Tom Wilkinson

Directed by Richard Eyre
Designed by Hayden Griffin
Lit by Rory Dempster

This revised edition of *The Churchill Play* was first performed by the Royal Shakespeare Company on 8 August 1978 with the following cast:

Prisoners

Ted Barker	Geoffrey Freshwater
Furry Keegan	Bill Dean
George Lamacraft	Bill Buffery
Mike McCulloch	Hilton McRae
Joby Peake	Raymond Westwell
Peter Reese	David Bradley
Jimmy Umpleby	Malcolm Storry
Jack Williams	Philip McGough

Guards and Wives

Colonel Ball	Paul Webster
Mrs Glenda Ball	Valerie Lush
Sergeant Baxter	Paul Moriarty
Corporal Taylor	John Bowe
Captain Thompson	John Nettles
Caroline Thompson	Juliet Stevenson
Private	James Griffin
Private	Ian Reddington
Roger	Skippy

The Committee

Gerald Morn M.P.	George Raistrick
Julia Richmond	Darlene Johnson
Jonathan St. John	Donald Douglas

In The Play

Winston Churchill	Raymond Westwell
A Private	Geoffrey Freshwater
A Marine	Philip McGough
An Airman	Malcolm Storry
A Seaman	Hilton McRae
A Black Dog	David Bradley
A Dervish	Bill Buffery
Uncle Ernie	Bill Dean
Auntie Annie	Malcolm Storry

Directed by Barry Kyle
Designed by Kit Surrey
Lit by Leo Leibovici

Act One

A dim light. Above, a huge stained glass window of medieval knights in prayer. Below, candles round a huge catafalque, which is draped with the Union Jack. At each corner a SERVICEMAN *stands guard, head lowered in mourning. They are an Army Private, a Naval Marine, an Airman and an Ordinary Seaman. The Private is a Londoner, the Marine is Welsh, the Seaman is a Scot and the Airman is a Yorkshireman. They are young.*

A long silence.

PRIVATE (*roaring his lines. Choked, awkwardly*). Body! (*A pause.*) Body a! (*A pause.*) Body a Sir Winston! Churchill! (*A pause.*) Laid in State! (*A pause.*) West-minster Pal-ace 'All! (*A pause.*) January Nineteen-'un-dred an' Sixty-five! (*A pause.*) An' 'ere we are! (*A pause.*) Three A.M.! (*A pause.*) Filthy wevver! (*A pause.*) England! Filthy wevver! Three A.M.! Back 'ere! Inna nineteen-bloody-sixties! Be-fore Eng-land fell a-part!

A silence.

An' back here! Be-'ind me, anme mates! Why! Wha's left a' the greatest, the biggest, 'blood-y most monument-al Englishman that ever lived! (*A pause.*) Daddy of 'em all! (*A pause.*) An' I a poor sold-i-er! Guardin' 'is re-mains! (*A pause.*) Great 'onour! (*A pause.*) M'Mum cried when I told 'er. Loved 'im! Loved 'im, she cried. M'Mum cried. (*A pause.*) Yeah. Dyin' ferra fag.

SEAMAN (*to the* AIRMAN). Eh. Mate. (*A pause.*). Eh.

AIRMAN. Shush.

SEAMAN (*a pause*). Oh my Godfather.

AIRMAN. What?

SEAMAN (*trying to look behind him, eyes flickering*). Nothing. (*A pause.*) Oh, Jesus Christ.

AIRMAN. What is 'bloody matter with ya?

SEAMAN (*a fierce whisper*). Dunye hear?

AIRMAN. 'Ear? (*A slight pause.*) Wha'?

SEAMAN. Knocking.

AIRMAN. Knockin'?

SEAMAN. Knockin'. (*Slight pause.*) Front . . . (*Jerking his head back, indicating the coffin.*)

AIRMAN. The Coffin?

A silence. Dead still.

(*Scornful.*) Nuthin'.

SEAMAN. I tellye, the old bugger knocked.

AIRMAN. Ye're one under.

SEAMAN. He wants to get out.

PRIVATE. Eh, you two. Shut it.

AIRMAN. Sailor boy, heard a knock.

PRIVATE (*a slight pause*). A knock?

AIRMAN. Fromt behind.

PRIVATE. What yer tryin' to do?

SEAMAN. I tellye, there was a knock. A knocking.

AIRMAN. I tells ye, there were a knock. A knockin'.

PRIVATE. Lesall just shut it. Eh?

AIRMAN. Why? There is no NCO present among us.

PRIVATE. Thassa nuff a that, you.

AIRMAN. Ha!

A silence.

Wha' can it be? Keeps is all standing here, bloody sailors and soldier boys?

PRIVATE. It's a great 'onour, so shut yer face, Jock.

SEAMAN (*at once, blithely*). A very close bosom friend a' mine, a Guardsman. Had an experience wi' a crowd a yankee school-girls while on Guard Duty at St James Palace . . .

PRIVATE. You 'eard me. You 'eard me . . .

SEAMAN. . . . Left 'im, totally exposed . . .

PRIVATE. Shut . . .

SEAMAN. To cold winds an' tourists' cameras . . .

PRIVATE. Shut up!

At once a loud knocking from inside the catafalque. The
SERVICEMEN *rigid. A silence.*

A rat. Or . . . Bird caught under the (*Falters.*) lid. Lads?

A loud knocking. The catafalque trembles.

(*Cries out in panic*). 'E can't come out!

MARINE. He'll come out, he'll come out, I do believe that of
him. Capable of anything, that one. (*Fiercely.*) To bugger
working people. (*He coughs. Recovers. Fiercely.*) We have
never forgiven him in Wales. He sent soldiers against us, bloody
man. He sent soldiers against Welsh mining men in 1910. Three
were shot. The working people of Wales know their enemies.
He was our enemy. We hated his gut. The fat English upper-
class gut of the man. When they had the collection, for the
statue front of Parliament . . . All over Wales town and county
councils would not collect. No Welsh pennies for the brutal
man to stand there. In metal. (*He coughs, a bad attack.*)

The knocking from within the catafalque again.

PRIVATE. But 'e won a war. 'E did that, 'e won a war.

MARINE. People won the War. He just got pissed with Stalin . . .

CHURCHILL (*from within his coffin*). England!

The catafalque shudders. Knocking.

MARINE. People won the War! (*He coughs. Doubles up. He is
racked by silent coughs.*)

CHURCHILL (*from within his coffin*). England! Y' stupid old
woman. Clapped out. Undeserving. Unthankful. After all I.
did for you. You bloody tramp!

CHURCHILL *bursts out of his coffin, swirling the Union Jack.*
The Churchill actor must assume an exact replica. His face
is a mask. He holds an unlit cigar.

The SERVICEMEN *turn round and back away, rifles at the*
ready.

It was my ninetieth birthday. The 30th of November. A dirty
Autumn. Was old. Out of power. Spit on the lip. Was led to
the window. Saw the English people in the street. Saw how

they waved and cheered. (*Angry.*) Ingratitude! (*A slight pause. Wearily.*) The blood was denied to my brain. I sat by the fire for hours, never speaking. Set myself little feeble tasks. When did I first (*A slight pause.*) see a man with a stomach wound? Memory. Hours. (*Lowers his head. A slight pause. Raises his head.*) I went from High Office without grace. There was an Empire. Is it burnt? Drowned? Dust. Ash. Cast away. Like on the edge of some hellhole, of some mining area. Those bitter men. Today I may as well be scattered there. (*A slight pause. Then again, enthusiasm.*) Still, I can say I bludgeoned my way, through many jarring blows and shocks, bludgeoned. (*With a great pout of his jaw and a gesture with his cigar hand.*) Onto . . . History's stage! (*Sees the cigar isn't lit. Then to the* SAILOR.) Lad. Give us a light, lad. (*With unsuccessful jollity.*) Sailor boy!

The SAILOR *hesitates.*

(*Pathetically.*) Don't worry. On m'way to Bladon Churchyard. English graveyard. Sod. Eh? Eh? English elms. Larch. Oak. Eh? Choc-box last resting for the old man. Bloody sentimentality. Dogpiss on my grave, more like. (*To the* SAILOR, *cheerfully.*) Light! Light, lad!

A pause. Then the SAILOR *gingerly puts his rifle down. He fumbles in his pocket and takes out a lighter. He approaches* CHURCHILL. *His lighter flares.*

(*Ignores the light. Imploringly.*) Give us a kiss, Jolly Jack Tar.

COLONEL BALL (*unseen*). Sergeant Baxter.

SERGEANT (*unseen*). Suh!

BALL (*unseen*). Could we stop. Could we have light. Could we get all this out of the way please.

The SEAMAN *hesitates and looks round into the darkness.* CHURCHILL *hesitates for a moment. Then leans forward and aggressively puffs on the cigar.*

SERGEANT (*unclear, then*). 'Uckin' cigar OUT! (*Unclear, then.*) 'Uckin' lights there ON!

CHURCHILL. Winnie's back! (*He makes a 'V' sign.*)

SERGEANT (*unseen*). Corporal Taylor!

CORPORAL (*unseen*). Yes, Sergeant!

SERGEANT (*unseen*). That man's cigar! (*Unclear, then.*) Anna lights!

CORPORAL (*unseen*). Yes, Sergeant!

CHURCHILL. Signal the fleet!

> CORPORAL TAYLOR, *carrying a Sten gun comes into the light.*

CORPORAL (*wearily*). Come on, Joby. Don't arse about. An' give us that.

Neon strip-lights flicker and come on above. It's an aircraft hangar. The stained-glass window is seen to be a flimsy, paper construction. There is a wind machine, an improvised thing operated by an internee — 'FURRY' KEEGAN. He is a gentle, middle-aged man, a Liverpudlian. He is dressed in the mixture of internee uniform and bits and pieces against the cold. There are TWO GUARDS at the back, very alert, with sten-guns. COLONEL BALL, 60, small and youthful for his age, though running to a little fat. He has large, soft hands, whose gestures often betray uncertainty. CAPTAIN THOMPSON, 29, a florid, thick-set young man. He is an Army doctor. BALL and THOMPSON are seen coming forward. PETER REESE is to one side with a broom. The Churchill actor — JOBY PEAKE, a Derby man — looks up at the lights. Vibrates his lips. He hands the cigar carefully to the CORPORAL. BALL and THOMPSON stop coming forward, BALL turning from THOMPSON in irritation. JOBY pulls off Churchill's face. His own is puckered, shifty, hangdog and sly. He is 45.

JOBY. Give us another drag on that, lad.

CORPORAL. Shut up, Joby. You dirty 'orrible old man. An' get out a' that bloody coffin.

SERGEANT. Corporal Taylor, when you have shook this lot up you will tell me. (*He stands immobile, waiting.*)

CORPORAL. Yes, Sergeant. (*To the* PRISONERS.) Get out a that tat.

'SAILOR' (*real name* MIKE McCULLOCH, *a bony, tough little man, 25, but seeming older*). D'ye like me as a poofdah actor boy, Corporal?

CORPORAL. Shut up, McCulloch.

MIKE (*adopting a mocking whine*). Sergeant, canna we change back in our huts? It's cutting cold here . . .

CORPORAL. Don't be stupid, McCulloch, don't be stupid . . .

FURRY. Do you want the wind now?

He starts the wind machine.

CORPORAL. Switch that fucker off!

FURRY. Do y' want the flags now? (*He throws handfuls of flags in the air.*)

CORPORAL. Switch . . . (*Gives up. He strides over and switches off the wind machine.*) Play's over, Furry. No more play.

FURRY. Said they wanted wind. For 'play.

CORPORAL. Are you as stupid as you say you are?

FURRY. Aye. (*Looks down then up.*) Joby said it were for wind of history. Or summat.

JOBY (*gives a wave*). Thank you. Corporal that cigar . . .

SERGEANT (*evenly*). I am waiting, Corporal. Get this rabble sorted. Then we can all go home for our tea.

CORPORAL. Sergeant! (*He looks at the cigar which he holds still, gingerly, smouldering end upwards.*)

The 'PRIVATE' laughs, then stops laughing. They are all suddenly tense. The CORPORAL stares, then stamps on the cigar.

Right!

He realizes they are all staring at the stamped cigar on the ground. He looks at it. A pause.

(*Gently.*) Get back in yer right togs. Get lined up, and we'll get bact to 'uts.

The PRIVATE makes a farting noise. The CORPORAL steps smartly forward and slaps him on the face and points at him. All stock still. Then slowly they change into their prisoner clothes.

BALL *and* THOMPSON *in mid-argument.*

BALL. Impossible. Out of the question. To present such a spectacle to Members of Parliament? Here as a select committee officially inspecting the Camp? No.

THOMPSON. The men have worked hard preparing the

entertainment for the Select Committee. It has raised morale. The costumes, the props, the words of the text . . . They have taken six months to prepare.

BALL (*shaking his head*). Not a chance.

THOMPSON. At least see the rest of the performance. This was the introduction . . . Preface.

BALL. Giant pisstake. Grow up. (*Turns away.*) Not a hope, not the sliver of a chance, Captain Thompson. More than my command's worth. Sergeant Baxter!

SERGEANT. Suh!

BALL. Have that done away with. (*Points to the catafalque, the window.*)

SERGEANT. Suh! Two men, this gear . . . Out!

GUARDS *dismantling the catafalque and the stained glass window.*

THOMPSON *puts his hand on* BALL's *arm, to turn him back to the argument.* BALL *stares at the hand.* THOMPSON *removes it and steps back.*

THOMPSON. Sir.

BALL. This is an Internment Camp. Not a school, for schoolboys.

THOMPSON (*tight*). I know what place this is, Sir. The men need recreation. They'll go down, otherwise. Deteriorate, already. Some have. In a few months. Keegan over there.

BALL *turns and looks at* FURRY KEEGAN. *He is standing turned away from the others stroking a piece of fur he has taken from his pocket.*

SERGEANT (*realizes whom* COLONEL BALL *is looking at. Roars.*) That man!

KEEGAN *does not respond.*

MIKE. Furry!

FURRY (*to himself*). Nip the wire. Wi' her little teeth. But in my pocket, quiet as a babe . . .

SERGEANT. That man, Corporal!

CORPORAL. Sergeant!

The CORPORAL *rushes over to* FURRY *and swings him*

round into line. FURRY *doesn't seem to understand.*

Come on Furry, cut it out.

JOBY. Bloody ferrets.

JOBY *knocks* FURRY's *hand down, shrugs at the* CORPORAL, *does a little curtsey.*

CORPORAL. Joby . . . (*Shakes his head. He walks down the line of changing* PRISONERS, *who blow kisses to him.*) Get on, get on. (*He blows on his hands against the cold.*)

On the stage during BALL's *speech . . . the* MEN *climbing into their prison clothes . . . the* SOLDIERS *smashing up the window and the catafalque . . . the huge Union Jack being lifted.*

BALL (*privately and passionately*). Doctor. (*Sarcasm.*) 'Doctor' Thompson. It is attrition. Quoting the Shorter Oxford English Dictionary at you, here. Attrition . . . A rubbing away. Wearing down. Grinding down. Excoriation. Abrasion. Or, theological . . . 'An imperfect sorrow for sin, not amounting to contrition or utter crushing, and having its motive not in love of God, but in fear of punishment.' Quote done. Doctor, this is the twenty-eighth internment camp in the British Isles.

THOMPSON. Sir . . .

BALL (*cutting him*). No, let *my* bleeding heart bleed to *you* for once, Dr Thompson. Forget that. (*He thinks. Then formally.*) No, Captain. The men may not perform this play to the Select Committee of The House of Commons on their visit to this camp.

THOMPSON. Sir, I . . .

BALL (*privately. Furious*). You what! What, you!

A pause. The props are wrecked. The PRISONERS *stand, bored, in a ragged row. A* GUARD *picks his nose and eats his snot.*

CORPORAL. Don't pick yer nose an' eat it, lad.

GUARD. Sorry, Corporal.

THOMPSON (*stiffly*). The men put the play together themselves. It is recreation. I am Recreation Officer. The Parliamentary Committee has the brief of looking at the recreational facilities of the camp, Sir.

A pause.

BALL (*sighs*). I am not an insensitive man, Thompson. I often think will my name be blackened? Will I be blackened? At some future date. Huh? (*Change.*) Very well. We'll have your Churchill nonsense. But I have to say . . . (*Viciously.*) That you're quite a big young man, Thompson. But there's a little worm in you. (*As if he has not said that.*) But . . . Water it down, cut it about. (*Stares.*) Put a few (*Irritated gesture.*) patriotic remarks . . . About England . . . In it. That is an order.

THOMPSON. Yes, Sir.

BALL. Winston Churchill saved this country from one thousand years of barbarism. So no disrespect to the memory of that great man. (*He turns and walks the line of* PRISONERS. *Wearily.*) Yes, yes, thank you, Sergeant.

Before the SERGEANT *can reply, a* YOUNG MAN, *blacked up, stands from amidst the wreckage of the catafalque. He is dressed in blood-stained rags. His left arm is fearfully wounded, hanging by a sliver of flesh. He clutches the arm. With a spine-curving twist he pulls. The wounded arm comes away in his hand. He screams.*

SERGEANT. Who are you, lad?

DERVISH. Dying wounded Dervish, Sergeant. At the Battle of Omdurman. Tenth of September 1898.

SERGEANT. Shut up! Shut up, you!

DERVISH (*at once, fast*). Strong hot wind, foul and tainted . . . The Dervish Army, slaughtered there . . . Churchill young sightseer rode across us . . . Quote . . .

In unison with JOBY.

JOBY. ⎱ Can you imagine the postures in which a man,
DERVISH. ⎰ once created in the image of his maker, had been
twisted? Do not try, for you would ask yourself with me 'Can I ever forget?'

The DERVISH *throws the arm at* COLONEL BALL.

BALL (*momentarily the arm is in his hands. He throws it to the ground*). Serg . . .

SERGEANT. Suh! Corporal, that . . .

CORPORAL ⎱ Sergeant!
SERGEANT. ⎰ Man!

CORPORAL. Douglas! Peters!

FIRST GUARD. Corporal!

SECOND GUARD. Corp!

JOBY (*casually*). End quote. (*He sniffs.*) Young Winston's early prose. Wonderful, wonderful. Bloom of ambition upon it.

The GUARDS *coming forward.*

DERVISH. Butchery! Flies! (*Holds out his wrists for a set of handcuffs wielded by one of the* GUARDS.) Under th' imperial canopy a never settin' sun.

CORPORAL. All right! All right!

BALL *turns and looks at* THOMPSON.

BALL. I trust Captain Thompson.

THOMPSON. No, Sir.

BALL. Carry on Sergeant Baxter.

BALL *goes out.*

SERGEANT. Suh!

THOMPSON (*hesitates, then*). Sergeant Baxter . . .

SERGEANT (*a little too sharp, he hates* THOMPSON). Suh!

THOMPSON. I would like to see the entertainment committee . . .

SERGEANT. Suh!

THOMPSON. . . . And anyone else, eh . . .

SERGEANT. Suh!

THOMPSON. Interested in the Churchill play, at . . .

SERGEANT. Suh!

A pause. Both men looking at each other.

THOMPSON (*stiffened*). During evening recreation. I think in the compound. It looks like it will be a fine evening, don't you think so, Sergeant Baxter?

SERGEANT (*holds a pause as long as he dare*). Suh!

THOMPSON. Thank you.

SERGEANT. Suh!

THOMPSON. Don't harm the . . .

They're all looking at him. Pause.

Flag.

THOMPSON *goes out.* JOBY *smacks his lips, looks up to heaven, rolls his eyes.*

SERGEANT. What do you mean by that, Peake?

JOBY. Nothin', nothin'. Just . . . (*Repeats the gesture.*)

MIKE. 'Ate 'im, dunye, Tom Baxter?

SERGEANT. Sergeant please, Mr McCulloch.

JOBY (*skittishly, to get the* SERGEANT *screwed into the chit-chat*). Thought y' liked cheeks o' me old arse, Sarge. Didna know yer 'ated me.

MIKE. Don't be daft, not you. (*To the* SERGEANT.) Captain, the boy Captain that was here just now. All rubbed up an' gleamin'. (*Quick, sharp.*) 'Ate 'im, dunye, Tom. Man to man, get to you, did he, Tom? Some way or other? Abuse ye? Under th' foreskin.

SERGEANT (*calm. They've been through this kind of exchange many times*). Never let go, do yer, Michael? Agitate, agitate. Worse than a berserk washin' machine, tumble, tumble, always stuck in there, froth an' suds flying about all over the place.

MIKE. I have my convictions.

SERGEANT. Well, yeah . . . You play with 'em, quietly. In your corner.

MIKE. I was a union man. I had dignity. I was a union man.

SERGEANT. And what are you now, Michael?

MIKE. Now. (*A slight pause.*) A crank behind the wire. (*A slight pause.*) Sergeant.

SERGEANT. Why, so you are, Michael. (*Publicly.*) We'll 'ave all of you pickin' this stuff up an' carryin' it to the woodsheds. Where it can do fer stoves in the huts. Waste not, grieve not.

JOBY (*sadly*). True, true.

The PRISONERS, *picking up debris, loading it on their backs, balancing it on their heads. The coffin is intact.*

GEORGE LAMACRAFT (*the young man who is dressed as a Dervish*). Joby, that Cap'n. What school y' reckon he went to?

FIRST GUARD. Shut up.

SECOND GUARD. Shut up.

FIRST GUARD. Shut . . .

SECOND GUARD. . . . . Up.

They shove him. GEORGE gives a gasp of pain as he goes down on one knee and the handcuffs jerk.

JOBY (*deliberately ignoring the guards' violence*). Public School.

JACK (JACK WILLIAMS, *who was the Marine*). Who are you kidding? That was a jumped up English Grammar School boy. Not the genuine thing at all. You can see the cracks round the edges if you look.

JOBY. Spot 'em can yer, Jack?

JACK. As a foreigner I'm very sensitive to the English class system.

JOBY. With a talent like that yer could set up 'booth, at a Fair Ground. Like reading bumps.

TED (TED BARKER, *who was the Private*). I'd ha' said that Captain was yer actual public school. Talks like 'es eatin' a peach.

JACK. Wetly.

JOBY. Thought Stowe m'sel. Second rate, but . . . Socially plush. I know that bilious kind of rosebud in 'is throat.

JACK (*coughs. Fights it down*). Fake. He's outright make-believe. He's got to be.

SERGEANT. All right.

CAPTAIN THOMPSON *walks back on. They stop and stare at him. All of the prisoners are loaded with debris. Bits of the broken knights of armour. Splinters of wood.*

THOMPSON. I apologize.

Stares. Embarrassment.

It's my fault. (*A pause.*) We all wanted this play. You have put yourselves into it.

JIMMY UMPLEBY, *who played the* AIRMAN, *giggles.*

SERGEANT. Sh.

THOMPSON (*he hasn't noticed that*). I blame myself. The Colonel has made it clear that he disapproves of the, eh . . . Elements. (*Takes a deep breath.*) Of the presentation.

TED. Gotta clean it up then 'ave we, Sir.

THOMPSON. I'd like you to think of that.

A pause. Suddenly he realizes they are all opening their eyes at him.

Soldiers. This makes for tensions. I would like to alleviate.

The SERGEANT *seethes.*

So I would make it clear to you . . . That if I get my way, we will have a little fun with the play about Sir Winston, yet.

SERGEANT. Sure you will Suh!

THOMPSON (*startled by that. A pause*). I thought I'd pop back to tell you that.

SERGEANT. Thank you *Suh!*

THOMPSON. I want to say. (*He fails.*) Anyway. A gesture of good faith, on *my* part. We will meet at nineteen hundred hours. (*A pause.*)

The SERGEANT *turns his head slightly and eyes him.*

We live . . .

SERGEANT. Thank you SUH!

THOMPSON. I have not finished, Sergeant.

SERGEANT. No Suh.

THOMPSON. I was going to say . . . We live in difficult times. Times . . . (*Failing.*) Difficult for . . . (*He fails.*) All of us. (*A slight pause. Then he turns quickly to go out.*)

TED. Sir.

THOMPSON (*stops*). Barker?

TED. Did you go to a Public School, Sir?

A slight pause.

THOMPSON. ⎱ I . . .
CORPORAL. ⎰ Shu' yer lip!

GEORGE. Fag for yer, Sir. Gotta black face here, but m'arse be English white.

CORPORAL. Private hit that man.

The FIRST GUARD *hits* LAMACRAFT *in his stomach.* LAMACRAFT *doubles up.*

THOMPSON. Corporal! How dare . . .

SERGEANT. Don't worry, Sir . . .

SERGEANT (*leading* THOMPSON *off*). This will be alright, Sir. This will be nothin' 'ere, Sir. May I suggest the Sergeants' Mess, Sir. A grog before dinner, Sir . . .

THOMPSON. Thank you, Sergeant Baxter. (*Stops dead still, breaks away from the* SERGEANT.) Corporal Taylor.

SERGEANT. Corporal Taylor!

CORPORAL. Sergeant!

SERGEANT. Twostepsaforward! Double mark time!

The CORPORAL *steps forward two steps.*

Andoneandoneandoneandone.

The CORPORAL *running on the spot.*

Attention and Officer 'ere! Now!

The CORPORAL *comes to attention and salutes.*

(*Sotto to* THOMPSON.) May I suggest not in front of the internees, Sir . . .

THOMPSON (*ignores that*). Corporal Taylor, did I hear you tell this soldier to hit this man. Suh!

A pause.

CORPORAL. No, Sir.

SERGEANT (*sotto to* THOMPSON). May I suggest not in front of the internees, Sir . . .

THOMPSON (*ignores that. He's flushed*). Sergeant Baxter.

SERGEANT. Yessuh.

THOMPSON. Did I hear Corporal Taylor tell this soldier to hit this man?

SERGEANT (*sotto to* THOMPSON). Not in front of the internees . . .

THOMPSON. Sergeant Baxter did I hear Corporal Taylor tell this soldier to hit this man?

SERGEANT (*fast*). Don't know, Suh! Corporal Taylor!

CORPORAL. Yes, Sergeant!

SERGEANT. Did you order this soldier to 'it this man!

CORPORAL. No, Sergeant!

JOBY. Bubble bubble . . .

SERGEANT. Shut up Joby, no Suh! Corporal Taylor did not tell this soldier to hit this man. Suh!

THOMPSON. Sergeant Baxter! (*A pause. He controls himself.*) Did *you* hear . . . Corporal Taylor . . . Tell this soldier . . . To hit this man?

SERGEANT. No Suh! (*At once sotto.*) Best not in front of the internees, Sir. (*To the* CORPORAL.) Get these men to huts. All that, gear, back a' the woodsheds. (*He turns smiling to* THOMPSON.) It's like tinder, Sir. Tinder and woodshavings. I hope you will forgive me, Sir.

MIKE. Aggro, aggro.

JOBY. Lovely, lovely.

CORPORAL. Be quiet.

The CORPORAL *and the internees, but for* PETER REESE, *go off.*

SERGEANT. What you up to lad?

REESE. The Corporal told me to sweep up.

SERGEANT. Then sweep up, lad. (*And personally, to* THOMPSON.) If you want, Sir, I will place myself on a disciplinary report for this Sir.

THOMPSON. I don't know, Sergeant Baxter. I don't know at all.

SERGEANT (*quietly*). Is that a threat, Sir?

THOMPSON. Why should I have to threaten you, Sergeant Baxter?

SERGEANT. I'm sorry Sir, I don't understand.

THOMPSON. I need have no fear that you may not carry out my orders. Need I?

SERGEANT. God forbid Sir, if I may use the phrase. But . . .

THOMPSON. But what, Sergeant Baxter?

SERGEANT. Nothing, Sir. I was a lad in the Army in Ulster, did you know that, Sir?

THOMPSON (*guarded*). No. No I . . . Did not know that.

SERGEANT. Oh yes, Sir.

THOMPSON. Then you have . . .

SERGEANT. Seen a lot of pigs stuck. In English streets too, Sir.

THOMPSON. And?

SERGEANT. I know you're a liberal man, Sir.

THOMPSON. But?

SERGEANT. But the men think you're a (*Deliberately.*) fucking namby pamby Sunday school do-gooder fucking lily-white bleeding heart. Soft on the internees. Soldiers don't like that, Sir.

THOMPSON *opens his mouth to say something.*

And you have egged 'em on. Egged the scum on to take the piss out of a great Englishman. The soldier lads o' this camp don't take that very well, Sir. They take that, coming from you, like a cup of cold sick.

THOMPSON. Sergeant, I will have you put upon a charge.

SERGEANT. Doctor Thompson, right now in this camp you could not charge your grandma's pussy cat.

THOMPSON. You are a conspicuous bastard, Baxter.

SERGEANT. Conspicuous, Sir?

THOMPSON. I can see you. I can see what you are.

SERGEANT. We could run this place like sweet music. Double 'em all day, A to B, B to C an' back to A again. That's all. No plays against a-bout Sir Winston Churchill. Drop it Sir. You would be very popular. It's in all our interests.

THOMPSON. No.

SERGEANT. I'm sorry you take that attitude, Sir.

THOMPSON. I bet you bloody well are.

SERGEANT. I hope you don't get injured, Sir. Grenade on an

exercise. At any moment a nasty moment. Men have killed
officers many times over many years. Many wars, many ways.
As an NCO I don't like that, particularly.

THOMPSON. No officer would believe the way you are speaking
to me here.

SERGEANT (*blithe*). I'm pretty sure every officer has had an
NCO whisper in his pinky-piggy little ear'ole. One time or
another. Read a lot of military 'istory do you, Sir?

THOMPSON. No.

SERGEANT. I read a lot of military history. Do you know
what it tells me? In medieval times before a defeated city, they
cried havoc. And for three days the city was the common
soldier's. Rape. Burn. Loot. Dance in the blood, wine, stuff
yourself. Disgustin', eh? Morning of the fourth day, king'd
send 'is aristocrat officers in with staves, an' dogs. Clear out
the common soldier. And then send in the Archbishops to
consecrate the place . . . So the king and his retinue, a fat
ermine-robed lot, politicians all, could ride in. Unsullied. To
thank God for their delivery and freedom. The point of
my story is that the running amok, the havoc, the sacking
of the city, why that was the soldier's pay.

THOMPSON. Getting (*A breath.*) one's rocks off.

SERGEANT. Why yes.

THOMPSON. Dear God. In the officers' mess you've regarded as
a fair decent man. One of the least . . . bull-necked of our NCO
strength.

SERGEANT. Then you should pay attention to what I say, you
puffy ponce.

THOMPSON *starts.*

Don't try to hit me. I've killed men. Have you killed men? Then
don't try to hit me. Ten years the ordinary soldier has scrubbed
your bedpan. That you may not smell the terrorist in the
street. Soldier Tom doorway to doorway, bullet in the jugular,
bullet in the crotch. Ten years down Ulster way then English
streets. Soldier boys at the picket line, working men his own
kind, coming at him yelling 'Scab, Scab'. I went down a mine,
a corporal then, in the strike of nineteen eighty. The miners
of that pit tried to kill us, y'know that? A lot of soldiers are
thinking — if we got to run the mines, if we got to run the

prisons, why not the whole bloody country? I know what I would do if there was a military rebellion in England. Do you know what you would do? Or can't you do your duty? Or are you a real liar, a real self-deceiver, eh? I mean really washed up? All spent, are you? The British Army's got politicized you see, sir. You should be very glad we've not gone red.

THOMPSON. What have you gone? Black?

SERGEANT. Way o' putting it, Sir.

THOMPSON. God help us then.

SERGEANT (*snap*). Suh. (*Change*). Don't push the men, sir. Don't let this Churchill shennanigans get off the ground, Sir. The men . . . I had to speak to you, in all fairness, Sir.

THOMPSON. I will report you, Sergeant. I will break your balls.

SERGEANT. Suh!

THOMPSON. Go away.

SERGEANT. Suh!

He marches off strictly.

THOMPSON (*quietly, to himself*). Go away. Go away. Go away. Go away. Go away.

PETER REESE *approaches* THOMPSON *from upstage, broom in hand.*

REESE. Excuse me please. I arrived in this camp this morning. Perhaps you remember you asked me about my health, and told me I would have a medical examination later. At another date.

THOMPSON *looks at him blankly. He turns and walks about the hangar, self-obsessed.*

(*A slight pause.*) I come from a very small . . . Small place just on the outside of Aberdare. (*A slight pause.*) I was arrested this morning. But just before dawn, you see. When I arrived at work. Anyway. (*He swallows, a slight pause.*) I have been looking for an opportunity to speak to someone in authority. I was put in a *lorry* you see. And driven. Here, to this place. Which, I am told, is called Camp Churchill. Is that . . . Not so? (*Nothing from* THOMPSON.) In the lorry it was bad. There was an incident. We were allowed, after some time, to get out for a piss. A very bleak landscape it was. But no longer Wales.

Perhaps it was Wiltshire? Limestone, I believe. We pissed, and there was the incident. The soldier who had charge of us was a boy, over grown men. One man, not Welsh, an Irishman, Convery his name . . . Pushed the boy. In the lorry, then in the open air . . . Ran for it. Oh, we were chained. (*Raises his wrists, looks from one to the other, a pause.*) Convery pushed the soldier lad, and the soldier lad fired. Through Convery's foot. It was so . . . trivial. But Convery was a brave fellow. For both the soldier and the driver, also armed, were lads . . . And hysterical . . . And Convery calmed them down. Despite a wound that was ugly. Convery, he said . . . (*He hesitates.*) In any case, I had the impression he had been . . . to a camp before.

THOMPSON, *walking.*

Please, what worries me is my family.

THOMPSON *stands still.*

All I know is I am detained, I am somewhere in England, I have a broom in my hand and I have been asked . . . to sweep this aircraft hangar. (*Change.*) No, that is . . . false of me. I know I am in a camp. I am detained. Please, let my family know where I am. That I'm well. I have three children. Let my wife know. Can you help me?

THOMPSON (*quietly*). Go away.

REESE. I'm sorry?

THOMPSON. Go away. Go away. Go away.

He walks off briskly, a straight back.

REESE *smashes the broom, breaks it twice, throwing the head high into the flies. It falls back onto the stage, yards upstage of him. He speaks passionately, alone in the huge aircraft hangar.*

REESE. That man with his shattered, bloody foot. Said. Degradation. That there'll be no end to it. The soldier guards they'll be like gods to us. Half a cigarette from their hands, and we'll cry with wonder, and happiness . . . Never, I said. We'll never come to that. But we will, oh we will. Read every flicker of our captors, every gesture, for meaning. Said the man with the terrible wound in his foot . . . We are going lower than the lower depths. And this is how we will survive. Leave our real selves by the gate of the camp. Like old coats. And it's not us in here, daily going lower, more terrified, more craven. We are only the hearts and lives and kidneys, the bodies of those beautiful, brave and free men. And though we do terrible things, eat each other's shit, it's not our real selves here. God knows, there's no difficulty in degrading the human animal, it's vulnerable enough. A few blows, a few weeks' starvation, a few nights without sleep. And man? Would slander a slug under a stone to call him animal. And there's no shame, Convery said. There's no shame, my comrades, there's no shame in what we will be driven to. (*He raises his arms wide. A pause. His arms flop. He sags.*) Not even the time of day. (*A gesture with his wrist.*) Had my Omega . . . (*He shrugs.*)

He goes upstage, picks up the head of the broom, comes down stage, sweeps with it as best he can.

GEORGE LAMACRAFT *is whirled across the back of the stage by the* GUARDS, *handcuffed to one. They beat him, all three men running.*

GEORGE. Canopy . . . Canopy . . . Under the British Empire's Canopy . . . Never settin' sun . . . Thick so thickly they lay . . . As t'hide the ground . . . All was filthy corruption . . .

They're off. For a few seconds REESE *sweeps alone.*

FURRY KEEGAN *comes on, surreptitiously.*

FURRY. Don't sweep tha'.

REESE. Pardon?

FURRY. Cigar.

REESE. I'm sorry?

FURRY. 'Cigar tha'. Don't sweep tha'. 'Ere, mate. (*He takes out a crumpled paper bag.*) Give us 'hand.

They pinch the crumpled leaves and put them in the paper bag.

New in, ain't yer?

REESE. Yes.

FURRY. After mess call t'neet, sidle up t'me. In compound.

REESE. Yes.

FURRY. I put on I'm a hopeless case, y'know all over 'place.

Remember tha'. Treat me like I'm gone in 'ead, reet?

REESE. Right. (*Slight pause.*) My name is Peter Reese.

FURRY *ignores that.*

FURRY. I go on like I've got a ferret in my pocket. (*He takes out the piece of fur.*) See? Like I were really 'alf cut. But I let 'em know I'm good with me 'ands. Put that together. (*He points at the wind machine. Casually.*) Learnt a trade. See, I were in their Army.

REESE. 'Their' Army?

FURRY (*looks blank*). Ruling Class.

REESE. Oh.

FURRY. Yank, that. (*The wind machine.*) Engine fan, off a Tornado.

REESE. Oh.

A pause. Then FURRY *has collected the cigar tobacco and seems about to go.*

Is there a man in here called Convery?

FURRY. Convery? Na.

REESE. We were in the same lorry. He had an injured foot. Shot.

FURRY (*shakes his head*). Na. (*Going.*) T'neet.

REESE. Yes.

FURRY. Call me Furry. 'Count a fuckin' ferrets. Okey doke?

REESE *looking away.*

Pete?

REESE. Yes.

FURRY. Toodle-oo.

He scuttles off.

REESE (*a pause. He stares out into the auditorium*). Peter Reese. Hung like an old coat on the wire. Waiting. Somewhere in England, in 1984.

A pause. The lights fade out.

Act Two

The aircraft hangar. Early evening. Through the opened doors a mackerel sky with the yellow beginning of a sunset. The camp compound. Ordered wire. The flat landscape goes for miles. English hedgerows, copses, cabbage fields.

The lamps are not lit.

There are a few old oil drums downstage to one side. There is a pile of oil drums upstage.

A football match is in progress with old drums for goal posts. TED, JIMMY and JACK are in the game. MIKE stands nearby, occasionally joining in. It's a free-for-all knockabout. FURRY is in goal.

JACK (*scuffing hard with* TED). All they want . . . (*Scuffs.*) To humiliate us. (*Scuffs.*) Make us look daft.

JIMMY. Me! Me! Give it 'me.

JACK. Entertainment for Members of the English Parliament? That what they want us to be?

JIMMY. To me! Now!

TED dribbles the ball away from JACK who suddenly stands still. TED turns, ball at his feet.

Now as I do my run in . . . (*He steps back then running toward the goal.*) Oh, 'e carves 'defence apart w'is cannonball shot.

FURRY. Don't bump inta me, I 'ate it when y'bump inta me . . .

JIMMY makes his dummy run. TED fails to pass the ball, turns round with a bit of fancy work.

JIMMY. 'Og it, 'og it. Go on, 'og it. (*He stands and glares at* TED.)

JACK. I'm no puppet scarecrow. To be stood up before ladies and gents of the House of bloody Commons. What do they think I am? Want me to get up and do a turn 'bout Winston Churchill do they? Oh what a funny little man, they'll say. But how happy he must be, to stand up there. Jerk his arms about. He must almost like it, they'll say. And they'll think I'm being rehabilitated. Which is the word of the Government for total, abysmal humiliation. I mean what are we? Performing bears? To stand up in our chains? Our great paws held out to say . . . (*He adopts a pathetic posture, hands held out like a beggar.*) Look we're not savage after all. We're in chains. And we won't hug you to death. For we're silly bears. W' grins on our muzzles.

TED *flicks the ball up on his knee, then cradles it in the hollow of his foot.*

Recreational Activity? Rehabilitation? Winston Churchill? We should stuff the whole ragbag right up their throats. Eh? Mike?

Nothing from MIKE, *who merely puts his hands in his pockets.*

Ted?

TED (*intent on balancing the ball*). Dunno. Give it a whirl.

JACK. Don't you care? Being made mock of?

TED. I'm all for peace and quiet. And what you can get, on the side. So . . . (*Shrugs.*) Give it a whirl. See what crops up.

A slight pause. Then JACK *rushes at* TED. TED *side-steps with the ball and passes to* JIMMY.

JIMMY (*tees the ball up*). Y'ready, Furry? Fer me bone-breakin' cannonball?

FURRY. Don't kick it on me 'ead. Y'always kick it on me 'ead.

JIMMY takes a run up. FURRY *turns his back.* JIMMY *gently taps the ball past* FURRY.

What 'appened? What 'appened?

JACK (*sotto, bitterly, turning away*). What happened, what happened?

FURRY (*looks round*). Y' young bugger.

JIMMY. Tha's twenty-nine nil.

FURRY. But tha's only wunside, thy side. Y're not playin' agin anywun.

JIMMY. Playin' agin ye, Furry. (*He collects the ball, dribbles with it.*)

FURRY. But I ain't gorra goal t'kick inta, even.

> TED *and* JIMMY *run off with the ball.*

MIKE. Difficult, eh Jack?

JACK (*spiky*). What's that?

MIKE. To keep angry.

JACK. How d'you mean?

MIKE. Keep y'bile flowing. The 'ate topped up. Keep . . . going at the world. Eh, Jack?

JACK. I have a go, Michael. (*He coughs. A pause. He breathes deeply.*)

MIKE (*a kind of contempt*). Ay, don't you just, Jack.

JACK. We should be hard. Go at them, again and again. No respite. (*He swallows back his phlegm.*)

MIKE (*shrugs. Smiles. Spits precisely*). Ptt.

> *The game comes back on.*

JIMMY. Leeds! Leeds! 'Appy an glorious! Leeds victorious!

TED. Rubbish.

MIKE. Halfway down the League — Division Three.

JIMMY. Yeah but they're 'ard. Y'gorra admit they are 'ard.

TED. Assassins.

JIMMY. But 'ard.

FURRY (*dodging about nervously in the goal*). Don't kick it too 'ard, I waint see it. I waint see.

> JIMMY *with the ball at his insteps, looking down at it.*

TED. We gonna chuck it then? The Churchill kick.

MIKE. Y' want to do that, Ted?

TED. Look at it like this. We get up an' do a turn for these nobs . . . Well, maybe there's something in it for us.

JACK. Humiliation.

TED. I was thinking of a few crates a Guinness.

JACK. Don't let's get into booze again.

TED. No. (*Slight pause.*) Though what is very nice . . . Pint a draught Guinness . . . wi' a bottle a Barley Wine. Mixed.

MIKE. Chaser man mesel. Irish Whiskey flowin' after the cheapest bitter in the 'ouse.. Very, very fast. (*Smiles at* JACK.)

TED. Yeah, but what yer *really* want from booze, speakin' personally, is the bulk and the smoothness.

FURRY. Tell y'wha'. Red wine drunk 'ard. So 'ard it 'urts. Betwixt 'alf bottles a light ale. It were 'art student, taught me t' drink like that, years ago. We drank like that all night. Then I 'it 'im, the pansy. (*Sadly.*) Still, I say this. Makes look a things very bright and shiny. Mind ye, morning after's pretty rough. Bomb damage in yer head.

JACK. Booze talk, booze talk. I'm sick of booze talk in this place.

JIMMY. Know what they're inta, over in 'ut eleven?

TED. Dressin' up as women again, are they? Got right outta 'and that did, last time. You'd go in there . . . Long Nissen 'ut, of an evenin' . . . Fifty odd big grown men, lot a Durham lads . . . Sittin' there in frocks they'd made. I dunno. (*Shakes his head.*)

JIMMY. Na, it's electricity they're on, now.

They all look at JIMMY.

Made a resistor. Wi' wire. So to carry strength a current. Plugged the 'ole thing int' light socket. An' two terminals wi' paper clips t' put on earlobes.

FURRY. Earlobes?

JIMMY. Fromt mains. Switch 'light on, an', and ye light up, all inside. Whee. Zonk. Twinkle twinkle.

FURRY. Ay well. Takes all kinds.

TED. 'Ut eleven. Always goin' out on a limb.

JIMMY (*adolescent*). I were thinkin' of 'aving a go.

FURRY. Fryin' yer brains?

JIMMY. Why not?

FURRY (*eyes* JIMMY. *Shrugs*). Why not?

JIMMY. Ay. Why not. Neo-Luddite that'd be.

TED. You and the neo-Luddites, Leeds Chapter . . .

JIMMY. We 'ad every telephone kiosk out in a radius a twenty mile from Leeds Town Hall.

TED. Mindless.

JIMMY. Righteous.

TED. That Neo-Luddite talk . . .

JIMMY. 'Smash the World . . .'

TED. 'To make it beautiful . . . Smash the beautiful . . .'

JIMMY. 'To make it real.'

TED. Art School twaddle.

JIMMY. Yeah.

TED. Hooligan gangs.

JIMMY. Yeah, yeah . . .

TED. Smashing computers, yer dreamed of . . .

JIMMY. Let circuitry bleed.

TED. Not one computer yer ever reached. Too many guard dogs and olde English barbed wire round the real hardware.

JIMMY. We brought down Post . . .

TED. Post Office Tower, oh yes. And they put it up again and clamped down on you. You were the last . . . farts of the age of Aquarius.

JIMMY. Yeah we were stupid. Yeah we were mindless.
Yeah we tore things apart just . . . for the rippin' sound. 'Long the fault lines of the world. Rip. Rip. But give us this, we really did 'ave it in fer 'world, eh? Y'got to give us that. We really . . . had it in for the world.

TED (*with a shrug turning away*). You really had it in for the world.

FURRY. Y'gonna kick that ball at me?

A slight pause. Then JIMMY *turns and kicks the ball off. He looks at* TED. *A slight pause. Then they dash off after the ball miles away.*

Thar they go. Lose ball, they will. Did, only a week ago. Kicked ball over wire. An' soldier boy in 'tower shot leather t' pieces. Like 'e were shootin' pigeon. (*Raising his hands like a gun.*) Splat. An' leather ball . . . all shredded. On grass, 'other side a wire.

JACK. Dream of pints. Sit in a hut done up as a woman. Reminisce on a shot-down football.

FURRY *looking off at the game swaying a little.*

(*Shouting at* FURRY.) You are decrepit. Look at you. You are falling apart.

FURRY (*concentrating on the game. Blandly*). Well, y'know. Y' get by as best y' can.

JACK. Do you think that boy will really burn his brain?

MIKE. Prison talk.

The ball comes on the stage to MIKE. *He traps it, passes it to* JACK. FURRY *follows the game. But* JACK *turns and boots the ball angrily offstage.*

JACK. Hard. Hard. Go at them hard. No respite. A stone in the mouth, spat at them. Stone in the gut, spewed out at them.

MIKE. An' tha's just prison talk. And y' know it, Jack Williams.

JOBY *enters at the back. The game between* TED *and* JIMMY *comes back on.* MIKE *joins in.*

TED. Backs to the wall, boys. 'Ere comes Winston Churchill.

JOBY *gives him a V-sign.*

Really think you are 'im, don't yer, Joby. Dear oh dear. Bet you think yer standin' on the White Cliffs a Dover right now. (*The ball comes to him. He lines it up to kick at* JOBY.)

JOBY. Don't kick 'bloody thing at me.

TED. Not going to dazzle us with a bit a thigh down a right wing, then, Joby?

JOBY. Always 'ated sport. (*He sniffs.*) All them beautiful bodies. It's not 'ealthy. (*He sits down on the oil drums.*)

PETER REESE *comes on. The game being played well, seriously.*

TED (*to* PETER). Game?

PETER. Pardon?

MIKE. Get in the game?

PETER. No thank you, very much. Not just now.

TED. As yer like.

The game goes offstage. A pause. Upstage JACK WILLIAMS, *back to the audience, scuffing the ground with his foot in a corner.* FURRY *keeping goal.* JOBY *and* PETER *sitting on the oil drums.*

JOBY (*suddenly*). 'Ad y' chocolate?

PETER. Beg pardon?

JOBY. Chocolate ration.

PETER. No.

JOBY. Then you've been done.

PETER. I should have had chocolate . . .?

JOBY. Don't sneer at that.

PETER. I'm not sneering . . .

JOBY. You'll not sneer at that in a week or two.

PETER. I wasn't . . . sneering.

JOBY. 'Ard currency, chocolate. Bar a chocolate in 'ere is worth more than the Governor of the Bank of England's own knickers . . . Signed by the Governor a 'Bank of England himself. Believe me.

PETER. Yes, I do. Of course.

JOBY. Na y'don't. Y' don't 'cos y'not felt it yet. The weight of it. That's 'ow these places, can flourish. In England. Suddenly, w' no trouble at all. Shove troublemakers behind wire. 'Cos people have not felt the weight of it. For 'emselves. (*He sniffs. A slight pause.*) Funny in't it.

PETER. Yes. What?

JOBY. 'Ow freedom goes. When did freedom go? (*Snaps his fingers.*) Thar, then, was it then? Or some ev'nin', way back in 'nineteen seventies. Wun ev'nin'. Y'were in 'pub. Or local Odeon. Or in 'bed w' your Mrs. Or watchin' telly. An' freedom went. Ay, y'look back and y'ask . . . When did freedom go?

PETER. I have been given this letter form. (*He takes a buff letter form out of his pocket.*) I am told I can write one letter a month. I don't have a pencil . . .

JOBY· *takes out a pencil and gives it to* PETER.

Thank you.

PETER *doesn't write, he stares at the paper, turning it over and over.* JOBY *stares out into the auditorium.*

JOBY. What y'in 'ere for?

PETER. Conspiracy, they said.

JOBY. Conspiracy they do say, usually. (*Malevolently.*) What did y' do?

PETER. I . . . Became angry.

JOBY. Ay.

PETER. I committed an act of vandalism.

JOBY. Ay. (*Eyes* PETER.) What did y'vandalize?

PETER. I would rather not say. Petty vandalism.

JOBY. Ay.

PETER. I'm ashamed. I've a wife and three children. And I've been hauled off, to this place. And I'm ashamed.

JOBY (*sniffs. Lightly*). I were a journalist, on Derby evenin' paper. No militant, not by a million mile. (*Chuckles.*) Strike a 1980 I were a scab. Went on workin'. I were reportin' picket line at pit gate. There were a punch-up. Like there can be, on such occasions. When men get lathered up . . . 'bout world, 'bout life . . . Usually is a punch-up. Anyway, upshot were I 'it a po-liceman. Dunno why. I'm not a violent man. Summat must a come over me.

PETER. Passion.

JOBY. What? (*Stares.*) Oh, ay. (*A slight pause.*) I 'it the policeman. And the upshot a that were . . . 'policeman 'it me. And the upshot a that were . . . They did me under 'Emergency Provisions Act. As they did us all. Ordered to be detained. Till further notice. (*He sniffs.*)

PETER. You've not appealed to the Home Secretary? I'm told you can appeal to the Home Secretary.

JOBY. Na. I seen men write long letters, pour out their 'earts t'Ome Secretary. I've 'eard men, cryin' in their sleep t'Ome Secretary. Na. (*A malevolent glance.*) Y'not 'oardin' that chocolate.

PETER. No.

JOBY. Fer bunce, eh?

PETER No.

JOBY. I remember when chocolate were ten pence a bar. (*Sniffs.*) Inflation. In-flammation. Schubert, t'composer, died a the clap, y'know.

PETER. I didn't know that.

JOBY. Inflames the brain. Makes artist think a weird an' wonderul tunes an' shapes. Inflation does 'same for a country. Weird an' wonderful, till 'backbone rots. (*A slight pause.*) Anyroad, that's my contribution t'economic theory. (*Sniffs.*)

The ball flies on. FURRY *catches it.*

FURRY. Eh, I caught 'ball. (*He squeezes it.*)

At the back of the hangar the CORPORAL *comes on. He carries a tin bath. He goes to a light fitting and switches the lamps on.*

(*Looking at the ball.*) Eh it's goin' down. Sumwun'll 'ave t'sell their arse fer 'bicycle repair kit.

JIMMY. What's up?

FURRY. Ball's goin' down. Eh it's all pitted.

The CORPORAL *has come downstage with the tin bath.*

CORPORAL. Joby. One bath.

JOBY. Many thanks.

CORPORAL. Won't take anythin' fer it. (*Touches his nose.*)

JOBY. I won't ask where it comes from. (*Touches his nose.*)

CORPORAL. Officers' kitchens actually. They keep it 'andy fer restin' champagne bottles in ice, when they 'ave a do. *In* the Officers' Mess.

They look at the bath in wonder.

MIKE. Jesus.

TED. Pigs.

JOBY. They won't be using it fer visitin' Members a Parliament t'morrow?

CORPORAL. Spoil the 'ole image wouldn't it. Na, it's austerity kick tomorrow. Be a few cans a lager an' a slosh a medium sherry. (*Nods at the bath.*) Fer the play, eh? Bubble bath. Hurr.

FURRY. Tommy. Could y'gerr'us new ball?

CORPORAL. That will cost yer.

FURRY. 'Ow much?

CORPORAL. 'Ow about a ferret sandwich? Ferret sandwich, hurr hurr.

No one laughs.

FURRY (*seriously*). I dunno.

TED. Could do, eh . . . (*Looks round the group. Shrugs.*) Fifty Senior Service? Or cash?

CORPORAL. I'll take the fags.

MIKE *nods.* JOBY *waves his hand.* JACK *shrugs.*

FURRY. Ay.

TED. Done.

CORPORAL. One match-play football. Wembley.

No response. He turns to go.

MIKE (*at once*). Oh Tommy.

CORPORAL. Yeah?

MIKE. Georgie.

CORPORAL. Georgie?

MIKE. Lad with the face done up black this afternoon.

CORPORAL. Oh yeah, Georgie.

MIKE. How is he gettin' along?

CORPORAL. Oh. Very . . . very perky.

MIKE. Glad to hear of it. Where is he?

CORPORAL. Cooling.

MIKE. Under guard is he?

CORPORAL. 'E's cooling.

MIKE. Cooling off?

CORPORAL. Down. Cooling down.

MIKE. I have him on my mind, y'see, Tommy.

CORPORAL. Yeah. (*He backs away.*) One football. Match-play, Wembley football. (*He goes.*)

TED. They not dumped Georgie, 'ave they? They not dumped 'im.

A pause.

JOBY. Right. (*He takes a big lump of sheaves of paper from inside his coat pocket.*) Yalta Conference.

TED. Y'what?

JOBY. Yalta Conference. President Franklin D. Roosevelt. Churchill. Stalin. On 'shore a Black Sea. February Fourth 1945. Carved up modern world. And Roosevelt dyin'. Churchill pissed out a 'is mind. An' Joe Stalin, Joe Stalin ah ha! Sayin' nowt. (*Handing out lumps of paper.*)

PETER. Beg pardon, but I . . .

JACK. But you what?

PETER. I am not very good at reading aloud.

JACK. You can read, brother.

PETER. Not very well aloud. Not . . . absolutely with conviction.

MIKE. What's the bath symbolic of then, eh Joby?

JOBY (*he thinks. Then he kicks the bath*). Europe. Europe, sat upon by 'bums a Super Powers.

MIKE. And the bathwater? What's the bathwater symbolical of?

JOBY (*he thinks. Then*). People a Europe! Displaced by . . .

MIKE . . . Great bums . . .

JOBY. Ay.

MIKE. An' soap?

JOBY. Soap? (*Sniffs. A slight pause.*) Truth.

MIKE (*groans*). Ah, come on . . .

JOBY. Bar a soap. (*Points fiercely at* PETER's *navel.*) Stands for historical truth. In all 'er vulnerability.

PETER (*lost*). Am I to be a woman, then?

MIKE. Bar a soap . . .

JOBY (*intense*). Y'see, worn away by brutal 'ands. Now a mere slither, a pale thing. Cleansin' fragrance, floatin' away. Easily lost at bottom a bath. In danger a goin' down (*Points into bath.*) plug'ole a Fascism altogether. (*Change. Lyrically.*) Jus' a scent . . . jus' a whiff . . . On 'dirty bath water.

TED. Oh my gawd.

JOBY (*to* PETER). Truth! I mean . . . soap!

PETER. Pardon?

JOBY. Read.

PETER (*deeply unhappy. He reads*). I was a bar of soap, in between the thighs . . . of Winston Churchill and Joseph Sta-lin . . .

JOBY (*interrupting*). All right you'll do. Let's do it in 'bath. I'm Churchill a course.

TED. A course.

JOBY. Who wants t'be Joe Stalin? Sumwun 'eavy . . .

FURRY *turns to slouch off at once.*

Furry Keegan come back 'ere.

FURRY. Do I 'ave ter?

JOBY. We won't do it in 'nude fer rehearsal. (*He settles in the bath with some difficulty.*)

FURRY. In me bare pelt?

JOBY (*waves his hand about*). Add t'effect . . .

FURRY. I don't wanna be Joe Stalin in 'altogether. I don't wanna be Joe Stalin, even.

JOBY. 'Ere's ya famous droopy moustache. (*From his pocket. Hands it to* FURRY.)

FURRY. I'll jus' look after me wind machine . . .

TED. Come on Furry. Y'need a bath.

JOBY. Just you get in bath wi' Winston Churchill. (*He sighs.*)

FURRY (*climbing into the bath*). Recreational activity they call it. Gerrin' up a play. Reckon it's good fer ye. Well it's not. It's bloody murder. (*He puts the moustache on. Large, clown-like. Big black elastic band.*) Takes ye back, years. Bloody school. Bloody poetry bein' read at ye. Bloody daffodils wavin' in 'wind. An' Jesus walkin' on dark Satanic Mills. All I can remember a school. Daffodils bloody wavin', an' Jesus walkin' on bloody dark Satanic Mills. An' daring girls t'run in boys' bog.

JIMMY *turns away and crouches down on his haunches, back to the audience.* JACK *and* TED *look at each other and shrug.* MIKE *turns aside and cleans his nails with a split match.*

JOBY. Furry.

FURRY. What?

JOBY. Shut up.

FURRY. Right.

JOBY. Just be Stalin.

FURRY. Right. (*At once to* PETER REESE, *who listens politely.*) What y'remember, all y'days? When y'were a kid. What were all that about? An' gerrin' married. An' first kid, an' flowers in 'ospital. Wha' were all that about? Dunno. Not the faintest. Jus . . . sunk down. Sediment. Silt. Mud. An' world changin'. An' money goin' mad. An' a strikes. And when Union said . . . Leave y' back door open tonight. Fer lads t'pop in. Jus fer night. Y'did. I did. Left door on 'latch. Beer out. Camp bed, eiderdown and blankets in' parlour. We 'eard 'em, down there. One came up t'door and said thanks. Sounded a lad. Southern. (*A pause.*)

JOBY *takes a breath.*

(*Continues oblivious.*) Indus'tr'l saboteurs, they said. Arbourin' an' abettin', they said. Detained, they said. Why? Dunno. Put it down t'experience, me old Dad'ld say. Daft old sod. What you do is . . . Get yerself a bit a cunnin' in world. What y'can. And the rest . . . sediment. Silt. Mud (*A pause.*)

JOBY. Done?

FURRY *lost in reverie.* JOBY *sighs. The lamps are bright now. The daylight has gone. The light is dirty rich yellow pools, shadows.* JIMMY *springs up and kicks the oil cans that were goal posts over. He pauses, breathing, tensing himself. Then he runs to the back of the stage and kicks into the pile of oil drums. The pile collapses, they bounce and spin on the stage. Then a silence. Then he shouts from the back of the stage:*

JIMMY. Old men! Rot old men! Chop old men up! Chop up dead old men! Chop up dead old men's England! Chop! Chop!

JACK. I agree, I say no to humiliation. I say we go down their throats. Hard.

The CORPORAL *walks out of a shadow. A nasty silence.*

CORPORAL. Alright, gents?

MIKE. We're fine, Tommy.

CORPORAL. Oh Michael, a word.

MIKE. Sure, Tommy.

CORPORAL (*falters, unable to ask for privacy. A pause.*) That lad with the black face.

MIKE. Georgie.

CORPORAL. Georgie. 'E's 'urt.

MIKE. Hurt, is he.

CORPORAL. Yeah. I tell you out a friendship.

MIKE. I fully understand that Tommy.

CORPORAL. What wiv the . . . arrangement we 'ave.

MIKE. Y'mean the stuff y'steal for us an' we pay ye for.

CORPORAL. Yeah.

MIKE. Why should that come to an end, Tommy?

CORPORAL. No reason.

MIKE. Then . . . (*He shrugs.*)

CORPORAL. Good. (*Uncertain.*) Very good then.

MIKE (*deadly*). Tommy, where is the lad?

CORPORAL. We dumped 'im, Michael.

A pause.

MIKE. That'll be the third ye've dumped this month, Tommy.

CORPORAL. The lads are very . . . nervy. Tell yer, out a friendship.

MIKE. That's alright. (*A slight pause.*) Then.

CORPORAL. Yeah. (*He hesitates. Then goes off fast.*)

PETER (*a pause*). What's dumped? (*A pause.*) What's dumped mean?

All the others dead still. PETER *looks around at them, then realizes 'dumped' means 'murdered'.*

CAPTAIN THOMPSON *comes on. He is out of uniform in a*

good sensible coat. He wears a brown felt, affectedly brimmed hat. He has a large, lovely fluffy dog with him. It wags its tail and pants eagerly. (N.B. A real dog.)

THOMPSON. Evening, lads. (*A pause.*) Take the dog for a walk. In the woods . . . And the wife, eh? (*Chuckles. Stops chuckling. A pause.*) Well. (*A pause.*) Ah. A bath. Yalta? Churchill? Stalin? Very, eh. Yes. And. (*To* REESE.) Who are you?

JACK (*viciously*). He's the bloody soap.

THOMPSON. The soap? Oh. (*A slight pause.*) Must be off. Take the dog for a walk. And the wife . . . Good night, everyone. (*He hesitates. Then goes off quickly.*)

MIKE. We'll do Churchill for 'em tomorrow, Jack. And we will. (*A slight pause.*) To them. At them.

JACK *and* JIMMY *coming towards* MIKE.

JACK. What you got in mind, Michael?

MIKE. Breakout. (JIMMY *and* JACK *stop dead.*) Breakout.

Blackout.

Act Three

A copse near the camp. Night. A dog barking. THOMPSON *and his wife,* CAROLINE. *They are shining torches at each other.*

CAROLINE. Mummy will give us money for the house, Julian. (*A slight pause.*) Julian? Say yes.

THOMPSON. I don't know, Caroline. I just don't know.

CAROLINE. It's not actually in Maidstone. More on the outskirts of Maidstone.

THOMPSON. Near your Mother.

CAROLINE. Julian, Mummy's put a deposit down.

THOMPSON. Mummy's put a desposit down.

CAROLINE. Don't be angry.

THOMPSON *shakes his head, turns his light away. Her light plays on him anxiously.*

Don't be hurt. Don't be upset. Don't go cold on me.

THOMPSON (*upset, hurt, cold*). No.

CAROLINE (*bitterly*). I don't know why you have to feel so guilty.

THOMPSON. I don't 'Feel guilty'.

CAROLINE. You feel guilty. Because you're in the Army and because you're a doctor. In a prison camp.

THOMPSON. I do not 'Feel guilty'.

CAROLINE. Guilt. It drips off you. Like a runny nose.

THOMPSON. All right. I feel guilty. Yes, wonderful, fine. That's me. The English leper.

CAROLINE (*irritated*). For Godsake.

THOMPSON. Unclean, unclean, along the English lanes. (*Change.*) I have to stay here, Caroline.

CAROLINE. You don't.

THOMPSON (*at once*). What's the matter with our bloody dog? (*He calls into the dark.*) Roger? Here!

CAROLINE. Roger! (*She slides the beam of the torch along the stage.*) Roger, here boy!

THOMPSON. Don't shine that at him. You know he's nervy.

The barking stops suddenly. They look at each other, momentarily startled.

(*He shrugs.*) Rabbit? Stoat track? (*Playfully.*) Roger, all sniffy, zig-zagging along some lovely smell.

CAROLINE. Happy dogs.

THOMPSON. Happy dogs.

Both sad.

CAROLINE. I look out of the window. The window of our married quarters. At the rain. And the mud. And the huts. And the men, going from hut to hut, on the duckboards. This morning I saw a man stumble. He stumbled off the boards, into the mud. It came up to his knee. Where does the mud come from? The ever-deepening mud. And when there is a fine day the men light fires. You look across the compounds . . . and the men are stooping, by little fires . . . I've never understood why they do that. What do they have to burn? It's not only to keep warm. At the height of summer there will be little fires, the men stooped over them. It seems for miles. The prison is so strange. Another thing, why do the men stuff the windows of the huts with rags? Nail the rags over the glass, where they can. I'm so frightened. So deeply frightened of this place. I want to go back down South. I want you out of the Army and a real doctor again. Worrying about little girls' tonsils and little boys' acne. Not crucifying yourself for being half doctor, half prison guard. Tearing yourself apart. Crying in your sleep. I'm frightened, I'm sick scared. Julian? Julian? (*Nothing from* THOMPSON.) You were going to do research. Heart diseases? You loved heart diseases. You'd talk for hours, into the night, about heart diseases. Julian?

Nothing from THOMPSON.

(*Bitterly.*) Oh, I know that silence. That stiff neck. Go on, go on . . . flick your neck! Jerk your head, like a little boy.

A slight pause. Involuntarily, for she's caught him, he flicks his head.

That's it! The I am so innocent, sensitive and delicate gesture. (*Savagely.*) The little flick. (*A slight pause.*) Julian?

Nothing from THOMPSON.

It's not bad, what I want, is it? It's no disgrace? A house, with a garden, in the south of England. Decent. Mild. Safe. Away from this . . . rural slum. Slum landscape, slum fen . . . Cabbage fields for miles. Derelict airfields . . . On the horizon, barbed wire . . . Men by little fires . . . (*She is near tears.*) Julian?

Nothing from THOMPSON.

No disgrace. Not wanting to be the English wife. Of the English Doctor. Of an English concentration camp.

A pause.

That's what you are, my love.

THOMPSON. I know! I know! I know that's what I am! (*A pause, then speaking fast, evenly, looking at the ground six feet before him.*) I remember, as a student. Driving in Spain. We went deep into a poor region. We drove down a track. Up over a little ridge, quickly, down into a hollow. And there before us, a gate. Wire. And in the . . . gentle slope of the hillside . . . holes. Sheets of corrugated iron over them. And pushing the sheets of corrugated iron aside, and crawling out of the holes . . . Men. Who looked grey, and like sticks. And running towards us, soldiers, waving, shouting, 'Fuck off! Fuck off!' We tore the car round. And drove all that day and most of the night, out of Spain. Never in England, we said. Never in England.

A long silence.

Tell her . . .

At once, COLONEL BALL *in the dark.*

BALL. That anyone there?

THOMPSON. Thompson, Sir.

CAROLINE (*anxious*). Julian?

THOMPSON (*ignroes her*). Captain and Mrs Thompson, Sir.

BALL. Ah! Walking the dog?

THOMPSON. Yes, Sir. (*He shines the light at* BALL. BALL *is in civilian clothes.*)

BALL. Likewise. Wife and dog, eh? She's got somewhere. Wife I mean. (*He calls out.*) Glenda? Glenda, where are you? Come here! (*A slight pause.*) Well. (*He nods to* CAROLINE.)

Nothing from CAROLINE.

Don't want to go on about work, but the heating situation is worrying the daylights out of me. The bloody huts should be insulated. But then the damp's got into the concrete prefab sections . . . It's all bloody. Chew it around from the medical view, would you, Thompson.

THOMPSON. Yes, Sir.

CAROLINE. Julian . . .

A dog howls.

BALL. That's our Alfred.

THOMPSON. Our Roger, I think, Sir.

BALL. What good English names we have for our dogs.

The howling stops abruptly. He looks at THOMPSON, *and he draws a pistol.*

Your light. Over there. Now.

THOMPSON *flicks his light straight at* MRS BALL.

GLENDA (*distressed*). A young man. Over there.

THOMPSON (*to* CAROLINE). Look after her.

GLENDA. He's got black on his face.

THOMPSON *and* BALL *run forward and find* GEORGE LAMACRAFT.

CAROLINE (*leading* MRS BALL *to one side*). Glenda, don't . . .

GLENDA. But he's . . . On his face.

LAMACRAFT. Did it to me. Behind a woodshed thurr . . . Then dumped me in the dustbin, an' took me out. Wi' the refuse, come nightfall.

THOMPSON. Who? Who did?

LAMACRAFT. Be fool t'say, wouldn't I?

THOMPSON (*to* BALL). I know him. Hut nine. George Lamacraft.

LAMACRAFT. Doctor Thompson.

THOMPSON (*lifts him round the shoulders*). Yes, George. What?

LAMACRAFT. Killed your dog, Doctor.

THOMPSON *looks away and sees the dog.* BALL *goes and picks the dog up, then throws it down in disgust.*

Poor savage. Eh? Eh? English soldiers? Poor savage Dervish, lover of God. (*Pain.*) Dyin' in a sand. One a Winston's Wars weren't it, when he was a young man. Young blood. Inna sand. (*He lifts himself a little.*) Can you imagine the postures in which a man . . . (*He dies.*)

A pause. The actors switch their lamps out.

Act Four

The aircraft hangar. The doors open. Bright afternoon sunlight. In the hangar a stage has been erected. It has a Union Jack curtain. Comfortable chairs are set before it. Its crude lighting rig is in sight, with a lighting board to one side. FURRY sits by it, carefully smoking.

A raucous version of 'Puppet on a String' by a brass band is being played over the loudspeakers. Outside the doors there is the sound of a helicopter landing. A blast of air across the hangar rocks the little stage. FURRY unconcerned shelters his cigarette.

The blast dies down. FURRY stubs his cigarette out. The Select Committe, COLONEL and MRS BALL, CAPTAIN and MRS THOMPSON, SERGEANT BAXTER and CORPORAL TAYLOR come on. The Select Committee are MR JONATHAN ST JOHN (Con-Lab ruling National Government coalition), MR GERALD MORN (Soc. Lab) and MRS JULIA RICHMOND, a young Civil Service Secretary to the Committee. They are all well dressed, the camel hair, the woollen suit, MRS RICHMOND's pastel shaded suit, coat and hat. They sweep on to before the stage. From across the hangar a SOLDIER approaches with a tray stacked with drinks. A PRIVATE closes the doors of the hangar. The music of the loudspeakers stops.

BALL. Sherry?

They all take a glass politely. Not the SERGEANT and the CORPORAL.

Ladies and gentlemen. The Queen.

SERGEANT. Detail. Attention!

ALL. The Queen.

They all drain their glasses. A moment's hesitation. Then they all put the drinks back on the tray.

SERGEANT. Detail: Stand at ease.

BALL. On behalf of the officers, other ranks and men, and the detainees, I am pleased to welcome you to Churchill.

ST JOHN. I am Jonathan St John. I am Chairman of this sub-committee of the Committee of Ways and Means and I am very thankful.

BALL. Thank you sir. (*Salutes.*)

BALL *shakes hands with* ST JOHN.

ST JOHN. This is the right honourable Mr Gerald Morn of the Socialist Labour opposition. He is vice-chairman of the committee.

MORN. How do you do?

BALL (*salutes*). Sir.

BALL *shakes hands with* MORN.

ST JOHN. This is Mrs Julia Richmond. On loan from the Min of Defence think tank.

JULIA. How do you do?

BALL. Ma'am.

ST JOHN. As Chairman of the Committee I am, of course, of the party of the Government of the Day. But since that Government is a coalition of the Conservative Party and part of the Labour Party . . . not the part to which Mr Morn still stubbornly adheres to . . .

MORN *gives a little wave.*

Since we have a Con-Lab Government, I think it only right to tell you I am more Con than Lab. Very much more.

Polite titters.

MORN. The Mother of Parliaments is in an on-going cock up situation. 'Nother sherry, soldier.

Polite titters. MORN *takes another drink.*

BALL. This is Captain Thompson, our Medical Officer and Recreational Duties Officer, responsible for the prisoners' . . . the detainees' . . . Bodily and psychological welfare.

THOMPSON (*salutes*). Sir.

Shakes hands with ST JOHN.

ST JOHN. Pleasure, Captain.

THOMPSON (*salutes*). Sir.

MORN. How are you?

> THOMPSON *and* MORN *shake hands.* MORN *takes another sherry and wanders away looking at the* SOLDIERS *and the hangar.*

JULIA. You were at Clare College, a little before me.

THOMPSON. How did you know?

JULIA. I read a file on you.

THOMPSON. Ah.

JULIA. Do you go back to Cambridge?

THOMPSON. No. Do you?

JULIA. I use the psychology lab. from time to time.

THOMPSON. How are the experimental rats?

JULIA (*staring him out calmly*). Happily out of their minds.

BALL (*eyeing* THOMPSON *and* RICHMOND *warily*). And how is London, Sir?

ST JOHN. Oh, you know. Squalid as ever.

BALL. Yes Sir.

ST JOHN. Metropolitan life. The paranoia and the glory.

THOMPSON. What exactly is your research at the Ministry of Defence?

JULIA. It is for a new kind of imprisonment. That's humane.

THOMPSON. Humane?

JULIA. Drugs, surgery, control. Kinder than your prison wire. We're on the same side, Captain Thompson.

THOMPSON. Good, good.

CAROLINE. And what side is that?

JULIA. Humanity.

CAROLINE. Oh, humanity. (*She sips her drink carefully.*)

BALL. If I can kick off formally now . . .

GLENDA. Philip. Could . . .?

BALL. Oh yes. This is my wife.

ST JOHN. How do you do?

He shakes hands with MRS BALL.

GLENDA. Very well thank you.

JULIA. How do you do?

She shakes hands with MRS BALL.

MORN. Hello there.

THOMPSON. This is my wife, Caroline.

ST JOHN. How do you do?

CAROLINE. Very well, thank you.

ST JOHN *shakes hands with* CAROLINE.

JULIA. How do you do?

CAROLINE. Very well thank you.

JULIA *shakes hands with* CAROLINE.

MORN. Hello.

MORN *is now very close to* SERGEANT BAXTER, *staring at him.*

Hello to you too, Sergeant.

SERGEANT. Suh.

MORN *drinks his sherry, right in the* SERGEANT'*s face.*

GLENDA. If, during your inspection time here, you are at any time dirty . . . and would like a shower, or a bath, you are very welcome to use our bathroom. (*She smiles at* JULIA.)

JULIA. Thank you.

A difficult pause.

BALL. Kick off. As the Committee you are welcome to inspect what you will. However, I would ask you to remain accompanied by an NCO . . . Sergeant Baxter here has a detailed rota of the Sergeants' Mess to accompany you.

MORN. Accompany?

BALL. Merely if you would please be accompanied, we would be grateful. We think it would be best and . . . We would like to insist.

MORN. Would you?

ST JOHN. I think that's reasonable. We do not know the moods, the ins and outs, the ups and downs . . . of the camp. A body of men is continually changing, day to day. And, I'm sure, that we should accept very good advice.

MORN. As I see it . . . AND I don't see why we shouldn't go hammer and tongs at this from the start, this committee is a dead alley cat. Slung from garden to garden. Stomach well on the rot.

ST JOHN. My colleague has a love of the lurid phrase.

MORN. It's our terms of reference from which the stench rises. God knows my party did what it could, bless its little red socks. But being a left wing MP in the British Parliament's like being an enema up an arseful of piles.

GLENDA. Oh.

ST JOHN. Gerald . . .

MORN. We can't ask should there be a place like this? How come there's a place like this? Just 'health and recreation'. See how pink the prisoners' tongues are. And are there enough footballs and cricket pads for the inmates of the English Dachau.

ST JOHN. } Oh God.

BALL. } I'm sure.

CAROLINE. You don't think enemies of society, terrorists, should be locked away?

A silence. All still.

You don't think they flout basic human rights . . . themselves forfeit human rights?

All still. FURRY *looking down at the floor. He sees the butt he trod out. He stoops and picks it up. Stares at it. Sniffs it.*

SERGEANT (*sotto*). Don't do that, don't you do that, don't do that.

FURRY (*loudly*). Butt, on the floor.

He puts the butt behind his ear then removes it, and picks at the burnt end. The SERGEANT *loses his patience and strides over, slaps the butt out of* FURRY's *hand. All but for* MORN *and* CAROLINE, *looking at the* SERGEANT.

SERGEANT (*embarrassed*). Detainee. Fiddling, Suh! Fiddlin' with a cigarette butt, Suh! Very unhealthy habit. Suh! Pick anything up off the floor they would, Suh!

BALL. Yes. Thank you, Sergeant.

SERGEANT. Suh.

CAROLINE. Or are you a secret sympathiser with any criminal with a gun who shouts 'Change the world'?

THOMPSON (*low*). Caroline, shut up, just shut up.

CAROLINE *ignores him.*

MORN. I don't know, Lady. We're all caught in some vast conspiracy of obedience. Who is responsible? None of us. All of us.

BALL. If . . . a more appropriate time could be found. For a wide ranging discussion in depth. (*He waves at the little stage.*) The men have prepared an entertainment, in the nature of something like a play. Since your Committee's terms of reference are to look at the welfare of thé detainees . . . this may be of interest to you.

MORN *looks pissed off. He goes back to staring in the* SERGEANT's *face. He flows on.*

The aircraft hangar here, we use as a recreation and leisure area. In itself, something of a marvel of a building. Second World War. And way back there in the nineteen forties, very hush hush. Frank Whittle's early, first jet engine was test flown here. Two of 'em . . . slung under the wings of a Wellington bomber. A great secret, over the villages. How many land-girls looked up and saw the impossible in the sky? But no one said a word. Shall we sit on the chairs?

ST JOHN. Mrs Ball?

GLENDA. Oh, thank you, Mr St John.

All of them settling on the chairs but for MORN.

MORN. And what do you feel?

SERGEANT. 'Feel' Sir?

MORN. About shoving your social enemies into internment camps.

SERGEANT. Personally Sir?

MORN. Why not?

SERGEANT. Personally. Put it like this, Sir. What do you do with a slobbering rabid dog? Don't let it go round infecting us all, do you Sir? Y'take it out and shoot it, don't you Sir? Like, in the end, we did to the micks in Ireland.

MORN. Why, a social philosopher in Army boots.

SERGEANT. Just one of freedom's professionals, Sir.

MORN (*low, at the* SERGEANT). You sods. Oh you sods.

ST JOHN. Gerald, please. (*Lightly to* BALL.) This committee is a bitch to chair.

MORN. I come, I come.

MORN *goes to a chair, passing the* PRIVATE *with the drinks tray, taking another on his way.*

BALL (*angry*). Yes. Do please top up.

THOMPSON *standing before the little audience, gangly, awkward.*

THOMPSON. The entertainment, by the men, has been entitled by them 'The Other Second World War', or 'You won't believe where I'm going to put my cigar!'

The little audience look blank.

Er, the men devised the entertainment themselves, making their own speeches. They made the costumes and the props. It is their own expression.

THOMPSON *goes to his chair.*

ST JOHN. Encouraging.

GLENDA. Very jolly.

BALL (*privately to* THOMPSON). Going smoothly I think, Thompson.

THOMPSON. My wife was . . .

BALL. No No. Hope to God you've cleaned this up, though. Cut out the abuse, and the bits about Welsh miners.

THOMPSON. All above board now Sir.

BALL. How did you manage that? Or should I be deaf and blind?

THOMPSON. Promised the men a perk. Five crates of Guinness, Sir.

BALL. I am deaf and blind.

THOMPSON. Thank you, Sir. Right Keegan.

FURRY *steps forward with a dustbin lid. He hits it with a
hammer.*

FURRY (*aggressively*). I jus' wanna say this. 'Bout dirty words.
When there's a dirty word, in play . . . Stead of yer gerrin'
dirty word in yer face, I hit my gong. This (*Brandishing
the dustbin lid.*) is my gong. (*He hits the dustbin lid with the
hammer.*) Right? .Right. Jus' so yer know. An' ladies present
won't get their knickers in a twist by foul language. So (*He
hits the dustbin lid.*) to you all.

Uncertain applause. A silence with occasional coughs. FURRY
at the little electrical board.

One. Two. Three. Go.

*Light on the little stage. The Union Jack curtain rises. The
'scene' is the same as that at the beginning of Act One, but
the whole presentation is coarser. A dim light. Above, a huge
stained glass window of medieval knights in prayer. Below,
candles round a huge catafalque which is draped with the
Union Jack. At each corner a* SERVICEMAN *stands guard,
head lowered in mourning. The parts are played as before.*
JACK WILLIAMS *as the Marine,* TED. BARKER *as the
Private,* MIKE McCULLOCH *as the Seaman,* JIMMY
UMPLEBY *as the Airman.*

TED. Body of Sir Winston Churchill. And I a poor soldier
guarding his remains. My Mum cried when I told her. Loved
him, loved him, she cried. My Mum cried. Yes, something
to write home about. To say I was there, night they laid
him, there in the dark.

MIKE (*aside*). Standing guard you get to thinking. And
imagining. The general public come up to you and torment
you. Dogs pass. It rains. It sleets. It snows. Sun comes
out, sweat runs down your nose. And your mind . . . drifts.
Night jobs like this are worst. Spots before your eyes. Planets.
Moons and stars. You fall through the floor. Thinking of your
life, and just what the (FURRY *hits the dustbin lid.*) you're
doing. And you fall. Toecaps . . . spats . . . the crease of your
uniform slices through the stone. And you fall. Through
England.

JIMMY. Hey, mate.

MIKE. Hush.

JIMMY. Oh my Godfather. Mate.

MIKE. What?

JIMMY. Oh Jesus Christ.

MIKE. What is the bloody matter with you?

JIMMY. Don't you hear?

MIKE. Hear what?

JIMMY. Knocking.

MIKE. Knocking?

JIMMY. He knocked.

MIKE. You're one under.

JIMMY. He wants to get out.

TED. Hey, you two. Shut it.

MIKE. Sonny boy, he heard a knock.

TED. Knock?

MIKE. From behind.

A knocking heard from inside the coffin.

TED. A bird, caught under the lid.

A knocking from inside the coffin. CHURCHILL *forces the lid off and sits up, swirled with the flag. He has an unlit cigar.*

JACK. Don't look now, but I think we've got a problem.

They look round.

JIMMY. Back from the dead!

TED. Back from the dead!

JACK. Back from the dead!

MIKE. That's not decent. To come back from the dead like that!

A pause. Whispers.

JACK. That's what he looked like, close up to.

TED. Wait till my Mum hears about this.

JACK. That's what's on the stamps. And the Memorial Five Bob bit in Presentation Case.

TED. Do you think a corpse can sign an autograph?

CHURCHILL, *a massive victory sign with cigar.*

JACK. Victory from the grave. That's what that is, victory from the grave.

JIMMY. I think I've cottoned on. The living dead.

TED. Living dead?

JIMMY. Straight case. Like Dracula, come back for blood and young women's necks. Take a stake through the heart to get him back in the grave. Or a cross. Or a twig of wolfbane. Or sunlight, the first rays of dawn. And there's something else.

TED. Surprise me.

JIMMY. The way you get to being a vampire is by being bit by another vampire. Your blood is . . . translated.

TED. So?

JIMMY. So, who bit him?

JACK. Evens on General de Gaulle.

JIMMY. Maybe they're all the living dead. All the leaders of the world. Vampires. Imagine them in the Gents Toilet at the United Nations, sucking each other's necks.

CHURCHILL *yawns and stretches, then beckons to* SERVICEMEN.

TED. Don't like the look of that. I'm off.

JIMMY. Too right.

JACK. Me too.

TED. Guarding the remains of a great man is one thing, and all very well. But when he sits up and waves at you . . . no thank you.

JIMMY. First ray of the sun through the window, that'll see him off.

JACK. Dying for a fag just to calm my nerves.

JIMMY. Right.

TED. Right.

JACK. Coming, mate?

MIKE. I'll stay on here.

JACK. What, with that?

MIKE. I've got a bone to pick with him.

JACK. You? A bone to pick with that?

JIMMY. You got a bone to pick with Sir Winston (*The dustbin struck.*) Churchill?

TED. What can a scabby jock layabout like you have to pick over with the Man who Won the Second World War?

MIKE. I've got a (*Dustin lid.*) bone to (*Dustbin lid.*) pick here, so (*Dustbin lid.*) off.

A drum roll from FURRY, *on the dustbin lid.* JIMMY, TED *and* JACK *turn and shrug to the audience and go off.*

Eh. You. Mister.

CHURCHILL. Jack Tar. Give us a light, jolly Jack Tar.

MIKE *gives* CHURCHILL *a light.* CHURCHILL *smokes.*

Where am I?

MIKE. At your funeral.

CHURCHILL. Shovelling me away are they, after all these years?

MIKE. Shovelling you away.

CHURCHILL. Won't go! Won't! Won't, even now, let go.

MIKE. Want to be Prime Minister again?

CHURCHILL. Why not?

MIKE. You're dead, that's why not.

CHURCHILL. That has not stopped others.

MIKE. Britain ruled by a corpse?

CHURCHILL. I'm a fresh corpse. The country will get used to it. They were always fond of me. I always felt love rising to me from English crowds, sweet, sticky affection. Like your town.

MIKE. My town?

CHURCHILL. Glasgow lad, aren't you?

MIKE. I may be.

CHURCHILL. A grey, overcast day. The June of 1945. Spoke in the open air. Boys perched in the trees. Men stood in serried ranks on the roofs, round about. Wonderful sight. The beauty of so many human faces lit in a flash with welcome and joy.

Young women whose beauty charmed the eye, old ladies
brought out in chairs, or waved flags from windows. Dazzled
me. When I had said my few words they sang 'Will Ye No
Come back Agin'. Glasgow dazzled me.

MIKE. Dazzled you? Glasgow? Old man you don't know the half.
Clydebank, my father was born. Thirteenth of March, 1941.
Night of the first great German air raid. The people walked out
of the town. Out to the moors. Some stayed for weeks,
camped out in the open air. My father's first night alive was
on the moors. And the next night, fourteenth of March, came
the second great air raid. Of twelve thousand dwellings, seven
only not hit.

CHURCHILL. The lights went out and the bombs came down.
Out of the jaws of death.

MIKE. Old man, we don't live in the same world.

CHURCHILL. It's not all ermine robes to wipe your bottom
where I come from.

MIKE. Nor is it all cloth caps and waving flags where I come
from.

CHURCHILL. We're both of the Island Race. Out of the Celtic
mist. The Saxon fen. And bitter, dark green Normandy.

MIKE. I did not understand a word of that.

CHURCHILL. Blood. Heritage . . . (*He clutches his heart.*) Pain.

MIKE. What's the matter?

CHURCHILL. Pain. Help me out of this damn contraption. This
engine for dead war heroes.

MIKE *helps* CHURCHILL *out of the catafalque.*

MIKE. Don't like to touch you. You may fall apart. In my hands.
Bits a Sir Winston Churchill. I don't fancy that.

CHURCHILL. Don't be squeamish. First World War, saw
bits of men in the trenches, shovelled into bags with mud and
wet stone, the pink against the brown, to be blessed by the
Chaplain. We're all meat, laddy. Lit momentarily by the divine
spark. Or whatever it is makes us plough so brutally through
life.

CHURCHILL *is out of the coffin. He leans on* MIKE's *arm.*

What's in the corner . . . ?

MIKE. Nothin is in the corner.

CHURCHILL. A black dog?

MIKE. Churchill, you left us nothing. Few statues of you, in your boiler suit. Your name in a kid's skipping rhyme. Adventure story from some lost, colonial war. Bit a gas from our fathers about some darkest hour years ago. Gas only, not a single human thought. Not a single true, human remain.

CHURCHILL. Words! Words! Left you words! Listen, listen. I'm speaking to you from the grave. My words, hammered out. Sh.

JOBY (*at once the* CHURCHILL *manner dropped completely. To the* SELECT COMMITTEE). I just like t'put a word in 'ere. Speakin' as a man now, who's goin' t' do Blood, Sweat an' Tears speech up 'ere . . .

MIKE (*to himself*). Ah Joby, just get on wi' it.

JOBY. I'd jus' like t'say . . . (*Slight pause.*) This dead, great old man I'm tryin' t'put before ye. Fer a few laughs. I'd like t'put this in' play with special feelin'.

MIKE (*to himself*). Joby, you old clot.

JOBY. All right, I know me own mind. (*A pause.*) Gerron wi' it, then.

MIKE (*back in the play*). A one, two, three a rave from the grave.

FURRY *gives a drum roll on the dustbin lid.*

CHURCHILL (JOBY *composes himself, then*). In this crisis I hope I may be pardoned if I do not address the House at any length today. I would say to the House . . . 'I have nothing to offer but blood, toil, tears and sweat'. We have before us an ordeal of the most grievous kind. We have before us many, many long months of struggle and of suffering. You ask what is our policy? I will say: It is to wage war, by sea, land and air, with all our might and with all the strength that God can give us; to wage war against a monstrous tyranny, never surpassed in the dark, lamentable catalogue of human crime. That is our policy. You ask, what is our aim? I can answer that in one word — Victory, victory at all costs, victory in spite of all terror, victory, however long and hard the road may be; for without victory, there is no survival. Let that be realized;

no survival for the British Empire; no survival for all that the
British Empire has stood for, no survival for the urge and
impulse of the ages that mankind will move forward towards
its goal. But I take up my task with buoyancy and hope. I feel
sure that our case will not be suffered to fail amongst men.
At this time I feel entitled to claim the aid of all, and I say,
'Come, then, let us go forward together with our united
strength'.

A dog bowls from behind the little stage.

Black Dog! Throw something at it, quick, before it gets me.
Dogs dig up dead men.

FURRY *lets the Union Jack curtain down then shambles
onto the stage. He carries a piece of paper. He drops it.*

FURRY. Hang on. (*He stoops. Picks up the paper. Reads.*) An
   'istorical note. Sir Winston Churchill 'ad terrible fits a
   depression. He called these fits, Black Dog. When 'e 'ad the fit
   come on, 'e would cancel all appointments, and shut 'imself
   up. Not even Mrs Churchill could come into 'room, when
   Black Dog was upon 'im. So. (*He looks up.*) That's what's
   goin' on. (*He shambles off and pulls the Union Jack curtain
   up.*)

BLACK DOG, *played by* PETER REESE, *stands at*
CHURCHILL's *side. A shaggy, mangy dog.*

BLACK DOG. Woof! Winston, I'm still with you.

CHURCHILL. Black Dog . . . The very night London burned, the
   second great fire . . . I saw you, bounding along, among the
   fire hoses beneath St. Paul's.

BLACK DOG (*pants*). Tell it to us, Winston. (*Pants.*)

CHURCHILL. Of my childhood? Hedged by fears. As a young
   boy in the great Blenheim Palace Library, little Winston
   Churchill, me, took down the dark books of the Spanish
   Inquisition. Read of the whips, the racks, the brands.

BLACK DOG *bowls.*

Naked body on the wheel, over the fire. Naked young monks
at the side of the Saint, laid on the red hot irons of the
griddle . . .

BLACK DOG *bowls.*

Up in my room, high in the dark Palace of the Marlboroughs, my toy battlefield went for miles over the carpet. The carnage of leaden severed heads, little leaden groins shot away filled my imagination with terror. I was a sad little boy. Nine years old, brutally put to prep. school. The English Public School system is there for the brutalization of the Ruling Classes, not their benefit. And Harrow is an abattoir to hack out the sensitive spirit, the all too human meat of the shy, fat boy. Dogged. Dogged. (*He points at* BLACK DOG.)

BLACK DOG. His-tory. Fam-ily. Privil-ege. Duuuuu-ty. (*He howls.*)

CHURCHILL. A little shift of history . . . and I would be remembered as a minor English impressionist painter.

BLACK DOG. His-toreeeee . . . (*Pants.*) His daddy, his daddy . . .

CHURCHILL. Throw something at it, break its legs.

BLACK DOG *snarls and crouches.*

Of my father's syphilis. The tender secret my family has cherished, the terrible fact. Lord Randolph Churchill, brilliant meteor of his day, the man they said would run the English Twentieth Century . . . died of that filthy disease . . . I came home from India, to a quiet sitting-room. Out of the window the English countryside and warm, gentle rain. By the fireside my father. An English aristocrat, fine, arrogant. The honed grace of his class, ground and polished. The natural right of an English gentleman to rule . . . for there was a quality of History about him . . . shone about his very features. (*A pause.*) I cannot express, even to myself, the obscenity of what the disease had done to him. It had . . . scraped his brain. Despite the heavy cologne his nurses doused upon him, he smelt. His affections had putrefied. All his sense was of self-pity. One yearned, like one yearns for love, for a coherent remark. One scanned his dribble for a sign. For him to say, merely . . . It is the disease, it is the disease. But he was gentle. Lost in the vile, infected marsh of his illness. A marsh light. (BLACK DOG *whimpers.*) I have feared his disease all my life. When Black Dog came, thought . . . This is it! My Father's disease, visited upon me, as the Bible says, generation upon generation . . . In the lavatory would look at myself for chancres, little signs, eczemas, rashes, the slightest inflamed pimple . . . made me mad with fear! The bridge of my nose!

On the rot! Spent hours before mirrors. Should it ever come upon me, I resolved, I would kill myself. Took that resolve into the grave. Won't read that in the official biography.

FURRY *comes on. He speaks aside to the official audience.*

FURRY. Change a whar the scene's at, 'ere. (*He pulls a cord. A white sheet comes down. On it is the legend 'We can take it, Guv. Give it 'em back'.*) An' I'm goin' t'nip round back, 'cos I'm goin' t'do a bit a actin' in a jiffy. See yer, right? Right.

He gives a thumb-up sign, winks and goes off.

MIKE. Black Dog, take us back to 1940.

BLACK DOG. On my back, on my back.

CHURCHILL *and* MIKE *get on the back of the dog.*

CHURCHILL. Back through England!

Through the cloth, slides of post-war English history in reverse, starting with Churchill's funeral, the catafalque itself. Then the first Wilson government. Alec Douglas-Home. Macmillan. Profumo. Gaitskell. Eden. Suez. Eoka on a Cyprus wall. Churchill, early fifties. Attlee. Rationing. Bevan. Coal fields nationalized. Election 1945. Potsdam Conference with Truman. Yalta Conference with Roosevelt. Berlin bombed. Normandy invasion. Alamein. Hitler attacks Russia. Finally the photograph of St. Paul's in the 'Second Great Fire' 29th December 1940.

These slides are crudely done, as if with a domestic slide projector, distorted badly from the side on the cloth, spilling across the hangar to the far wall. Following exchanges over this.

Where are we going, lad?

MIKE. Meet my Uncle Ern!

CHURCHILL. Who?

MIKE. Don't you remember me Uncle Ern?

CHURCHILL. Cannot say, with any honesty, I do.

MIKE. You met my Uncle Ern in 1940!

CHURCHILL. Glasgow man?

MIKE. Not my Uncle Ern from Glasgow, my Uncle Ern from Liverpool!

CHURCHILL. I know no such Uncle Ern!

MIKE. December 30th, 1940. In the early morning.

CHURCHILL. Morning after . . .

MIKE. Morning after the Second Great Fire of London.

CHURCHILL. Don't remember. Back through the years . . .

MIKE. Peckham.

CHURCHILL. Peckham?

MIKE. You cried.

CHURCHILL. Did I cry?

MIKE. Winston Churchill cried. And an old woman said . . .

BLACK DOG. We can take it, Guv. Give it 'em back.

CHURCHILL. Did I cry?

The St. Paul's slide.

BLACK DOG. The second Great Fire of London!

MIKE *and* CHURCHILL *dismount from* BLACK DOG, *who retreats, backwards, into the wings of the little stage.*

CHURCHILL. Remember. Peckham landmine. Heard the bang in Ten Downing Street. Drove over to see what was cooking. And I saw these good people, at the side of the crater. And they cried out to me . . .

ERNIE *and* ANNIE *(played by* FURRY *and* JIMMY) *very cheerfully.*

ANNIE. Look. He's crying for us.

ERNIE. Good old Winnie.

ANNIE. We thought you'd come and see us.

ERNIE. We can take it.

ANNIE. Give it 'em back.

They wave, doll-like.

CHURCHILL. And I wept. Deeply moved.

MIKE. Not like my Uncle Ern told me it.

ERNIE. Yer dead right. That were 'myth. This is like it was.

He sags, sits down in the rubble. ANNIE *scuttles back to the rubble. CHURCHILL goes off. ANNIE scrabbles in the rubble, she finds a dinner-table chair. She puts it at the front of the stage. This way, going back and forth out of the dust and wreckage, she assembles a dinner-table suite and living-room. The table has two legs and is splintered. Three chairs, none of which stands. The charred remains of an easy chair. The delicate shell of a smashed china display cabinet, glass-fronted, all the glass gone. She finds pieces of glass and china, unrecognizable lumps, and carefully puts them in the cabinet. Then she sits on the ground, in the middle of the 'room' salvaged from her home.*

Wish you would not. (*A pause.*) Wish you would not, Annie.

A gentle, shocked gesture from her.

(*Aside.*) And he walked up.

CHURCHILL *comes on. He is in an overcoat, with Homburg and walking stick. He looks at* ERNIE.

Sir Winston Churchill. Just there. Oh aye, I thought, looking across. (*He looks across.*) Oh aye. I'll say this — he looked well. But then they do, don't they. Pay clerks upwards, they all look well. Difference between steak and mucky sausages, true meat and mashed up lung. Tells, in the end. Aye, I looked across. At the myth. Standing there. Like he'd come down from a cinema screen, out of a film show. Winnie. With a cigar. And I felt angry, suddenly, angry. Sat there with me life. Which is to do with being widowed and having a dicky lung. And coming to London to live with me sister Annie. For light work, you see. And getting it in a warehouse, Morleys gents outfitters, but the warehouse going early on in a daylight raid . . . y'know. Your life. And it were sick kind a anger . . . like water, mixed up with oil. Queasy. And I wanted to say . . . Go away from this hole that were my sister Annie's house. We're all right, we'll come through, what else is there for us? Just go away from this hole. And I made a gesture like this. (*A wave.*)

CHURCHILL *raises his hand in salute.*

And he waved back. And I said, I swear to this day I said . . . Thought you'd come and see us. (*Aside.*) This were like it really were, unzip yer ear'oles . . . (*A slight pause.*) Thought you'd come and see us.

CHURCHILL. Ah. Ah.

ERNIE. We can take it.

CHURCHILL. Ah.

ERNIE. But we just might give it back to you one day.

MIKE. We just might give it back to you one day.

ERNIE. And in his book on war he wrote it down as . . . Give it 'em back.

BLACK DOG. Give it 'em back. (*Howls.*)

MIKE. And my old Uncle Ern, in his cups, telling it for the ten thousandth, three hundred and eighty-fourth time.

ERNIE. God rot great men.

MIKE. God rot great men.

BLACK DOG. God rot great men.

CHURCHILL (*raises his stick in a fury*). Who won the war?

ERNIE. Didn't you know that? I did. And she did. People won the war.

MIKE. And for what?

CHURCHILL *sags*.

CHURCHILL. God bless you all. God bless you all.

ERNIE. And rot you too.

The Union Jack tumbles down at once on the little stage.

A silence, GLENDA *applauds. Stops applauding. A silence.*

MORN. I need a drink. (*He takes out a flask, and drinks from it.*)

ST JOHN. Yes. Well. The play's the thing in which to catch the conscience of an old bitch of a democracy we all love and live in, eh? (*He snorts.*)

GLENDA. Did Lord Randolph really . . . ?

BALL (*angry*). Yes. Yes.

GLENDA. How terrible for the family.

ST JOHN. Still. Very good. Very well got up.

THOMPSON (*stands*). I must make clear . . .

BALL. No you must not.

THOMPSON. In all conscience . . .

BALL. Captain Thompson! (*He stands.*) Sergeant Baxter.

SERGEANT. Suh.

BALL. See to that behind there.

SERGEANT. Suh.

The SERGEANT *ducks nimbly beneath the curtain of the small stage.*

BALL. Always be a sense of outrage, a lot of mess and abuse, in a little world like ours. May be a little play is no bad way of blowing it off. Into the deep blue yonder . . . Tea? In the Officers' Mess? And a look at our financial accounts?

All but MORN *stand.*

ST JOHN. Yes, get cracking. Gerald.

CAROLINE (*low, to* THOMPSON). You fool.

JULIA (*low*). Yes, your husband is a fool.

CAROLINE (*low*). Thank you very much.

THOMPSON (*low*). What exactly is your research, for Christ's sake.

JULIA *turns away.*

ST JOHN. Come on old son, take the plunge and stand up.

MORN. Sorrow and defeat. Deep, abiding personal guilt. Years and years of it.

GLENDA. Would you like an Anadin?

MORN *stares at her.*

ST JOHN. Please.

MORN (*stands*). In for a penny, in for a pound.

The party begins to drift towards an exit. MORN, *dabbing a finger.*

But I am going to go through this place like . . . like . . . a hot turd in an outside loo on a frosty morning.

ST JOHN. My colleague is often tired. 'Tired'.

BALL. Quite.

ST JOHN. We are all stressed. Trying to do what's for the good.

THOMPSON *breaks back.*

THOMPSON. I cannot let . . .

BALL. Captain Thompson!

ST JOHN. What is the matter now?

THOMPSON. Conscience. In all conscience I . . .

At once the Union Jack curtain goes up, the SERGEANT *is tied up in an ugly way.* MIKE *has his gun, and holds it to the* SERGEANT's *head. The prisoners who performed in the play stand round about.* JOBY *sits smoking, ignoring what's going on.* JIMMY *is still in drag.*

MIKE. You play ball wi' me and I'll play ball with you and na problem. All sweet and all a us getting along just fine.

JIMMY. It's happenin'! Happenin' to you, you fuckers!

MIKE. So we are going to think now. We are going to go moment to moment now. Are we not, Colonel?

A silence.

BALL. Yes, we are McCulloch.

ST JOHN (*to the prisoners*). I beg you, at once . . .

BALL. Please be silent, Sir. And all of us, absolutely still.

JACK. Let's get armed, now. Out. Now.

TED. The pisshead's got a noggin on him. Requisition that for a start . . .

MIKE. Moment by moment, we do this.

A silence.

One of your VIPs up here. Lady, a the Committee. The lady, up.

JIMMY *jumps down off the stage.*

JIMMY. Little island a freedom in here now love. Freedom to poke my little finger up your arsehole. All the way.

He grabs JULIA *by the hair and throws her down on the floor.*

MIKE. For fucksake, Jimmy . . .

JULIA. All right, Jimmy.

A silence.

I'll get up on the stage, all right?

JIMMY (*clenching his hands into fists, shaking them*). Fuck.
Oh fuck. It's strong.

JULIA. It's all right. I know how you will behave. Please?

JULIA *steps up on the stage,* TED *giving her a hand up.* MIKE
points the gun at her head.

MIKE. Your arms and Captain Thompson's arms, Colonel.

The COLONEL *moves his hand.*

No no. We are collecting.

JACK (*indicating* ST JOHN). That slimy bastard is armed.

MIKE. You carry a firearm, Sir?

ST JOHN *does,* FURRY *takes it.*

Now Colonel Ball, you carry a key to the armoury.

A silence.

You carry a key to the armoury. You do na leave it in your
office, which is sensible. You carry a key.

A silence.

The situation you have, moment t' moment.

BALL *pauses, then takes out a key from a wallet. He throws
it to* MIKE. MIKE *lets the key fall against him, not looking
at it.*

Pick that up for me, Jimmy.

JIMMY (*picks up the key*). Key t'Utopia. (*He holds it up.*)

ST JOHN. Atrocity? Upon us? Are you about . . . ?

BALL. Be quiet, Sir!

MIKE. Stick 'em up on the chairs!

JACK. Stand up on your chairs!

GLENDA. Oh no, no.

THOMPSON. Look.

JACK. At what?

THOMPSON. Doctor. Come with you.

JACK. You?

THOMPSON. I'm a doctor. You'll have to cross country. Have wounds.

BALL (*shouts*). Shut up, shut up, shut up, you ill-disciplined, selfish, self-regarding . . . (*Low.*) We all stand up on our chairs. Please. Now.

They stand on the chairs. MORN *is incapable.*

JACK. Their handbags and things now, right? Ladies, throw down your handbags. The men, don't go to your pockets. We'll do that.

TED. We need money for the journey. And your overcoats — we'll be sleeping rough.

FURRY (*to* MORN). Y'got to stand up now.

MORN (*rambling, to himself*). We should have done it. Years ago. Factory floor, street level. Taken means of production, given power into people's hands. '45. '64. '78. We had the democratic space. But somehow there were always good reasons. Day to day, little crises. For not. Not.

FURRY. Y'got to stand up now. On y'chair.

FURRY *takes* MORN's *flask and cigarettes.* JIMMY *rummages in the women's handbags. He takes a photograph from* CAROLINE's.

JIMMY. Picture of an 'ouse. (*He tears it up.*)

CAROLINE. A house? Why do you sneer at that? Not wrong to want that. In peace. Grow the vegetables. And children in bright clothes. On the swing. On the lawn. That's what I want. It's not obscene, is it? The house, the lawn, the plants, the children playing . . .

JIMMY. Want a house, do you lady? What, with a garden? Yeah and barbed wire round it t'stop dirty animals like me getting in? Oh lady, I'm coming out the dark. Right through plate glass window a your house. Kick in your colour telly. Paraffin on your fancy furniture. Redecorate your living room with you, nailed to the ceiling.

CAROLINE. Why? What have I ever?

JIMMY. Ever? Ever? What, ever done?

TED. Jimmy cut it out.

JIMMY. You put me in 'ere, lady. (*To* MIKE.) She put me in 'ere. (*Shouts at her.*) Lady!

MIKE. Jimmy, go carefully.

JIMMY runs about the hangar shouting. TED *and* JACK *run after him.*

JIMMY.   ⎫ No freedom! No fun! No future!
SERGEANT.   ⎬ Michael, out a your hands!
CORPORAL.   ⎭ You'll kill yourselves!

JACK. Jimmy . . . You've fucked it Jimmy.

JIMMY fires the gun offstage. He comes back on.

JIMMY (*quietly*). I fired through the wall at 'em. I fired through the wall.

A silence. All dead still.

MIKE. Jack. Go and look on the outside.

JACK. Right.

REESE. You had better give me that.

JIMMY gives REESE the gun.

A silence.

SERGEANT. What you gonna do? Walk out with hostages? Into the sunset and happy ever after? They'd not let you lot out, armed. Running into the woods? Into people's back gardens?

CORPORAL. Jack? Ted? Furry? You stay in 'ere, where they put you. I can get you a ping pong table. Bats, little net. Bulk load a ping pong balls. Yeah, you stay in 'ere. Out there . . . (*He shakes his head.*)

ST JOHN. Have men of your command orders for an incident like this? To shoot indiscriminately? Colonel?

BALL (*slowly, getting off his chair*). The huts. Always sinking. The damp. The men . . . rotting.

JACK. They're out there. In their glory. And we are tight now, in this tin can. (*A slight pause.*) Mike, they have searchlights.

MIKE. Right. Right. Get down.

The people on the chairs hesitate.

Concrete, concrete, on the concrete.

They get off the chairs and lie down gingerly. Little gasps, 'Obs' and 'No's' from them, as JOBY speaks.

JOBY. Never noticed. The bad temper. People's minds closing. Getting colder. The country sliding down. Guns. Barbed wire. The woods stripped clean a their leaves. Journalist I were. Good story that, but I never noticed.

JACK. I say we still go out.

TED. We make demands. Bargain.

JACK. We go. Eh? (*He looks round the group.*) Eh?

FURRY. We're like the plague. They'll not let us out of 'ere.

JIMMY. Why not? I fancy a career as a disease.

JACK. Joby?

JOBY (*taking the mask off*). Dunno. Na, I belong to another world.

JACK. Mike?

A silence.

MIKE. Breakout we thought. Freedom we thought. Get to a big city, lose ourselves among the people. Go to the hills. Or only . . . reach the sea, eh? Be on a beach in winter. Clean, in the clean air. Joby, Ted, Furry, Jimmy, Jack, Peter. But we all know. Nowhere to break out to, is there? They'll concrete the whole world over, any moment now. But either way, for me, I declared war on the bastards a long time ago.

REESE. Lower than the lowest.

MIKE. Yes, what do you say, Peter Reese?

REESE. I say survive. In the cracks. Inside or outside the wire. But not at any cost . . .

At once the lights go out.

TED (*shouts*). They cut the lights.

At once matches flare.

JACK. Get light, get light.

GLENDA. I don't want the future to be . . .

A great deep clang. The doors are opening. Outside the revving engines of motorbikes. Blinding light from searchlights. Loudspeakers all round the hangar call out.

LOUDSPEAKERS. PEAKE. BARKER. KEEGAN. UMPLEBY.
WILLIAMS. REESE. McCULLOUGH. PEAKE. BARKER.
KEEGAN. UMPLEBY. WILLIAMS. REESE. McCULLOUGH.

JOBY. The Third World War.

Blackout.

WEAPONS OF HAPPINESS

To Sam

A Note

The real Josef Frank was hanged in
Prague on the 3rd of December 1952

WEAPONS OF HAPPINESS was commissioned by the National Theatre, London, and first performed there, in the Lyttleton Theatre, on 14th July 1976. The cast was as follows:

Josef Frank	Frank Finlay
Ralph Makepeace	Michael Medwin
Billy	Derek Thompson
Ken	Billy Colvill
Stacky	Nick Brimble
Janice	Julie Covington
Liz	Annie Hayes
Alf	Frederick Radley
Sylvia Makepeace	Thelma Whiteley
Mr Stanley	Bernard Gallagher
Inspector Miller	Maurice O'Connell
Hicks	Matthew Guiness
Doubek *Interrogators*	Maurice O'Connell
Kohoutek	Matthew Guiness
Russian Adviser	Michael Medwin
Clementis	William Russell
NKVD Men	Pat Connell
	Martin Friend
	Shaun Scott
	Jeremy Truelove
Stalin	Geoffrey Bateman
Waiter	Chris Hunter
Commentator	Geoffrey Bateman
Guards	Martin Friend
	Chris Hunter
Constables	Pat Connell
	Martin Friend
	Jeremy Truelove

Director: David Hare
Designer: Hayden Griffin
Lighting: Rory Dempster

Act One

SCENE ONE

By the factory wall at night. JOSEF FRANK alone.

FRANK. I don't sleep. I walk about London. So many people, sleeping. Around you. For miles. After so many years, it is better to be tired. Not to think or remember. Ten million, asleep, around you, is warm. The ignorant English, like a warm overcoat. About me. It is better. While in the nightmare of the dark all the dogs of Europe bark.

A shaft of light from an opened door shines across the stage at the back. The light goes off. RALPH MAKEPEACE comes on. He is dressed in a fine coat and carries a briefcase. He has been drinking alone.

RALPH. Who's that there?

   JOSEF FRANK turns away.

   Mr Frank?

   RALPH MAKEPEACE walks towards him.

   It is you, Frank.

FRANK. Walking . . .

RALPH. What are you doing by the factory, this hour?

   A pause.

FRANK. Sleepless.

RALPH. Ah.

FRANK. I . . .

   RALPH MAKEPEACE waves his briefcase.

RALPH. Working late. On the books. Not a very good cook with numbers, eh?

   He tries to laugh and fails. A pause.

   How long have you been with us?

FRANK. A week. One week.

RALPH. Week isn't it? Yes. You don't find the work too heavy?

FRANK. I . . .

RALPH. Manual work. Man of your age, intelligence? Perhaps some clerking, filing in the office . . .

FRANK. No . . .

RALPH. We like to . . .

FRANK. I prefer . . .

RALPH. Prefer it?

FRANK. I . . . Yes.

RALPH. Funny thing to make really. Crisps.

A pause.

My father always made a point of sprinkling the workforce with foreigners, foreign people. And disabled . . . Disabled people. We get by, don't you think?

JOSEF FRANK *hesitates.*

The secret's in the crunch.

FRANK. Work is work.

RALPH. What? Ah, yes.

JOSEF FRANK *stumbles.*

RALPH. Are you . . . Not well?

FRANK. No.

RALPH. Cold night. Been threatening snow . . .

FRANK. I am well.

RALPH. Will you ever go back to Hungary?

FRANK. Czechoslovakia. The Czechoslovak Socialist Republic.

A pause.

RALPH. Goodnight then.

FRANK. Goodnight.

RALPH MAKEPEACE *walks away, jangling his car keys.*

RALPH. Tuck yourself up. Good book, hot drink and a packet of crisps. Ha!

YOUNG MAN'S VOICE (*off*). Mr Makepeace!

Three figures, dressed as YOUNG MEN, although one of them is a YOUNG WOMAN, with balaclavas pulled to the bridges of their noses, run on. They knock RALPH MAKEPEACE *over and kick him.*

YOUNG WOMAN. Tossing cunt.

FIRST YOUNG MAN. Get his keys.

RALPH. What are you?

SECOND YOUNG MAN. Here's the case. What I tell you? No chain.

The FIRST YOUNG MAN *picks up* RALPH MAKEPEACE'S *car keys.*

FIRST YOUNG MAN. Flash away in his flashy car!

SECOND YOUNG MAN. Case we want, idiot.

FIRST YOUNG MAN. Fucking Rolls, though.

YOUNG WOMAN. Split let's split.

The SECOND YOUNG MAN *points at* JOSEF FRANK.

SECOND YOUNG MAN. What about him?

YOUNG WOMAN. Foreign git.

The three figures run off. RALPH MAKEPEACE *crawls on the ground in pain.*

RALPH. Contact lens.

FRANK. I plead.

RALPH. If it comes on to snow I'll never find it. Frank!

FRANK. I plead.

RALPH. Help me, man!

JOSEF FRANK *shakes his head.*

FRANK. I plead.

RALPH. For godsake, what's the matter with you?

FRANK. I plead guilty of being a war criminal. And of committing a whole number of grave crimes for the benefit of the U.S. imperialists. To the detriment of the working people of Czechoslovakia and the whole peace camp. All the dogs of Europe.

SCENE TWO

Factory yard. Lunch break.
JOSEF FRANK takes a pack of sandwiches out of his pocket.
There is a wall at the back. Cricket stumps are chalked upon it.
Two young women, JANICE and LIZ, lean against the wall.
They are in working clothes. They wear plastic coats and their
hair is bound up in muslin cloth.
An old man, ALF, sits on a cooking oil drum. He has a plastic
lunch box and a thermos flask.
Three young men, BILLY, KEN and STACKY, are playing cricket
BILLY is batting. He has a guitar strung around his back. KEN is
bowling. STACKY, who is deaf and dumb and six and a half feet
tall, fields.
JANICE translates STACKY's sign language as a matter of course,
even when there is a large space between them.
KEN bowls to BILLY who strikes the ball. The ball runs off stage.

BILLY. Six!

KEN. What do you mean, six?

BILLY. Poetry poetry.

KEN. What do you mean, six?

BILLY. Went in the bog door, didn't it. Ball in the bog door's six.

KEN. But the bog door's open! Only six if it goes in under.

BILLY. You can't just change the rules.

KEN. I'm not changing rules.

    STACKY makes signals.

JANICE. Stacky says can he bowl now?

LIZ. Just like school. Work? Never know you'd left the bloody
playground.

    KEN, looking off.

KEN. Oh no. Who's gone and gone in the bog? Oy! You got our
ball in there!

    KEN runs off. BILLY swings the guitar to his front and fiddles
    with it. STACKY watches him.

JANICE. Like we're still running around in nappies. Wondering
where the smell's come from.

    STACKY is picking his nose. A pause.

LIZ. Ooh I know he's deaf and dumb, but I wish he wouldn't pick his nose and eat it. Oy Stacky!

STACKY has his back to her. He turns. JANICE catches his eye. They signal.

What's he say?

JANICE. He says one nostril is salt and vinegar and the other is cheese and onion, which do you prefer?

STACKY smiles.

LIZ. Sad.

ALF. Playing with a hard ball in the yard. Trying a prove something Billy?

BILLY: What do you know of it? Old man. Old old man.

LIZ. How old you then, Billy darling?

JANICE. Pretty ancient actually. Do you know he remembers Bob Dylan?

LIZ. Coo, bring out your dead.

JANICE and LIZ laugh.

BILLY. He could have changed the world, Dylan. Still could if we'd let him.

BILLY hits the guitar. A horrible chord.

JANICE. Sad.

LIZ. Make you weep.

A pause.

Age. I saw my Mum in the bath last night. You know, nude. Like curried chicken.

JANICE: Funny how their bodies fall apart when they're over thirty.

LIZ. Sad.

JANICE. It gets 'em.

ALF. Joey.

FRANK. Alfred

A slight pause.

Would . . . You like a sandwich?

ALF. Special are they?

ALF *lifts the bread, suspiciously.*

What's that white stuff in there?

FRANK. Cream . . . Cream cheese.

ALF. No thank you. You want a build yourself up. Look less of a dog's dinner. Give you a bit a my beef, if it weren't mine.

FRANK. I cannot . . . Take flesh.

ALF. Oh yeah?

ALF *eats and speaks with his mouth full.*

Rolled young Mr Ralph last night. Hear that?

FRANK: Rolled?

ALF. Knocked over. Bashed. Leant upon. Hit. Right outside the gate here.

FRANK. Who was responsible?

ALF. Hot heads. The wild ones, I ask you.

ALF *laughs.*

C.I.D.'s up the office right now.

BILLY *and* JANICE *start.*

FRANK. C.I.D.?

ALF. Coppers. Rozzers. Fuzzy wuzz. Bottle boys. The men in blue. Old Bill. Police.

FRANK. Police?

BILLY. Oh fuck.

JANICE. Shut up. What did you say, Alf?

ALF. Up the office with Mr Ralph. Right now.

BILLY. Why do they think it was us, eh? Why do they make that assumption?

JANICE *signals to* STACKY. *He goes off.*

FRANK. Police?

ALF. Back in the thirties I was in a dole queue. Bloke in front a me, took out a gun and shot the pay clerk dead. Just like that. Did no good though. Another one popped up in his place.

ALF *laughs and spits.* STACKY *comes on with* RALPH MAKEPEACE's *briefcase. He gives it to* JANICE. JANICE *makes a signal to* BILLY *then she runs to him, he gives her a*

*stirrup jump and she drops the briefcase over the wall. ALF
and JOSEF FRANK see this. They stare.*

LIZ. I hope you know what you're doing, Jan.

KEN (*off*). Catch!

> *The ball bounces back onto the stage. STACKY fields it.
> KEN comes on.*

> What's going on?

JANICE (*to KEN, unheard*). Police up the office. We dumped the
case over the wall.

> *A pause.*

KEN. Right. What we want's a bit a intimidation round here.
(*To JANICE.*) Tell Stacky a give him a bouncer.

BILLY. No bouncers.

> *JANICE is signalling to STACKY.*

> We not got pads on and it's a real ball.

KEN. Right little Mike Denness in't we.

> *STACKY signals to JANICE.*

BILLY. It's the rules!

KEN. Change the rules!

JANICE. Stacky says he'll take a long run up.

> *STACKY goes off, purposefully.*

BILLY. Bad light stops play.

KEN. Blinding sunlight. Look, blinding Australian sun.

BILLY. You change the rules, I'll change the weather.

KEN. Thousands a Aussies in their shirt sleeves. Stoned out a
their minds and baying for your blood.

> *SYLVIA MAKEPEACE walks on. All except JOSEF FRANK
> stare at her. She is well and sharply dressed with a knee-length
> hemline, sheer nylons and high heel shoes.*

KEN. Uh uh. Boss pussy.

LIZ. Look at the skirt. It lilts.

JANICE. Cow.

LIZ. Yeah.

> *KEN bars SYLVIA's way. She stops.*

KEN. Morning Mrs Makepeace. Come for lunchies?

SYLVIA MAKEPEACE *stares at him.*

LIZ. They do say she cuts her hairs. You know . . .

JANICE. What, her pubes?

LIZ. Yeah you know. In the shape of a heart.

JANICE. What for?

LIZ *shrugs.*

LIZ. Romance?

LIZ *and* JANICE *laugh.* SYLVIA *walks round* KEN.

KEN. Kiss kiss.

SYLVIA *goes off.*

Sometimes I think a all the places I'll never go. (*To* STACKY *off.*) Come on then Stacky. Thump your bollocks down the pitch.

STACKY *powers on to the stage. At that moment* JOSEF FRANK, *wandering across the stage, gets between batsman and bowler.* STACKY *restrains himself from bowling at the last moment.* BILLY *ducks instinctively.*

KEN. Joey! You stupid Ruskie!

BILLY. What happened?

KEN. Get out the way.

FRANK. I . . .

JANICE. Don't think he's Russian, Ken.

STACKY *has hurt his leg.*

BILLY. You all right, Stacky?

KEN. Now look what you gone and done. Stacky's going a miss the next Test.

KEN *laughs.*

FRANK. I do not understand cricket. What is short leg?

MR STANLEY *comes on.*

STANLEY. Frank?

BILLY. Here comes Big Brother.

KEN. Thought I heard his iron balls clanging together.

STANLEY. Alf. How's the window box?

ALF. The locusts are massing.

> MR STANLEY *stares at* ALF. ALF *smiles.*

STANLEY. Oh Joey, they want a see you up the office.

> KEN *and* BILLY *look at each other quickly.* JANICE *walks a few steps from the wall towards* KEN. *She looks at* BILLY, BILLY *looks at her.* BILLY *puts the bat down on the ground, carefully.*

FRANK. No. I would . . . Not. Prefer not.

STANLEY. Playing with a hard ball in the yard again, Ken?

KEN. Oh yeah, the real thing, Stanley.

STANLEY. Mr Stanley to you.

KEN. Since when?

STANLEY. Since now.

KEN. You're just the foreman here. Stan, old man.

STANLEY. Na, come on Kenneth.

> MR STANLEY *ruffles* KEN'S *hair. He is about to turn away when* KEN *hits his hand away.*

STANLEY. What's all that for?

KEN. Chummy.

STANLEY. Come on, Ken. You were a kid when your first came in here to work. Saturday mornings cleaning?

KEN. Chummy, that's all.

> MR STANLEY *makes a placating gesture.* BILLY, *choosing his moment, bumps goodnaturedly into* FRANK.

BILLY. Give us the ball then, Joey.

> BILLY *drops the ball between himself and* JOSEF FRANK.

FRANK. What . . .

> BILLY *stoops and picks up the ball. He shows it to* JOSEF FRANK, *smiling and standing near to him.*

STANLEY. All piss in't it Kenneth?

KEN. Yeah but management, in't you, Mr Stanley. Mr Ralph's finger, in't you. Winkling in there. Touching us up. Keeping us giggly.

STANLEY. Don't talk to me about fingers, lad.

KEN. We know, we know . . .

MR STANLEY holds up a mutilated hand.

STANLEY. Two fingers . . .

KEN
STANLEY } *(together)*. Half a thumb.

KEN. Yeah, yeah.

STANLEY. In the cutters. Thirty . . .

KEN. Yeah thirty years. Bits a Mr Stanley turning up in packets a crisps, Lands End a John A' Groats. Yeah, yeah. Should a started a new line. Specially enriched protein crisps, scab foreman flavour.

A pause.

STANLEY *(to FRANK)*. Get up those stairs, Joey. Mr Ralph's wanting a few words with you.

JANICE goes to BILLY and puts her arm across his shoulder as she says to JOSEF FRANK, suddenly . . .

JANCE. And keep your mouth shut.

JANICE walks away.

FRANK. What . . .

BILLY. Sh.

STANLEY *(to FRANK)*. Go on then. *(To KEN.)* Bugger, are you not, Ken?

KEN. Why that's what I must be then, Mr Stanley.

MR STANLEY takes out a Daily Mirror.

STANLEY. Want a read a the football?

KEN takes a step back.

KEN. Na . . .

STANLEY. West Ham did very well last night.

KEN. Na . . .

STANLEY. Racing page?

KEN. Bastard!

STANLEY. Garth?

KEN. You know I can't read!

STANLEY. Why, so you cannot, Kenneth.

KEN. All right!

   A pause.

   All right.

STANLEY. That's you in your place.

KEN. Oh yeah?

   A pause.

   Yeah that's me in my place.

   FRANK *walks away.* KEN, BILLY *and* JANICE *watch him going.* STANLEY *folds up the* Daily Mirror.

STANLEY. Just have to take the world on trust then, don't you.

   KEN *looks at* STANLEY.

KEN. You what?

SCENE THREE

Factory office.
The light is that of strip lighting, one strip on the blink.
RALPH MAKEPEACE, *who has a hand bandaged,* INSPECTOR
MILLER *and* BOB HICKS *stand round about* JOSEF FRANK
who has just risen from a plain wooden chair.

FRANK. The light, please . . .

RALPH. What are you thinking of, Frank?

FRANK. The light. A headache. It flickers.

MILLER. If you would sit down again, Mr Frank . . .

FRANK. The flicker . . .

RALPH. For godsake man, no need to be so nervy. You were not
   well last night. As for my eye thing, got a good pair of glasses.

   RALPH MAKEPEACE *takes out a pair of glasses and puts
   them on.*

   See? No harm done. And this is a policeman, only doing his
   job.

HICKS. Ralph, I don't think I really should be here for this.

RALPH. Do hang on, Bob. Lunch I said, lunch it will be.

MILLER (*to* JOSEF FRANK). All I need is a simple statement. Tell me what happened, I will write it down. You can read it through, in your own good time, and make any amendments . . . Changes . . . You wish, and sign it.

FRANK. No no, it is impossible. The light, my vision. Blinded . .

JOSEF FRANK *stumbles.*

I have a pressure. A hairline fracture. The bone thickened when it healed.

A pause.

RALPH. Here, sit down Frank.

JOSEF FRANK *sits.*

FRANK. A blow healed with time.

HICKS. Ralph I am here as the Labour Party . . .

RALPH. Don't go all ratty on me Bob . . .

HICKS. Your workforce has approached me with a view to advice about Union Representation here . . .

RALPH. All tight on me Bob . . .

HICKS. If you should take action against this employee here, Mr Frank here . . .

RALPH. There is no question of Mr Frank having action taken against him . . . Tight arsed on me, Bob . . .

HICKS. Don't want to be unseemly. Seen . . .

MILLER. Mr Makepeace, sir, I would like to complete this statement.

RALPH. Need you, Inspector?

MILLER. This man did see your briefcase stolen?

RALPH. There was nothing in it.

MILLER. No sir?

RALPH. Apple cores.

MILLER. What I really want to do . . . Set up a trestle table in your canteen. Have a Detective Sergeant and four DC's down here, going through every one of your employees.

FRANK. Flick flick.

HICKS *looks at* JOSEF FRANK.

RALPH. None of my workers knocked me over. That's flat. That's final.

MILLER. Not really your workers, are they. In this day and age. More the workers' workers. I get the impression you want to be a nice person, sir.

RALPH. I hope I am 'A nice person.'

MILLER. Oh we can all hope.

HICKS. Industrial relations your pitch is it, Inspector?

MILLER. I know I know I'm just a jack. But you take the word of a jack.

HICKS (*to* FRANK). You, er, all right, brother?

MILLER. You got a group of human beings here. And no group of human beings, in a big city, hangs together by niceness. Hate yes, love no.

RALPH. A thinking policeman.

MILLER. Yes yes. Just a public servant with his thumb in the dyke. Can I get on with my job Sir?

JOSEF FRANK stands, knocking the chair over. Suddenly the light . . .

SCENE FOUR

Suddenly the light changes to a fierce, overhead square, the rest of the stage in darkness. The beam of a film projector shines in JOSEF FRANK'S face. The shadows of the actors loom large at the back of the stage in the beam, which projects a photograph of a bare, dirty room with a naked light bulb. JOSEF FRANK holds his hands behind his back, in the manner of a handcuffed man.
MILLER *as* DOUBEK. HICKS *as* KOHOUTEK. RALPH MAKEPEACE *as* BESHCHASNOV.

FRANK. I appeal to the Secretary General of the Czech Communist Party Klement Gottwald . . .

DOUBEK. You are a criminal.

KOHOUTEK. Confess.

DOUBEK. You were a fascist collaborator.

KOHOUTEK. You are an American spy.

DOUBEK. You are a Trotskyist.

KOHOUTEK. Confess.

FRANK. I am a Communist.

KOHOUTEK. You are filth.

DOUBEK. What were your relations with the American Saboteur Noel Field?

FRANK. Just tell me what I've done, that's all . . .

KOHOUTEK. Do you think the Party would arrest you if you had done nothing? Confess.

FRANK. What? What?

KOHOUTEK. Confess.

DOUBEK. Confess.

KOHOUTEK. Confess.

FRANK (*aside*). Never allowed to sit.

KOHOUTEK. Now. Confess.

FRANK (*aside*). Walk, walk all the time. They give you little leather slippers . . .

KOHOUTEK. All the time you were a Government Minister you were an American spy. Your fellow conspirator, Clementis, has already confessed. Why do you not? Confess. Now.

FRANK. Eighteen, twenty hours a day they question you. You are cold. You are hungry. You sleep a few hours on a plank. They wake you every ten minutes you must stand and report. Detention prisoner 1274. Number in cell one. All in order. You are handcuffed. You drink the thin soup with your handcuffs on, on the floor. You are kicked blindfolded cell to cell. You walk for three days and nights in a cellar filthy mud to your ankles. Your feet are infected, the toenails bulge with pus. You are offered a sandwich they tear it from your mouth before you can swallow. And you are lied to. All your life is made a lie. Your head is beaten against the wall. You try to kill yourself. To starve yourself to death. They find out what you're up to, they force feed you. It goes on for a year.

KOHOUTEK. President Truman has ordered the attack upon the U.S.S.R.

A pause.

FRANK. What . . . Did you say?

KOHOUTEK. The war with America has begun.

FRANK. War?

KOHOUTEK. The war with America.

FRANK. W . . . When?

KOHOUTEK. It has begun.

FRANK. The . . . Third World War?

KOHOUTEK. Anyway, has not the socialist world been at war for decades?

FRANK. Are you telling the truth?

KOHOUTEK. You doubt that the socialist world is surrounded by enemies?

FRANK. No of course I don't . . .

KOHOUTEK. All we have struggled for, Joseph, since we were boys, they wish to wipe off the surface of the planet. And with such enemies, in such a crisis, is it not logical that they have penetrated the Party? At every level? We must preserve the Party, root out the enemy. Help the Party Joseph. Confess you are the enemy.

BESHCHASNOV, *in Russian, to* DOUBEK.

BESHCHASNOV. Shto tam vozítsya s étoi sobákoy? Pristrelítch yevó, i vsyo.

DOUBEK. The Soviet Comrade wishes to know . . .

He screams and spits at JOSEF FRANK.

Why we waste time with this filthy little Jew.

Suddenly the light . . .

SCENE FIVE

Suddenly the light reverts to that of the factory office. JOSEF FRANK *has just stood, knocking the chair over. They stare at him. A pause.*

FRANK. I wish to relieve myself. It is unreasonable that a man not be allowed to relieve himself. An inalienable human right, for all that's sacred, to let a man have a common piss.

JOSEF FRANK *weeps. A silence.* SYLVIA MAKEPEACE *comes on.*

SYLVIA (*to* RALPH): Are we going for lunch, or are we not?

FRANK. Don't you understand? A . . . A man could stand naked in such a room as this, his bowels open, the poor thin stinking stuff of his gut running down his leg.

A silence.

HICKS. Er . . .

RALPH. I . . .

SYLVIA. Ralph, what is this?

RALPH. Not now, my sweet.

MILLER. Why don't you sit down again, Mr Frank?

FRANK. Forgive me.

RALPH. No problem.

FRANK. A faintness.

RALPH. Of course.

FRANK. Forgive me.

JOSEF FRANK *sucks back a sob.*

SYLVIA. Is this the man who saw you attacked?

RALPH. Not now, my sweet.

SYLVIA. Want my lunch, that's all.

RALPH. All right? Darling? All right?

SYLVIA. I am an intelligent form of life. I too receive tax demands.

RALPH. Christsake. More than flesh and blood can stand.

RALPH MAKEPEACE *takes out a drinking flask.*

MILLER. Could we . . .

RALPH. Tot?

MILLER. Get on?

RALPH. Frank?

FRANK. No . . .

RALPH. Malt. Blend it myself. Bit of a hobby.

SYLVIA (*to* HICKS). It's true, he does all his own blending. All alone, up in his room.

HICKS. Really?

RALPH. Shut up Sylvia.

SYLVIA. I am a director of this firm. I mean I was put on the board.

RALPH. By your father, not mine.

A pause.

Yes. Yes or . . . Go home? Taxi? Or, Inspector Miller, you could run Mr Frank home?

MILLER. All things are possible. (*To* FRANK.) Are you a registered alien, sir, or do you hold a British passport?

FRANK. No no, I will work . . .

RALPH. He's ill and in another country . . . .

MILLER. Just tell me, just quickly, who attacked Mr Makepeace here?

FRANK. I was out walking. At night. In London. There was nothing.

INSPECTOR MILLER *sighs.*

SYLVIA. Just don't let him . . . (*To* JOSEF FRANK.) You're in this country on sufferance, know that?

FRANK. All I want . . . To work. In a place of reasonable height. And silence, in silence. Not speaking.

RALPH. Pointless . . .

HICKS. Where you come from, Party Member were you?

FRANK. Can I go now?

RALPH. If you're sure you're all right . . .

FRANK. Thank you.

FRANK *walks away. He stops as he hears* INSPECTOR MILLER *say* . . .

MILLER. The last man I saw frightened as that had just killed his wife and two little babies.

SCENE SIX

Street. Early evening. JOSEF FRANK *alone.*

FRANK. Too much lost.

A pause.

Too much blood.

JANICE *rides onto the stage on a motorcycle.* BILLY *is riding pillion.*

JANICE. Hello Joey.

BILLY. Walking home?

FRANK. Walking.

BILLY. Violence on the buses eh? Don't like to come out, do they. Stay in their nests. Seeing a bus round here's like seeing the abominable snowman.

JANICE. What did you say to them, Joey?

A pause.

To the Police.

FRANK. Nothing.

JANICE. Oh yeah?

FRANK. I was taken ill. In the room. The office. An oppressive air. I am a claustrophobe.

BILLY. Like going down the tube, eh?

JANICE. So what did you say?

FRANK. I'm deaf. I'm blind. I don't see anything. I don't hear. I'm a . . . Hole in the air. I'm dead to you. You're dead to me. I'm nothing. You want to beat up the owner of the pathetic little, grubby little capitalistic concern that hires you, do so. Why should I see or hear? I'm more mute than . . . Your fellow dumb workers in that place. I'm . . .

A slight pause.

A vacuum.

A pause.

BILLY. Tell you what you are, Joey. Spooky.

JANICE. Don't you want a know what's going down, back there at the factory?

FRANK. I do not.

JANICE. You work in the place. Look, we're having a meeting.

BILLY. Don't tell him that!

JANICE. Worker like the rest of us, isn't he?

BILLY. Can't trust him. He's old and all fucked. In't you Joey.

JANICE. Tonight. Half seven. Out the Rock Wharf Site. Know where that is? Going on out to Greenwich.

FRANK. Think of me as ill.

BILLY. Fucked inside.

FRANK. I'm going now.

JOSEF FRANK turns away.

JANICE. Come from a communist country, don't you?

FRANK. Forgive me.

BILLY. Said he's sick, Janice . . .

JANICE. Sick or ashamed. Workers' state over there. Stalinist, but a workers' state. What you do? Run away?

BILLY. Let him alone.

JANICE. I asked you a question! What you do, run away? I asked you a question!

JOSEF FRANK turns on her.

FRANK. Little girl. I have spoken to Stalin. In Moscow. At three in the morning, in 1947. He was as close to me as you.

A slight pause.

And you do not know the half of it.

BILLY. Stalin?

JANICE. Aren't you just full a shit.

BILLY. Funny how they do badges a all the others but not Stalin.

FRANK. Therefore I asked you, in all decency, do not ask me to play with you, little girl. In your games. I am going home.

JOSEF FRANK walks away. BILLY shouts after him.

BILLY. Spook.

JANICE guns the motorcycle and drives off. JOSEF FRANK is left alone on the stage.

SCENE SEVEN

JOSEF FRANK *alone. Night.*

FRANK. Spooky.

> *A pause.*

> Ghostly.

> *A pause.*

> Nineteen forty-seven.

> *A pause.*

> Moscow.

> VICTOR CLEMENTIS *comes on quickly at the back of the stage.*

CLEMENTIS. Joseph?

> JOSEF FRANK *turns to him. They embrace.*

> Joseph.

FRANK. Victor. The relief at seeing you!

CLEMENTIS. Yes?

FRANK. The flood of relief, Comrade Foreign Minister. Now that you will lead the delegation in my place.

> *A slight pause.*

> You will lead our trade delegation now?

CLEMENTIS. Not exactly.

FRANK. Victor, you must. Wasn't my report clear?

> *A slight pause.*

> My report on the deadlock?

CLEMENTIS. It was clear . . .

FRANK. Good Czech steel for Russian food. That should be a simple bargain. But the harshness of their demands . . . If they persist we will have to break off the negotiations altogether . . .

CLEMENTIS (*interrupting*). Joseph I . . . I asked for you at the hotel. They said you walked this way.

> CLEMENTIS *shivers.*

> Moscow nights. I'd forgotten the cold.

FRANK. Trade negotiations with the Soviet Comrades fast become nocturnal. But why wasn't I told the time of your arrival? I'd have been at the airport to meet you . . .

CLEMENTIS. We travelled from Prague by train. They feared the fuel would freeze in the plane's tanks. The Russian heartland, Joseph! Mile after mile. The devastation. One could hardly bear it, even from a train window.

A pause.

FRANK. You do agree with my report.

CLEMENTIS. Yes, I said. It is clear.

FRANK. As your junior I am not empowered to break off the trade talks with the Soviet Government. I had to ask for you to come from Prague. Surely that is understood, Comrade Minister.

CLEMENTIS. No, I agree absolutely. Joseph, a hundred yards away. There is a car parked.

A pause.

Why are you being watched by their security police?

FRANK. The Soviet comrades have a certain paranoid style. Night-time limousines?

CLEMENTIS. Yes?

FRANK. I meant . . .

CLEMENTIS. Did you? Joseph, I do feel sometimes you are a little . . . Overweening.

FRANK. For Godsake, Victor. I have bargained for the Czech Government. As I expected them to bargain for the Russian Government. It is my duty to argue in the interests of the Czechoslovak working class.

CLEMENTIS. Absolutely.

FRANK. But?

CLEMENTIS. Sorry?

FRANK. You were going to say 'But?'

CLEMENTIS. So I was.

CLEMENTIS *laughs.*

Absolutely. But. Joseph, you know the configuration of that 'But.'

FRANK. Yes.

CLEMENTIS. We are in Russia. We are not mere National

Governments, bargaining our national interests. We share a deeper responsibility . . .

FRANK. The communist nation is world wide.

CLEMENTIS. The communist nation is world wide. Yes.

FRANK. Yes!

A pause.

And that is why I saw the Soviet Minister of Trade last night at Party Level. Not as a mere trade delegate with a begging bowl. But as a fellow communist.

CLEMENTIS. You asked for a meeting with Mikoyan at Party Level?

FRANK. A young man came to my hotel room, just past midnight. He took me to a back street. A car was waiting. Mikoyan was in the back. We drove through Moscow slowly. The chains on the wheels slipped in the snow at street corners. We spoke for three hours. In a big black car, skulking through the streets of the socialist capital of the world, at dead of night. He shouted and scoffed at me. He was Soviet Minister of Trade. It was his duty to get the most advantageous terms possible. I told him of our Party's position. That we communists do not yet control the Czech government. That I am the official spokesman of a non-communist government. That it is vital that the trade agreement be seen as a generous act by Russia. Our harvest is a disaster. The foodstuff and grain we wish to purchase by exchange of kind, with rolled steel and iron, is desperately needed. Our people will starve within months if the food is not delivered. We must have the food, the grain, now. If the food and grain is not delivered now the Czech Communist Party will be blamed. The Czech Revolution will be threatened. As I spoke, Mikoyan scraped a face in the condensation of the car window. I thought then it was Winston Churchill. Later I thought was it the face of some old enemy, in the frost? (*A pause.*) This brutality. Brutal no. Don't they know we love this country? That it is an honour for us to stand here on the socialist earth of Soviet Russia? That the allegiance is to what happened here, always? A thousand miles that way, a thousand miles that way . . .

A pause.

Deadlock.

CLEMENTIS. Comrade Mikoyan met me at the Moscow

Station tonight.

A pause.

FRANK. He met you . . .

CLEMENTIS. An official reception. He has agreed to all the terms you asked for.

FRANK. Agreed?

CLEMENTIS. There was a band. And they gave me red roses. In midwinter!

FRANK. Agreed?

CLEMENTIS. Everything. And two hundred thousand tons of grain more than we asked for.

A pause.

FRANK. Stalin.

CLEMENTIS. Absolutely.

FRANK. Yes.

CLEMENTIS. Stalin intervened personally.

FRANK. I can see that is what happened.

CLEMENTIS. Yes.

FRANK. An enormous relief. Stalin.

CLEMENTIS. A very great man.

FRANK. Just like that.

JOSEF FRANK *laughs.*

I feel . . . Shaky!

CLEMENTIS. The relief is enormous.

CLEMENTIS *laughs. A pause.*

CLEMENTIS. We have done right. The right thing for the working class. It cannot be wrong. Not if Stalin has agreed.

A pause.

Can it.

The sound of a car's doors opening and slamming. Three YOUNG MEN *dressed in heavy black overcoats and black fur hats and gloves come on at the back.*

YOUNG MAN. Comrade Clementis! Comrade Frank! Comrade Stalin says . . . Why walk in the street, in the cold, at so late an hour? We are to take you to him.

He spreads his hands.

For a drink.

A choir sings. The portrait of STALIN, huge, glows through the snow. STALIN advances, smiling, smoking a pipe. A WAITER walks at his side, a step behind, carrying a tray set with glasses and a vodka bottle. Behind STALIN a crowd of men in a long line, all in dark suits and smiling and carrying vodka glasses, advances. STALIN stops. The entourage stops. The snow ceases to fall. A silence. STALIN takes a glass from the WAITER'S tray. He knocks the drink back in one. The entourage knock their drinks back in one. A silence.

STALIN. The Union of Soviet Socialist Republics.

A pause.

Has a very great.

A pause.

Ice-hockey team.

STALIN laughs. Everyone laughs. A silence. STALIN and his entourage as a tableau. It fades as JOSEF FRANK speaks aside.

FRANK. What do you expect me to see when I look in that mirror? The empty world. Like a room from which all human beings have fled. Leaving filth upon the walls, a few torn newspapers upon the floor. Oh we had the world to remake. The universe in our hands, history was water in a cup, we had only to drink. Who could have, then, imagined this dereliction. This filthy empty room, the broken doors, the exasperation. Too much lost, too much blood. Now, I do not even want revenge on all that I once believed in. I wish only to lie in the sludge of the debris, of what once was a fine building. Miles deep, stirring only for a little warmth.

The tableau has faded. JOSEF FRANK is alone. He stares out into the auditorium.

SCENE EIGHT

Street. Early evening. JOSEF FRANK alone. JANICE drives the motorcycle back on stage, BILLY riding pillion.

JANICE. Off you get, Billy.

BILLY. You what?

JANICE. I'm taking him out the Rock.

BILLY. You don't fancy him Janice.

JANICE. Get off.

BILLY. You can't fancy him. Look at him. He's all mangle-
worsy.

JANICE. You heard what I said.

BILLY sighs then gets off the pillion.

BILLY. You in't half a flashy chick sometimes, Jan. Whose
bloody bike is it anyway?

JANICE. Mr Never Never, I thought. Anyway disqualified from
driving it in't you.

BILLY. Yeah. I just love red wine.

JANICE. Give Joey the helmet.

BILLY. Here you are then, old chap.

BILLY takes off the helmet and puts it on JOSEF FRANK'S
head.

FRANK. What . . .

JANICE. Help him with the strap.

*JOSEF FRANK stands, slightly stooped, hands loose by his
sides while* BILLY *does up the straps.*

BILLY. Why were you born so gormless Joey? Ugh, you in't
half got bad breath. What you got at the back a your throat?
Dog that died?

The helmet fixed, BILLY *knocks on it.*

Wake up Joey. Your big chance. You want a climb out a
your wank pit for a touch a the real thing.

JOSEF FRANK *hesitates.*

Now don't say no to a lady.

FRANK. Do I . . . Put my turns-ups in my socks?

BILLY. That is really up to you, my friend.

JANICE. Get on Joey.

BILLY helps JOSEF FRANK *on to the pillion.*

BILLY. Lift up your leg. The throb a do you good.

FRANK. I protest! I am not involved!

   JANICE *guns the motorcycle.*

SCENE NINE

Dockland. A derelict site. JANICE *and* JOSEF FRANK *on the motorcycle.*

FRANK. What is this place?

   JANICE *gets off the motorcycle.*

JANICE. Wharf. Before they knocked it down.

   She shouts into the dark.

   Ken! Liz!

   A pause.

   Played here when we were kids. Mothers and fathers. Vietcong meet the Daleks. First boy I fucked was here.

   JANICE *laughs.*

   That's the River over there. Low tide. Tell by the smell. Sh!

   A slight pause.

   Hear the rats?

   A slight pause.

   Smashing London apart, you see. Ruins and holes.

   A pause.

   I'm a Communist too.

FRANK. You are a baby.

JANICE. I follow Trotsky.

   JOSEF FRANK *laughs.*

FRANK. You do *what?*

JANICE. Don't you believe me?

FRANK. Dear child.

JANICE. I'm dead serious.

FRANK. Dear little baby.

JANICE. That why they throw you out a Czechoslovakia?

FRANK. What do you mean?

JANICE. Trotsky.

> JOSEF FRANK *laughs.*

> Don't laugh at me!

FRANK. Is that why you stuck me upon this machine? Because you thought I was a fellow Trotskyite?

JANICE. Lot a you, wan't there? Slansky? Clementis?

> *A silence.*

FRANK. How did you get hold of those names?

JANICE. You one a them?

FRANK. How did a silly little girl in South London, get hold of those names?

JANICE. Prague Treason Trials. 1952. Conspiratorial Centre they called you, didn't they?

FRANK. A stupid adolescent, get those names in her mouth?

JANICE. Can read, can't I?

FRANK. You have no right to have those names in your mouth.

JANICE. What you been doing with yourself for twenty-five years? Been in prison?

FRANK. No right!

JANICE. First book I read 'bout Communism was called *The Evil That Was Lenin.* Think it was meant to put me off. 'Stead it put me on.

FRANK. No right!

JANICE. And I read and read. Shiny books you get from Moscow. And plastic covers, red, from Peking you know? All printed faint. Couldn't understand a word. But I believed in it.

> JOSEF FRANK *laughs.*

> I knew it was right!

FRANK (*to himself*). Filth on the walls. All torn.

JANICE. Then I got in with this crowd. Big flashy flats. Lots a cushions and booze. That's how I met Trotsky.

FRANK. The little girl met Trotsky. Oh God.

JANICE. I was their pet, in a way. Real, wan't I. The real stuff.
Proletarian. Na, they were all right I s'pose. Kept on wanting
a poke me rigid though, some of 'em. So I gave that lot up.
And I gave school up. Wanted me to do 'A' levels.

She laughs.

One teacher, woman, Mrs Banks . . . You know thirty and
raddled with groovy afro hair . . . Said I'd got a go a University.
Said if I didn't I'd ruin myself.

She laughs.

I mean, I may as well a been a hundred. And I left.

FRANK. Juvenile.

JANICE. Yeah I'm juvenile! But I'm working on it. See . . .
They're not going a get me.

FRANK. There is too much lost, too much blood. Can't you
understand?

JANICE. No I don't. Less you're saying you're a clapped out
old man.

FRANK. Yes, yes, say that. I am a clapped out old man.

JANICE. Well we're going a change this fucking country.

FRANK. Nothing will change in England. Decay, yes. Change,
no.

JANICE. We're going a have a revolution in England.

FRANK. There will never be a revolution in England.

JANICE. Who are you to say? You're a clapped out old man.

FRANK. Painful for me, I do not wish to continue the
discussion . . .

JANICE. No one's discussing mate, I'll telling you. Be bad for
you, eh? Run away to soft old, squidgy old England. And
then it breaks out here. What you ran away from. Be nowhere
for you to hide. Be a nothing.

FRANK. There was a violinist. A Jew. At the time of Hitler he
hid his race. One day he had to play, it was Beethoven's
Violin Concerto, at a concert with Hitler present. At the
entrance of the violin, after the orchestral introduction, the
violinist found he could not play. In the awful silence he
left the platform. After the war, after surviving the camps and
many sufferings, he lived obscurely in retirement. It was the

violinist's birthday when a friend gave him a gramophone and a record. It was Beethoven's Violin Concerto. The violinist put it on the gramophone. The orchestra played the introduction. The moment for the violin to play came . . . And went. No violin. It was a practice record. The music continued, a mockery. The violinist looked at his hands and killed himself.

A pause.

JANICE. Oh Joey, aren't you still a Communist?

FRANK. Cannot you understand? Will you not understand?

JANICE: Mum's the word.

KEN *and* LIZ, *unseen, set up whistles and catcalls.* JANICE *puts two fingers to her mouth and lets out a piercing whistle.*

JANICE (*to* JOSEF FRANK). Don't let on.

FRANK. About what?

JANICE. Tell 'em what I told you. 'Bout Trotsky.

FRANK. When I was fourteen I was already in prison. The police had found Young Communist leaflets under my bed.

JANICE. Don't you.

FRANK. Mum is the word?

JANICE. That's right!

JANICE *kisses* JOSEF FRANK *quickly.*

What's the smell?

FRANK. Garlic.

JANICE. Not your teeth?

FRANK. No, I . . .

JANICE. Great. I'm really happy.

JANICE *shouts into the dark.*

Over here Ken!

FRANK (*to himself*). Kindergarten.

KEN, STACKY, LIZ *and* ALF *come out of the dark.*

KEN. Where's Billy?

JANICE. Walking.

KEN. Well he ought a be here!

JANICE. He will be here!

KEN. We got a be all . . . All in on this!

>STACKY *makes signs.*

>Oh shut up Stacky.

>KEN *turns away.*

JANICE. What's a matter, Ken?

>KEN *kicks at the ground.*

ALF. Joey.

FRANK. Alfred.

ALF. Fun and games, eh?

FRANK. What are these children doing here?

ALF. Tearaways. Bloody hoodlums. I'm all for it myself.

>ALF *laughs and wanders away, rolling a cigarette.* KEN
>*shouts into the dark.*

KEN. Come on come on! Where are you?

LIZ. What you up to, Jan? (*She nods at* JOSEF FRANK.)
Nibbling old men?

JANICE. So?

LIZ. Ooh Jan, how could you. The boys say . . . You know in
the washroom . . . You could have his skin for breakfast
'stead a cornflakes.

JANICE. So?

LIZ. So don't be disgusting.

JANICE. Maybe I like being disgusting.

LIZ. Jan, you not . . .

JANICE. It's a meeting a minds.

LIZ. How horrible.

>BILLY *runs on, breathless.*

BILLY (*to* KEN). The man's got his car. Over by the boilers.

>*A slight pause.*

>Stanley's with him.

KEN. Stanley?

JANICE. Oh no.

KEN. What's he want with Stanley?

ALF. Stir, stir, nice and stinking.

ALF *laughs.* BOB HICKS *and* MR STANLEY *walk on.*
A pause.

STANLEY. Now you boys and girls. What's all this, dragging Mr
Hicks out here?

KEN. Piss off, Stanley.

STANLEY. I resent that, Kenneth.

HICKS. Now let's all have a calm, here.

JANICE. We want a talk with you.

BILLY. That's right . . .

LIZ. You're a Union man. You're meant a be on our side.
(*To* JANICE.) Or have I got it wrong?

BILLY. We talk to you.

KEN. Not the boss's bum boy.

STANLEY. Have you across my knee lad . . .

STACKY *makes signs to* JANICE. JANICE *replies by signs.*

KEN (*to* MR STANLEY). Yeah? Let me tell you something,
Mr Foreman. Mr come on boys and girls be good. It should
not a been your fingers got cut off in the machines, it should
a been your neck.

A silence.

HICKS. Now we are all working people here . . .

BILLY. You're not.

HICKS. Shush shush.

STANLEY. Personal abuse all you got to hand . . . ?

JANICE. Stacky says when are we going a have a strike then?

A silence.

STANLEY. Strike?

KEN. You heard what the dumb man said.

STANLEY. You kids . . . You want a get back in the pages a the
Beano where you belong.

HICKS. Shush shush Ted, no.

A slight pause.

But you . . . Young people . . . You had better get a bit of hard, real thinking done. Now.

HICKS *flexes his shoulders.*

I take it you represent the workforce at Makepeace's.

A silence.

All right I take it you are a representation. Now you want to unionise yourselves. And before we all go up in the air 'bout strikes that means discipline. That means all agreements you have evolved over the years with the Makepeace family, with the management, not only rates of pay but conditions, over-time practice, safety, sickness . . . All that will have to be put down. On paper.

BILLY. We don't want any of that shit . . .

HICKS. Everything. Think about it. Because you may not like it.

ALF. Here we go. Shoot one of 'em, another pops up in his place.

ALF laughs.

BILLY. What's he trying a say?

HICKS (*to* BILLY). It may not be worth your while.

STANLEY. Now listen, listen a Mr Hicks.

HICKS. I mean, I'll help you. Any time you want advice, always talk it over. Over a pint. Just give me a ring.

STANLEY. Now just listen a Mr Hicks. Someone older for a change.

HICKS. See, the best you can hope for in this world is to nudge. Give it a bit of a nudge.

HICKS *flexes his shoulders.*

Industrial relations, that's a mighty animal. Bit of a dinosaur. Or, to look at it another way, bit of a giant oil tanker . . .

BILLY. What the fuck is he talking about?

STANLEY. Billy Mason . . .

BILLY. I can't help it. He hurts my brain.

STANLEY. Why won't you listen, why won't you learn? Mr

Hicks is a respected man. Spent many years keeping the
wolf from the door a working men and women.

HICKS, *low.*

HICKS. 'Nough said, Ted.

STANLEY. And you do not know it, but Mr Hicks may one day
be your Union-sponsored MP.

BILLY. Wow. Let's all have a good wank.

STANLEY. Right. That's it. That's the remark I been waiting for.
All go home now. Strike? You're wet behind the ears, or
gaga. Yes I'm talking about you, Alfred Mallings.

ALF. Nice.

STANLEY. Silly old man. Go and warm your hands up 'front a
your telly set, 'fore you catch your death. Weed your window
box. And the rest a you. Go on. Get home to your Mums and
Dads.

A pause. No one moves.

ALF. If I kick the telly in and pour Harpic over the window box,
will things get any better? On the whole I'd say . . . Yes.

JANICE. Mr Hicks, the Makepeaces are going to sell the factory . . .

MR STANLEY *and* HICKS *look at each other. A slight pause.*

You do know that?

BILLY. Course he knows that.

HICKS. Look love, don't think I don't realise, but . . .

KEN. They're going a sell off the machines! Strip the whole place
out!

JANICE. You do know that?

A pause.

STANLEY. You got the wrong end a the stick.

KEN *goes into the dark.*

HICKS. Does look like it.

STANLEY. All along the line.

BILLY. Jan, do they know or don't they?

JANICE. Don't know . . .

BILLY. I look at 'em and I can't tell. (*At* HICKS.) He standing there, taking up air, lying to me?

HICKS. Now, now.

STANLEY. Way above your heads anyway. You're no better than kids out on the street. How you know what's going on? I mean in the head of a man like Mr Ralph.

KEN runs out of the dark whirling RALPH MAKEPEACE's *briefcase round his head. He throws the briefcase on the ground. A pause.*

Why, Mr Ralph's briefcase.

A pause.

Oh Kenneth.

KEN. Look inside.

STANLEY (*to* HICKS). I think we better leave, Bob.

HICKS. Sadly.

KEN. Take a look!

STANLEY. Criminal, Kenneth.

KEN. You can read. I can't. Go on. It's stuffed full of it.

JANICE. It's all there. Letters . . .

BILLY. Yeah. He writes poems too. All sex and death.

JANICE. He's going a screw us. Throw us away. Like we were nothing, you understand? That's why we got a, we got a . . .

A pause.

STANLEY. You got a what, girl?

KEN. Take hold. Got a take hold.

JANICE. Else, what is there for us?

STANLEY. I'm not going a argue another word. Ken, you go straight to Mr Makepeace first thing tomorrow morning. I'll put a word in for you, the bugger knows why.

KEN runs to the briefcase. He takes out a fistful of papers.

KEN. Words. Scribble. All over us. Lies and money. Why am I pig ignorant? Why can't I even read the name a the station on the fucking Underground?

STANLEY. Cos you want the whole world. Plop.

KEN clicks a flick knife open.

You will put yourself beyond the pale, Kenneth. For life.
Tomorrow morning.

He points at the briefcase.

With that. Bob . . .

JANICE. Dead end, in't we. The . . . Dead end. Grotty little
factory in a grotty hole. And working there . . . Few women,
few old age pensioners, yobbos and the deaf and dumb.
Don't want a know us, do you? No threat, are we?

HICKS. Clever little head you've got there. You could do better,
love.

A pause.

Takes years. Years. Ask your mothers and your fathers.

STANLEY. Get out a this area. Gracious. Rats big as cats.
(*To* KEN.) Tomorrow morning.

MR STANLEY *and* HICKS *go off. A pause.* BILLY *strikes
a nasty chord on his guitar.*

JANICE. What you show him the case for? What you do that
for?

KEN. Gesture?

ALF. My old Dad made a gesture, back in 1929. Drunk a whole
bottle a Dettol.

ALF *laughs.*

BILLY. Spose we could burn ourselves. Like them monks. But
I spose they'd just dial 999 and put the fire out.

LIZ. Oh let 'em close the place down. Crisps? Leaning over
stinking vats all day? Pushing bits a spuds through boiling oil?
Makes your skin all slime and your hair all seaweed.

A slight pause.

Think I'll go and get married.

STACKY *makes signals.*

JANICE. You're joking.

LIZ. No joke.

BILLY. What's he saying?

JANICE. Stacky says . . . We got a be happy.

BILLY. Highly profound, Stacky old son. Give him the Nobel

Prize.

KEN *sticks the knife into the briefcase several times.*

Better bury that. Give it to the rats . . . Big as cats.

BILLY *picks up a few of the papers, then looks at one.*

Don't seem right does it, your boss writing poems.

He reads.

'We live in an old con- (*he falters*) stituency of the sun
Or old de- (*he falters*) pendency of the day or night.'

He tears the paper up.

Let's get zonked.

JANICE. No . . .

BILLY. Sweet dreams.

KEN. Yeah. Bring out the little white powder Billy.

JANICE. No . . .

KEN. Sniff a fucking heaven.

BILLY. Rots your nose, you know.

KEN. Lovely.

BILLY. Dribbling snot in Nirvana.

JANICE. No . . .

ALF. Well you're all going a have drugs, I'll get on home for my
    Ovaltine.

BILLY. Actually I not got any stuff.

KEN. You what?

BILLY. Sold it. Payment on the bike came up.

KEN. It's up West then. Couple a dozen pints and a good sick
    on the tube.

LIZ. Ooh, am I getting took out?

ALF. See if I can get a 185. If they han't knifed the conductor.

JANICE (*to* FRANK). Why don't you help us? Why do you sit
    there like you were dead? You were a Communist, you said.
    Don't you care? We're in trouble. Tell us what a do.

    JOSEF FRANK *turns his head away.*

LIZ. Get married Jan. Han't you seen 'em, the old women? Old

tramp women? In the parks, on the tube. No home, living in
a bottle a ruby wine? We could be like that, easy as . . .
Nothing at all. Everything gone. Your body, your self-respect.
Yeah, on the whole, I'm going a get married. (*To* KEN.)
I warn you. I may leave you during the course a the evening
with my new husband.

JANICE *looks at them. Then she runs to the motorcycle
and gets on.*

BILLY. Oy Joey, that's my bike and that's my woman.

ALF. I used to be a like that. All that spunk gone a waste.

ALF *laughs.* JANICE *kicks the starter, the engine fails.*

BILLY. What you doing?

JANICE. Joey's taking me out.

LIZ. Jan his skin, it's horrible . . .

JANICE. You're going a have a good time, I'm going a have a
good time. I'm going a bring this old man back from the dead.

FRANK. I . . .

KEN. We had a go, Jan! Hate and anger! Wan't enough, that's all!

JANICE *starts the motorcycle.*

That's all.

SCENE TEN

*The London Planetarium.
A bare stage. But overhead and all round the spectacle of the
galaxies, stars and planets, unfolds above the London skyline.
A COMMENTATOR, dressed in a suit with the mannerisms of
a sentimental ballad singer, speaks into a hand microphone with
a cancerous, cold American accent.* JOSEF FRANK *and* JANICE
*stand, hand in hand, looking up.
Space. Millions of stars.*

COMMENTATOR. Look up from your city, see the aeons of
space. Cold and infinite. We pass a galaxy.

*With a whoosh the spiral nebula in Andromeda passes over
the stage.*

JANICE. London Planetarium!

COMMENTATOR. In such a cluster of a hundred thousand

million stars is our sun. A star is a sun.

JANICE. Come here as a kid. Sneak in the exit.

A comet zooms down from above.

COMMENTATOR. A comet. Lone ranger of the heavens.

JANICE. Put your hand up my skirt, if you want.

The comet goes down below the skyline.

COMMENTATOR. Trip now to the Solar System. Pluto. Ninth and furthest planet, most desolate of the Sun's family.

The dark form of Pluto looms.

JANICE. Nip in the ladies take my knickers off, if you want.

Pluto passes.

COMMENTATOR. We hurtle toward the sun.

JANICE. Undo your fly, if you want.

COMMENTATOR. Past the cold giants . . . Neptune, Uranus.

One after another, the huge dark forms of Neptune and Uranus loom and pass.

JANICE. I'll give your cock a blow, if you want.

COMMENTATOR. Dead worlds.

JANICE. I'll get a ice lolly a suck. Really make your balls zing.

COMMENTATOR. Deadly atmospheres of methane freeze there.

FRANK. Put me on a bus . . . I want to go home!

JANICE gestures to an unseen usherette.

JANICE. Oy miss, give us a rocket ice lolly.

FRANK. Let me alone!

JANICE. No!

FRANK. Please!

JANICE. I fancy you.

COMMENTATOR. Saturn.

Saturn with its rings looms, tilting slowly upon its axis.

The rings of ice and dust shine in the sunlight. The sun is eight hundred and eighty-six million miles away.

FRANK. I'm dead.

JANICE. Then get alive . . .

FRANK. It's not a personal matter . . .

JANICE. Least give me a cuddle!

Saturn passes.

Please?

COMMENTATOR., Jupiter.

JOSEF FRANK *and* JANICE *embrace, awkwardly. They still look up at the spectacle, now over each other's shoulders.*

JANICE. In't you stiff and knobbly.

COMMENTATOR. Giant of solar space. Here rage hydrogen and ammonia gales, the nightmare poison winds.

JANICE. Your spine's like cement. You need a massage.

Jupiter passes.

FRANK. I . . . Was broken.

JANICE. Here come the asteroids.

FRANK. Bone splintered. Marrow scraped. Brain beaten flat. Blood soiled with the rust of crumbling nails.

The asteroids, tumbling lumps of rock, hurtle forward and pass.

COMMENTATOR. Debris of space. A fistful of gravel thrown around our sun . . .

The COMMENTATOR *continues to mouth his commentary in dumbshow.*

FRANK. How cruel of the mindless stuff of which we're made to have nerves. To peel so easily. Lower the temperature a speck upon the scale. Put water and a few chemicals out of reach. And where's our humanism? Freud, Marx, Engels, our mighty systems? They are less than the yellow matter that blinds the eye of the sleepless prisoner. Ow.

JANICE. What's a matter?

FRANK. Boil on my elbow.

JANICE. Put a poultice on.

FRANK. Poultice? Poultice?

COMMENTATOR. Mars, red planet.

Mars looms.

JANICE. Or T.C.P. Got some in my handbag.

FRANK. T? T what?

COMMENTATOR. Mars.

JANICE. Or just give us a kiss.

JANICE *and* JOSEF FRANK *kiss.*

COMMENTATOR. World of red deserts. Fields of carbon dioxide snow. Thin, gentle winds.

JANICE *looks up.*

JANICE. Eh . . . If there's life on Mars, do you think it's communist? Even if it's only a bit a moss . . . Solid red. Serve the bloody Americans right when they get there.

JANICE *and* FRANK *kiss again. They go down on their knees. Meanwhile Mars passes, Earth and its Moon loom.*

COMMENTATOR. The sweet Earth and its milky bride.

FRANK *looks up.*

FRANK. I . . .

JANICE *kisses him again. They fumble.*

COMMENTATOR. We are ninety-two million, nine hundred and fifty-seven miles from the sun . . .

Suddenly the COMMENTATOR *lapses from American to London English. He waves his hand at* JANICE *and* FRANK.

Eh you, you down there. Get up off the floor. Sorry 'bout this, ladies and gents, get all kinds in here, don't care 'bout the universe. You in row . . .

The Sun rises over the horizon of the Earth. Beams of light strike across the stage. Music crashes in — quadraphonic, exultant. JANICE *and* JOSEF FRANK *stay kneeling in their embrace.*

SCENE ELEVEN

Factory yard. Morning. It is very cold. JOSEF FRANK *comes on to find* RALPH MAKEPEACE, SYLVIA MAKEPEACE *and* MR STANLEY *looking up. From high up offstage a sack of potatoes is thrown down on the stage.*

RALPH (*shouts*). Please!

STANLEY (*shouts*). You stupid hoodlums!

FRANK. Good morning. I . . .

KEN (*off*). Boo hoo Stanley.

Individual potatoes are thrown down on the stage. RALPH
MAKEPEACE *and* MR STANLEY *dodge them.* SYLVIA
MAKEPEACE *stands still.* JOSEF FRANK *walks toward
the side of the stage from where the potatoes were thrown.*

STANLEY. Oy Joey! What do you think you're doing?

FRANK. Work . . .

KEN (*off*). Joey's down there. Oy Joey!

JANICE (*off*). Joey!

BILLY (*off*). Come in out the cold, Joey!

JANICE (*off*). Joey run!

KEN (*off*). You Ruskie!

JANICE (*off*). Put the ladder down for him.

JOSEF FRANK *hesitates.* HICKS *comes on.*

STANLEY. Stay where you are, Frank.

RALPH (*shouts*). Whatever you do, don't hurt the machines.

BILLY (*off*). Have a crisp Ralphy.

*Three cardboard boxes full of loose crisps and open are
thrown down on the stage. The crisps cascade out.*

HICKS (*to* RALPH). Got your call, Ralph. What's up?

RALPH. They say they have occupied the factory or something . . .

STANLEY. Broke in last night. Barred the doors. Overturned the
small van in the loading bay. Barricaded it.

HICKS. Out on a limb eh?

Two potatoes are thrown down on the stage near HICKS.

Spuds?

STANLEY. Got ten tons in there.

HICKS. Bloody hell.

SYLVIA (*to* RALPH). Call them.

RALPH. There must be . . .

SYLVIA. Call the police.

RALPH. Sweet reason . . .

SYLVIA. Now. If you don't I will.

JANICE (*off*). Joseph Frank!

FRANK (*aside*). What are the weapons of happiness?

KEN (*off*). Give him covering fire.

Potatoes and boxes rain down upon the stage.

JANICE (*off*). Joseph Frank!

STANLEY. Don't you . . .

FRANK *hesitates.*

Bastard commie . . .

FRANK *makes the first step of his dash toward the factory.*
Blackout.

Act Two

SCENE ONE

Out of the dark JOSEF FRANK, *blindfolded, barefoot and dressed in trousers and shirt sleeves, is rushed to the front of the stage by two* GUARDS.

FIRST GUARD. Stand.

SECOND GUARD. Keep your thumbs by the seams of your trousers.

The two GUARDS *go off. A pause.* JOSEF FRANK *turns his head this way and that way listening. Out of the dark* VICTOR CLEMENTIS, *also blindfolded, barefoot and dressed in trousers and shirt sleeves, is rushed to the front of the stage by the two* GUARDS. *They speak to* CLEMENTIS.

FIRST GUARD. Stand.

SECOND GUARD. Keep your thumbs by the seams of your trousers.

The GUARDS *take the blindfolds off* JOSEF FRANK *and* CLEMENTIS.

FIRST GUARD (*to* JOSEF FRANK). Talk to him. It is a privilege.

SECOND GUARD (*to* CLEMENTIS). Talk to him. It is a privilege.

The GUARDS *turn to go off.*

FRANK. What is the date?

The GUARDS *stop.*

Tell us the date.

FIRST GUARD. That's a privilege.

The GUARDS *go off. A silence.*

CLEMENTIS. Joseph?

FRANK. Victor?

A pause.

CLEMENTIS. How do I look?

FRANK. How . . . Do I look?

They do not look at each other. A pause.

CLEMENTIS. They gave me a lamb chop today. With carrots.

FRANK. They offered me meat. But . . . I cannot.

CLEMENTIS. I asked for the lamb to be pureed. They said they'd see what they could do.

A pause.

They told me you were dead.

FRANK. They told me you were dead.

CLEMENTIS. You accused me.

FRANK. Yes.

CLEMENTIS. So far from Moscow. We were government ministers then, riding high! Weren't we fine ones then.

He giggles, then weeps a little.

Moscow that winter, was so beautiful. The black cars in the snow.

FRANK. Please . . . No.

CLEMENTIS. Forgive me.

FRANK. Display. Any emotional . . . Disturbs me.

CLEMENTIS. Poor Joseph. You must be so tired.

FRANK. Not . . . So much now.

CLEMENTIS. No.

FRANK. Now . . .

CLEMENTIS. No.

FRANK. No.

CLEMENTIS. They gave me the date. It is the 20th of August, 1952.

FRANK. Summer?

CLEMENTIS. They gave me the date this morning. And a cigarette. Things are good.

FRANK. Now.

CLEMENTIS. What?

A pause.

How's your learning going?

FRANK. Very well.

CLEMENTIS. I've learnt all the answers I will give but they want me to learn the prosecutor's questions too.

FRANK. I slide a bit of card down the sentences to test myself.

CLEMENTIS. That's . . . I'll try that too, if you don't mind.

FRANK. It helps.

CLEMENTIS. So much better to have a transcript of a trial before the trial begins, don't you think?

FRANK. You know where you were.

CLEMENTIS. Absolutely. Was it orange juice?

A pause.

They gave you. First thing. When the confession was complete.

FRANK. Tea.

A pause.

Sweet. We aren't human, are we.

CLEMENTIS. No?

FRANK. They are feeding us now, they are telling us the day of the year now, but we aren't human.

CLEMENTIS. They offered me tea but I have . . . The oesophagus. Throat. Raw.

FRANK. So you took the orange juice?

CLEMENTIS. They told me the Third World War had begun.

A pause.

They told me the Americans bombed Peking at Christmas. Atom bombed.

A pause.

They told me Paris is a desert! And they are eating dogs in London!

A pause.

They said . . . Aren't you ashamed? The decisive struggle has begun! And you are in prison. Starving. Filth on your body. Your mind, my mind breaking.

A pause.

And I was ashamed. So very much, Joseph.

A pause.

Help the Party! Be the enemy we must root out! Yes, yes I said. Yes.

A pause.

Yes, I have difficulty with hot things. Rasp. The lining of the . .

CLEMENTIS *touches his throat.*

FRANK. Yes.

CLEMENTIS. What torments me is . . . Did he know?

FRANK. Who?

CLEMENTIS. He can't have known. What they have done to us. What . . .

FRANK. Be silent!

CLEMENTIS. What they have done . . .

FRANK. Silent!

CLEMENTIS. To the Party. To socialism. To me. To my mind. He can't have known.

A pause.

Stalin.

A silence.

They are worried my voice will not carry. At the trial. They are giving me medicine. An anti-septic spray, every hour. I assure them I will speak loudly. I won't let them down.

FRANK. No.

CLEMENTIS. I am confident. Have they given you spinach?

FRANK. The Grand Inquisitor.

CLEMENTIS. I ate spinach once in Paris, with butter. And a little nutmeg.

FRANK. The story of the Grand Inquisitor. At the height of

the Spanish Inquisition, Christ appeared among the terrified people in a public place. A woman came to him with her dead son. Among the crowd, disguised as a poor monk, the Grand Inquisitor saw the miracle. He ordered Christ's arrest. That night the Grand Inquisitor went alone to Christ's cell. The Grand Inquisitor said to Christ . . . Why do you come? To give the people love and happiness now? Out of pity in a crowd restore that child's blindness, that woman's skin, that man's life? And the Grand Inquisitor argued . . . You left love. A few pure words of truth. But how can words of love become concrete, survive in the filth and tumult of earthy life? How often has truth been spoken on the earth only to be lost in war, riot, the massive movements of people? It is in the Church that your truth survives. The feared, cruel, impregnable Church. I am the Church. My dungeons, my racks and my tribunals endlessly purify the unbelievers so that the Church may survive. So that your truth may survive, through this dark age. But now you come with miracles. Sentimental gestures. Anarchy. Everything you taught will disappear in a morass of exultation and false hopes. My Lord, the Church is Christ on earth. I, the torturer, am Christ on earth. That is why, in the morning, I will hang you and burn you.

A pause.

Christ said nothing, but leant to the Grand Inquisitor and gave him his blessing and kissed him.

CLEMENTIS. Oh Joseph. Are you still a Communist?

The GUARDS come forward with a noose and blindfold.

FRANK. Victor Clementis. Hanged in Prague on the 3rd of December 1952.

The GUARDS blindfold CLEMENTIS.

CLEMENTIS. Last letter to Klement Gottwald, Chairman of the Communist Party of Czechoslovakia, President of the Czechoslovak Socialist Republic.

The GUARDS put the noose around CLEMENTIS'S neck and scuttle off into the dark.

A few hours before his death even the worst man speaks the truth. I declare that I have never been a traitor or a spy. I confessed only to fulfil my obligation to working people and the Communist Party. It was my duty. In order that the Party survive our days of lies and fear to lead the working people to full happiness. Long live the Communist Party of Czechoslovakia.

CAPITAL RADIO. Hello all you nightriders out there.

A snatch of music. Mina Ripperton sings 'Loving you'.
CLEMENTIS *begins to sink through the stage.*

JANICE (*off*). Joseph?

KEN (*off*). Oy Joey! Where you got to?

CLEMENTIS. I tried to keep my trousers up in court! I did not show my bum in disrespect!

CAPITAL RADIO. Insomniacs all, cold out there? Here comes Californian Sun.

The radio plays the Beach Boys singing 'Good Vibrations'.
CLEMENTIS *has sunk to his chest.* JOSEF FRANK *kneels beside him.*

CLEMENTIS. I've got a handful of raisins. In a matchbox. I'd give them to you if I were alive.

CLEMENTIS *disappears.* JOSEF FRANK *looks upstage as*
STALIN *comes out of the dark smoking his pipe.* KEN *comes out of the dark carrying a transistor radio.*

KEN (*to* JOSEF FRANK). What you doing? Sleep walking about the factory?

STALIN *walks away into the dark.* JOSEF FRANK *watches him go.*

Oh go and tuck him up, Jan. Or whatever you get up to.

FRANK. He wanted to give me raisins.

KEN. What?

FRANK. Victor Clementis. In a matchbox. The last thing he said to me, before he died, in a corridor. You see . . . To keep raisins all those months, through the interrogation, the trial, the winter . . . That was an áchievement.

A pause.

KEN. I don't know, old son. I just don't know what you're on about.

KEN *throws the transistor radio down the drain. A silence.*

JANICE. What you do that for?

KEN. Can't stand the Beach Boys, can I.

JANICE. Where's the grating to that drain gone, anyway?

KEN. Chucked it on the barricade didn't I. When I was pissed.

JANICE *about to say something.*

All right, all right! But the beer's run out. And I'm coming out all over in bleeding lumps, cos a eating bleeding crips all the time.

A pause.

The great idea, eh? I don't know. Zonked, weren't we. Night we went up West and had it. The great idea.

A pause.

Billy raving he could see the Milky Way, middle a Oxford Street. Liz making clucking noises at any man in a sharpish suit. Stacky with his dumbhead eyes going like a fruit machine. It was Piccadilly Circus the great idea came. I'd just had a very satisfying sick and was feeling wonderful. The adverts, all neon . . . Like you could put your hand out, pull 'em down off the buildings, put 'em on your coat like a badge. And suddenly we all got it. You only had to look at Stacky and you knew he had it too. Just like that. Out the air. Out the traffic. Bang. Occupy the place. Blew all our bread . . . Six crates a Guinness, three bottles a gin, piled in Stacky's van and straight down here. Broke in, built the barricade. Christ were we ill when dawn came round.

JANICE. Aren't you happy, Ken?

KEN. Course I'm happy. Taking over the world in't we? Workers' paradise in here, in't it?

A pause.

Floating away in a the sunset on a sea a crisps in't we?

A pause.

Yeah.

KEN *goes off.*

JANICE. And what you wandering off for?

FRANK. Nightmares, I . . . Figures. People I once knew.

JANICE. And that's another thing. Why you always go on about the dead? You go on for hours. Names with 'K' and 'Z' in 'em.

FRANK. They died.

JANICE. Good.

FRANK. Suffered.

JANICE. Don't care.

FRANK. They hold my hands when I eat. They tie my shoes when I dress. When I speak they hold my tongue. They turn my head to see a dead bird in a garden. They pull open the lids of my eyes when I wake.

JANICE. Oh what you carry around. Wads a rotting stuff. All in your pockets, all stuffed down your shirt, urrgh.

FRANK. History . . .

JANICE. Don't care about history.

FRANK. I thought the little girl was a Marxist . . .

JANICE. Don't you try and frighten me, Mr Dracula. Half in half out your grave . . . Or so you'd like me a think . . .

FRANK. Jan, I . . .

JANICE. No history. Right? Wipe it out.

FRANK. Wiped.

JANICE. And don't forget it. And don't forget what you are.

FRANK. Count Dracula?

JANICE. A dirty old man. What are you?

JOSEF FRANK *shrugs.*

FRANK. Dirty old man.

JANICE. Child fingerer.

FRANK. Child fingerer.

JANICE. Right.

FRANK. Right.

JANICE. And there in't no history. Never happened. And if it did, make it go away.

She claps her hands.

There, it went away. Goodbye history.

She claps her hands.

Now is what I want. Now . . . That's what I love. The now. My now. Lovely sexy here and now. Perhaps we just been made.

A second ago. The world came into existence . . . Pop! Last time you blinked. And here we are now. Think so?

JOSEF FRANK *smiles.*

FRANK. Not a chance.

A pause.

JANICE. You don't make me feel sick you know. I mean you don't physically revolt me.

FRANK. Ah.

JANICE. I like your body.

JANICE *touches him.*

Poor body.

He brushes JANICE'S *hand away.*

Give us a cuddle? Now? Middle a the night? Middle of a dirty old factory? Middle a London? England? Europe? World?

JANICE *pauses, then touches* JOSEF FRANK *again.*

SCENE TWO

Factory yard. Night. It is very cold. Powerful lights are rigged up shining into the wings at the factory. Two of the lights swivel and are manned by POLICE CONSTABLES — *other* CONSTABLES *are on the edge of the scene.*
Upstage, swathed in fur coats and scarves, RALPH MAKEPEACE *and* SYLVIA MAKEPEACE *sit before a burning brazier in deck chairs, their backs to the audience.* RALPH MAKEPEACE *is asleep. A champagne bottle stands in a silver champagne bucket which is on an ornate tripod with wheels.*
INSPECTOR MILLER *and* HICKS *stand nearby.*
JOSEF FRANK, *barefoot his shoes hanging round his neck, is being led onto the stage by* MR STANLEY.

FRANK. I do not wish to leave the factory . . .

INSPECTOR MILLER *and* HICKS *turn.*

MILLER. Light over there, lads.

The POLICE CONSTABLES *swing the beams of the lights upon* JOSEF FRANK *and* MR STANLEY. *A pause,* JOSEF FRANK *blinking.*

FRANK. ⎫   I do not wish to leave the factory.

MILLER ⎬ (*together*).   Got him.

HICKS. ⎭   Very well done, Ted.

MILLER. Thank the Lord for that.

INSPECTOR MILLER *walks upstage to* RALPH MAKEPEACE

STANLEY. Huddled up in filth in there! Gracious.

HICKS. Bad, is it?

STANLEY. Slime all over. Condensation from the vats. Ought a been hosed down days ago.

MILLER. Mr Makepeace?

STANLEY. And doing their business in corners. (*To* FRANK.) Barricades? Pissing on the floor a your place a work? Makes me sick a my bones.

HICKS. Mr Frank . . .

(HICKS *sees* JOSEF FRANK's *feet*.)

There's nothing on your feet.

FRANK. I was asleep.

MILLER. Mr Makepeace?

STANLEY (*to* FRANK). Known these kids from the cradle. And their Mums and Dads. Then of a sudden they are spitting at me. Who got at 'em? You?

FRANK. You dragged me out.

HICKS. I feel . . . The time is really ripe for sweet reason.

STANLEY. Or a smashed upper plate. (*To* FRANK.) Smell a bad news about you. Go home, foreigner.

FRANK. I know nothing. I am an exile.

MILLER. Mr Makepeace, please . . .

SYLVIA. Ralph. Wake up.

RALPH MAKEPEACE *wakes*.

RALPH. What? Oh. Where were we?

SYLVIA. your mistress. The J-cloth I found in the glove compartment of the car. Soggy with it.

RALPH. Ah, that's where we were.

RALPH MAKEPEACE *stands, lifting the champagne bucket, with its bottle, from the tripod.*

MILLER. Mr Makepeace . . .

HICKS. Ralph. Ted has got Mr Frank out. For a discussion.

SYLVIA. I would like you all back there to know he never liked me to touch my own breasts.

MILLER (*to* HICKS). Sacred Arthur, give me patience! People in charge living in a bottle! Not even physically fit!

HICKS. I know I know . . .

MILLER (*to* RALPH). Eight uniform men and two C.I.D. on roster round your . . . Little empire, sir. Meanwhile in the big world they are still parking on yellow lines and knocking over old ladies in the parks. Now are you or are you not going to press a high court order?

A pause.

RALPH. Frank you've come out of your hole. Ho . . . Ole.

HICKS. It has been seven days, Ralph. I feel compromised.

RALPH (*to* JOSEF FRANK). Out your burrow. Like a weasel. To gloat. (*To* HICKS.) Do weasels have burrows? Do weasels gloat?

HICKS. After seven days, at least . . . Weigh their grievances. We have Mr Frank from in there, as a maturer and an older man. Reasonable behaviour cannot be dying out. Can it?

STANLEY. Court order and bang. For their good, if not ours.

SYLVIA. I am taking the children to mother in the morning. You can come for Antonia's birthday. After that . . . I am told the tides off Brighton West Pier are blessedly strong.

RALPH. I asked you all a question about a common animal!

A silence.

Don't you know him? Little feet? Pitter patter?

A silence.

HICKS. I . . .

RALPH. Enemy of man. Little alien brain. Poking through little red a . . . alien eyes. In and out the ground. Nick nick, little teeth. Rabid with it too.

A silence.

(*To* HICKS.) Livid!

HICKS. ?

RALPH. The word I want.

HICKS. I . . .

RALPH. To describe how a weasel must see the world, livid meat.

HICKS. Ah.

RALPH. That's what we are to that animal, to our little enemy. Red going on to purplish stuff to bite. And his day's coming, oh. Hang ourselves up on butcher's hooks eh? Dripping a little eh? Waiting for the precise little teeth.

A pause.

STANLEY. Your father would drop down dead, if he were alive.

MILLER. You're tired, sir.

STANLEY (*to* HICKS). I had to say it.

HICKS. Yes Ralph, you're tired.

STANLEY. Would a killed that lovely old man.

RALPH. I am . . .

A pause. They bang on his next word.

Tired.

They sigh.

MILLER.		All a bit dyspeptic round here.
STANLEY.	(*together*).	Right now, Joey. Mr Hicks, Inspector Miller and I will not haggle.
FRANK		Hag . . . ?
HICKS		Perhaps if you lie down, Ralph, and try not to, eh . . .

RALPH. Haggle? (*A pause.*) I'll haggle.

MILLER. Oh my God.

HICKS. I think that's not the good idea we need right now.

RALPH. Haggle. Waggle. Woggle.

MILLER. Oh dear oh dear.

RALPH. Wiggle my life away! I will I do, my life away. So all you . . . Lackeys.

A slight pause.

Go away.

STANLEY (*to* RALPH). Your father, that saintly man . . . Even in his last years, in his wheelchair, still ruled with a rod a iron. He'd never have let it come to this. Dear oh dear! (*To the others.*) Sick a my bones! Human doo-dahs in the machines, goodness gracious! Thirty years at work. And what now? The little I hold dear gets murdered. Sneer if you like, but with me it's pigeons on my roof. I been getting a dream. One day they are all dead. (*To* JOSEF FRANK.) And whose fault will that be, eh? Whose fault will that be?

RALPH. Will you all get off my property?

STANLEY (*to* JOSEF FRANK). I was in the desert!

FRANK. I was in Ruzyne prison.

STANLEY. Never heard of it.

FRANK. Have the children in that factory, asleep, heard of your desert?

STANLEY. Don't you talk about our children! Fucking foreigner!

RALPH. It is my livelihood in ruins! My creditworthiness that's bacon rind for the birds!

A slight pause.

MILLER (*to* HICKS *and* MR STANLEY). There's a panda car round the corner with a bottle of scotch in the boot. Noggin?

HICKS. Came prepared?

MILLER. You do these days. (*To* RALPH MAKEPEACE.) Lackeys, eh? Well . . . You carry on running the country then, sir. Just let us heavies know when it really gets out of hand eh? Before it's too late and hoodlums rule the whole kerboodle, eh? Come on Bob, Ted.

INSPECTOR MILLER, HICKS *and* MR STANLEY *go off,* INSPECTOR MILLER *beckoning the* CONSTABLES *off with him.* JOSEF FRANK *and* RALPH MAKEPEACE *look at each other. A silence.* RALPH MAKEPEACE *puts his hand in his coat pocket.*

RALPH. Ping?

FRANK. I'm sorry?

RALPH. Sh.

RALPH MAKEPEACE *takes a champagne glass out of his pocket. He holds it up and pings it with a finger.*

Ping.

RALPH MAKEPEACE *walks sideways to* JOSEF FRANK, *glass in one hand, the other clutching the champagne bucket with its bottle.*

Take one.

FRANK. What?

RALPH. Pocket.

JOSEF FRANK *takes a champagne glass from* RALPH MAKEPEACE'S *other pocket.* JOSEF FRANK *looks at the glass.*

Are you a religious man?

FRANK. Why?

RALPH. The feet.

FRANK. No.

RALPH. Thought perhaps it was remorse.

FRANK. I do not think so.

RALPH. Self disgust?

FRANK. No.

RALPH. No.

A pause.

Do you mind putting your shoes and socks on? The colour of your feet is bothering me.

FRANK. What do you want of me?

RALPH. Pour the champagne, obviously.

FRANK. I don't drink alcohol.

RALPH. You know, old man, you really are something of a perpetual absence.

FRANK. If I am to put my shoes and socks on, I will have to hold your sleeve.

RALPH. Be my guest.

JOSEF FRANK holds RALPH MAKEPEACE'S sleeve. He raises a foot. He looks helplessly from his foot to his other hand, holding the champagne glass. RALPH MAKEPEACE and JOSEF FRANK sway.

FRANK. Balance . . .

RALPH. Give me the bloody thing.

RALPH MAKEPEACE takes the glass and throws it into the wings. He takes the champagne bottle out of the bucket and throws the bucket into the wings.

Come the dawn will we find ourselves . . . Returned to our senses? Wake up lying in a pool of liquid . . . On the floor of our garden shed? And will we look out of the window and say . . . Why are there red flags on our chimney pots? Why are there young men and women shouting from our windows? (*To* FRANK.) Is that what they want in there?

FRANK. They are sleeping.

RALPH MAKEPEACE struggles to open the champagne bottle.

RALPH. The young in one another's arms? I mean . . . Are you all writhing in the liberated area?

The champagne cork pops out.

A far country. Birds in the trees. I am utterly ruined. Do they know that? Your sweet youths? Your sweet limbed, snotty hoodlums? Have you noticed how the oil from the vats makes the girls . . . Glisten . . .

A pause.

Don't they know they are wrecking a wreck? Your shitty little change-the-worlders? I am a drowned man. Why hold my head down the toilet?

He hiccups.

Bloody hiccups now. Just know the night's going to end in physical indignity. Ruptured stomach wall?

He hiccups. He waves the champagne bottle.

Want some of this?

Nothing from JOSEF FRANK.

It was the pork chop flavour that finally did for me. The Makepeace crisp is, anyway, deeply obscure. The monoliths of the crunch world long wanted to bite me. Bite me . . .

He biccups.

Out. The pork chop flavour was a last fling. But . . . Too much capital expenditure. Too little return. Sacks of pork chop powder piled up, going soggy in the rain. My accountant advised me to sell it fast, for cash, as fertiliser. Conducted a feasibility test. Tried it on my lawn. The lawn died.

He biccups.

Frank, I plead with you!

SYLVIA. All I wanted was a family. A good life in a good house. A few trees in the garden. And to go south in the summer. Perhaps to Tuscany. And in my marriage, and with my friends, all I wanted was . . . Certain moments of ease. Silence and smiles. Not this endless grubbing around. Lunchtime drinking. Hysterical calls to accountants. My husband with his back to me in bed at night, sobbing. All because a few pubs are going over to sausage and mash and will no longer take a gross of packets of crisps oh god! I've got crisps in my knickers. Little bits of crisps under my eyelids. The debt. The bad temper. The nightmare audits. Life should be . . . Sun on the wall, children on a swing in the shade. Not this guilt.

RALPH (*to* JOSEF FRANK). Get them back to work in there. I'll take my heart out and give it to you. I'll lay my bowels upon the floor. I'll crawl . . .

He biccups. A pause. He biccups again. JOSEF FRANK *turns away.*

Where are you going? You've not had a drink. You've not put your shoes . . . Stop, let me help you . . . With your socks . . .

JOSEF FRANK *stops.*

FRANK. Reason. Reason. Reason. Violence!

A silence.

What are you people? All I wanted . . . Was nothing. My need was . . . A crack in the wall in this country. In which to vegetate, moulder away, so quietly to rack and ruin. Be . . . Tired. Burn a little self-pity in the grate. I would have drunk, if I had something of a liver left. When I came here they wanted me to teach at your Cambridge University. Modern History.

He laughs.

Teach the slow movement of corpses, sinking in a graveyard?

A pause.

For, if I told you what was done to me, you would say it is a
miracle that I survived. But I did not survive. It is cruel!
When the worst thing that can be done to a man has been
done to you . . . To your body, to the valves of your heart,
your skin, the molars of your jaw . . . Why do they want you
to be a saint?

RALPH. God. If I'd known we'd have had you round to dinner.

A pause.

FRANK. I will tell the workers you employ what you said.

JOSEF FRANK *turns away.*

RALPH. I am not a bad man! I write poems!

FRANK. So?

SCENE THREE

The factory by the drain, night. JOSEF FRANK *alone.*

FRANK. So you're a fine human being? So there's a strip of
carpet in Ruzyne Gaol, blood and human hair in its pile. So,
you wish no one harm? Love gardens? Autumn? The city of
Venice, the music of Debussy? So, tonight the trains in Russia
go for thousands of miles, each with a prison coach . . . the
blacked out windows, seen on any station in that country . . .
There are mothers alive, tonight, who have murdered babies
rather than take them upon those trains . . . So. So. So what?

A pause.

The Soviet poet Mayakovsky, the last year of his life, before
he blew out his brains . . . Took to carrying a little bit of
soap about. To wash his hands, everywhere, even in the snow
in the street. So? So I know how he felt.

He laughs. A pause.

And Rudolph Slansky in his cell in Prague, ran his head at the
rim, rim of the lavatory in his cell . . . To beat his tortured
mind into some kind of peace. And they took him to hospital
to dress his wound . . . And three days later returned him to
his cell . . . Where he found the lavatory padded, with
steel strips and sacking. So, so he could not leave. So what?

Catalogues of horrors, fine feelings mangled, betrayal, generations lost, tyranny. So what?

JANICE (*off*). Joseph, where are you?

KEN (*off*). What you doing, Joey?

BILLY (*off*). Saw you out in the yard, Joey!

KEN (*off*) You creeping about in here Joey?

FRANK. I thought I could leave that bloodstained room. Be English. Anonymous, in a gentle climate?

KEN (*off*). Joey!

BILLY (*off*). Joey!

LIZ (*off*). Joey!

KEN (*off*). Where you at, Joey?

LIZ (*off*). Dirty old man!

FRANK. Right. If I am not to be left alone, all right. Right. I'll drag out all I once believed in.

STACKY *runs on, sees* JOSEF FRANK *and skids to a halt.*

(*Aside.*) Let the old melodrama hit the road again.

STACKY, *trying to call the others.*

STACKY. Huh! Huh!

JANICE, LIZ *and* BILLY *carrying* ALF *on an improvised stretcher and* KEN *come on. A silence.*

FRANK. Mr Makepeace wants you all to go back to work.

KEN. Oh great.

BILLY. News.

KEN. And what did you say to him?

FRANK. Nothing.

JANICE. Nothing?

BILLY. Never trust an old man.

ALF. I agree. I'm an old man and I don't trust me.

BILLY. What he offer you? Breakfast in a flash hotel? Silk underwear for your dirty old arse?

LIZ. Or just a wash. Wouldn't blame him. My blackheads are coming alive.

JANICE. Nothing, Joseph? Oh why? Why not tell 'em . . . We liberated the machines. The machines are free now. But you said nothing?

KEN. Course he said nothing! Cos he's a nothing man!

FRANK. Oh baby boy. You cannot even suck back your dribble.

A pause.

KEN. What you call me?

FRANK. A baby boy. Who has fouled his cradle a little and is proud of that. But really can do nothing for himself.

KEN *giggles.*

KEN. Think you rule do you Mister?

JANICE. Be careful, Joseph . . .

KEN *runs at* JOSEF FRANK.

BILLY. No don't . . .

BILLY *steps across* KEN's *path.* KEN *skids and falls.* FRANK *takes hold of* KEN's *ears from behind and puts his knee in his back.*

KEN. Let go my ears.

FRANK. Old lag's trick.

KEN. I said let go my ears.

FRANK. Hold a violent comrade for hours.

KEN. Get him a let go my ears!

FRANK. I am puffing out.

ALF. Puffed. Just puffed. That's English.

JANICE *and* LIZ *laugh.*

KEN. All right. All right.

A pause.

What do you want?

FRANK. No. What do you want?

KEN. Come all the way out the iron curtain, just a pull a bloke's earhole . . .

FRANK. Ken, the great idea.

KEN. Occupy the place.

FRANK. And?

KEN. No fucking 'and' about it ow!

LIZ. Steal, that's what we want a do in't it?

BILLY. Rip it all off!

JANICE. Run it ourselves.

BILLY. Liberate it. The lot! For us!

FRANK. And?

LIZ. And revenge. I don't mind saying it.

FRANK. Revenge and?

BILLY. Yeah! Sheds, machines yeah! Vats a oil!

FRANK. And?

BILLY. And chuck it at 'em!

FRANK. And?

BILLY. Yeah!

FRANK. And?

BILLY. Shut up saying 'and'!

FRANK. And how do you run the factory? And how do you buy the potatoes? And the cellophane, for the packets? And pay the printers, for the funny faces in pretty colours, upon the packets? And the oil in the vats?

JANICE. What you saying?

LIZ. 'Let go,' he's saying.

BILLY. Course he's saying 'let go'. They all say 'let go' in the end. Even Dylan, his last three LP's . . . He's said 'let go'.

FRANK (to KEN). You do not have the chance for revolt often. And, often, it is ridiculous. Fleeting. Difficult to think through. But it is rare. And not to be thrown away. It is the most precious thing on earth.

JOSEF FRANK *releases* KEN. *A pause.*

Revolt.

KEN. If we could take things all apart. Put 'em all agether again. There is a way, sometimes I do see it, like with words. And it goes blurred.

A pause.

Right. We go out the drain.

JANICE. What . . .

BILLY. What do you mean?

KEN. We chuck the factory.

A pause.

We get out.

A pause.

Only us we got, you see. (*To* JANICE.) Stacky's van. Parked out the back a Poppy Street, in't it?

JANICE. Yeah . . .

KEN. We go down the drain, out under the yard, out under the wall and . . . Away.

JANICE. Just walk out?

A pause.

ALF. In the war, last war, they walked out the cities. During the blitz. Thousands, just walked out. All over the countryside. 'Trekkers' they called 'em. Portsmouth, Coventry, Glasgow. You could see the camp fires for miles at night. Did it myself once. Visiting my sister in Pompey. One very bad night, just walked out on Portsdown. Out a that experience, I'll tell you what you need. Load a bog paper.

A pause. They look at the drain.

BILLY. Why not?

LIZ. Down there . . .

JANICE. Why not?

LIZ. Why not?

ALF gets up.

ALF. Don't know what I'm lying on this bleeding thing for, like a leper! Right, I'll go first.

ALF jumps down the drain and disappears.

BILLY. Fucking hell!

KEN. Oy, Alf!

KEN, BILLY and JANICE run to the drain. ALF shouts from down the drain.

ALF. Just hurt my leg a bit, that's all. Come on in, it's only muck

Blackout.

SCENE FOUR

In the blackout LIZ, KEN, BILLY, STACKY and ALF are heard passing along the drain.

BILLY. Lot a gunge down here!

LIZ. There's a smell, like seaweed.

ALF. Don't drop me in it, whatever you do don't do that. I got stiff knees.

LIZ. Didn't ought a jumped down the hole, ought you!

ALF. It was an impulse.

LIZ. Silly old man.

ALF. I'll be all right. I can look after myself. I been in brothels in Port Said. If you seen a woman going with a donkey you can put up with anything.

JANICE. Where's Joseph?

KEN. Don't know. Joey?

A silence.

Joey, keep behind us.

A silence.

JANICE. I'll find him.

KEN. Don't be stupid!

JANICE. Joseph?

Light appears at the mouth of the drain, revealing the same scene as the factory floor. JOSEF FRANK is sitting, shoulders rounded, legs dangling into the drain. JANICE climbs up holding a lamp.

JANICE. Joseph? They're waiting for us down there.

A pause.

Joseph?

FRANK. Excuse.

JANICE. What?

FRANK. You will have to excuse me.

JANICE. What's the matter? What is it?

FRANK. Something inside. A strange . . .

JANICE. Where?

FRANK. In. Inside.

JANICE. I'll get you to a hospital.

FRANK. No no, sh. Sh.

JANICE. I'll take you to the hospital.

FRANK. No be quiet.

JANICE. Don't be fucking stupid!

FRANK. No. Sh. Quiet. You will leave me here and go with the others.

JANICE. No.

FRANK. Look, 1968. I went back to Prague. Spring? Remember? The day I got back, tanks rolled down the Prague streets. Russian tanks?

He laughs.

I took a train to the Austrian border. I was lucky. Slipped back into the West, back into sweet nothing.

JANICE. Come on love.

FRANK. Do not ask me to move, I cannot move.

A pause.

After my trial, it was somewhen in the fifties, somewhere in the years, in the grey time . . . I met one of my interrogators. Kohoutek. A man who had told me that the Third World War had begun and that Paris was a radio-active desert. I was sitting at a cafe in a square and he walked up to me. He said . . . I too was arrested. And he offered to buy me a drink. I could not speak! And then he said . . . I'm sorry it was so bad for you. The old man.

JANICE. Alf?

FRANK. Put him in a doctor's waiting room. First opportunity.

JANICE. But . . .

FRANK. Elizabeth.

A slight pause.

JANICE. What about her?

FRANK. Put her on a bus back home.

JANICE. Why . . .

FRANK. Look they put me in a cellar. There were icicles on the bricks. I had to walk in mud. I suffered frostbite. They were trying to make a new human being.

JANICE. Don't tell me anymore . . .

FRANK. That young fool!

A slight pause.

JANICE. Who?

FRANK. Ken. Get him to read. And Billy. He has utopian tendencies. Squash them. Jan . . .

JANICE. What, love?

FRANK. Just that when I was on trial, injected with vitamins after the months of being starved . . . Glowing with a sunlamp tan . . . Parroting my confession, taught me by heart . . . I agreed.

JANICE. No.

FRANK. I agreed with what had been done to me!

JANICE. No.

FRANK. I was at peace.

He laughs.

JANICE. No.

FRANK. Plead a whole number of grave crimes!

JANICE. No don't . . .

FRANK. Only when my health returned, a little warmth creeping back . . . That the old pain began again. The old so, so what of the ugly world.

He laughs.

Don't stay in the countryside. Nothing revolutionary comes from agriculture, not in Western Europe. Make for another city

JANICE. And what about me, eh Joseph?

A pause.

FRANK. Don't get pregnant.

JANICE. Now the old man says so.

FRANK. And don't . . .

A slight pause.

JANICE. What?

FRANK. Waste yourself.

JANICE. No.

FRANK. I cannot come with you, for you see the new human being, I do believe his liver is finally about to explode.

JANICE. Will you be . . . ?

FRANK. I will go to a hospital.

JANICE. You will.

FRANK. I will.

JANICE. Cos I . . . Got a go with the others.

FRANK. Yes.

JANICE kisses JOSEF FRANK. He runs a hand down her face.

Go. My ignorant little English girl.

They smile. JANICE disappears down the drain. As the light of the lamp disappears he holds his forearms against his body in pain. The blackout is almost restored when brilliant light snaps on all over the stage. At the back stands a tank with Russian insignia. STALIN stands beside it. JOSEF FRANK stands and takes off his coat. He runs at the tank, leaps and flings his coat over the end of the barrel of the tank's gun. He sinks to his knees, exhausted. STALIN laughs.

STALIN. Incurable romantic.

A blackout and, at once, MR STANLEY, INSPECTOR MILLER and HICKS come on with powerful torches. JOSEF FRANK lies where he fell. He is dead.

MILLER. All right in here! Where you are, please!

STANLEY. Come on boys and girls.

A pause.

HICKS. Not here.

STANLEY. The bloody drain. Out in a Poppy Street. They got out the bloody drain.

HICKS. Sneaky buggers.

INSPECTOR MILLER *finds* JOSEF FRANK'S *body.*

MILLER. Mr Makepeace Sir! Over here, please.

RALPH MAKEPEACE *and* SYLVIA MAKEPEACE *come on. They gather around* JOSEF FRANK'S *body.* SYLVIA *looks, turns away and lights a cigarette.*

RALPH. Is . . . ?

MILLER. Yes, I do think so.

RALPH. Some sort of . . .

MILLER. Heart failure, or . . . Yes sir.

He calls off.

Oh Sergeant . . .

RALPH. He once was in the Government of his country, you know

SYLVIA. Just gone have they? Your workers?

RALPH. It would look like that.

SYLVIA. And what does that leave you with?

RALPH. Oh I don't know. Potato cutters, heating system. Metal value in the machines. And a divorce? And a course of aversion therapy for the booze . . . And who knows what will happen?

SYLVIA. We do.

RALPH. Yes? Yes. God, the little shits! Children of the Revolution? I want them to . . . To bleed like pigs in a ditch.

SYLVIA. Wherever they are.

RALPH. Wherever they are.

Blackout.

SCENE FIVE

Wales. Snow. Brilliant light. A winter orchard. An envelope is nailed to a tree. JANICE *and* LIZ *come on.*

LIZ. It in't Wales. It's the middle a the moon.

JANICE. We got here.

LIZ. But nearly dead.

JANICE. Should a left you with Alf.

LIZ. Middle of a doctor's waiting room in Swindon? Thank you very much.

JANICE *turns away.*

I want a be in the warm. I want a be under a hairdryer, a bit too warm, you know? Trickle a sweat between the shoulder blades. And everything fuggy and safe.

JANICE. Catch a bus then.

LIZ. You been trying a get rid of me, Jan, ever since we left London

JANICE. Just get on a bus. Out of here. Back home.

LIZ. See what I mean?

BILLY, KEN *and* STACKY *come on.*

KEN. No one in the house.

BILLY. Boarded up.

KEN. Not much in there. Empty deep freeze. Make a fire in there, though.

BILLY. Abandoned the place, looks like.

STACKY *has found the envelope pinned to the tree.*

What they grow here?

KEN. Be sheep wouldn't it? Yeah, baa baas.

BILLY. There's trees there. Apples eh? Or pears?

STACKY. Huh.

STACKY *gives* KEN *the envelope.*

KEN. What's this, then?

JANICE. Looks like a letter.

KEN. Read it, then.

JANICE. You read it.

KEN. Don't mess about.

JANICE. Least tell us what's the first word.

A pause. KEN *stares at the envelope.*

KEN. It's a 'T'. All right? All right?

JANICE *takes the envelope and reads.*

JANICE. 'To the Inspector of Taxes'.

> JANICE *opens the envelope and reads the letter.*

> It's from the farmer. 'Dear Sir. You do come from a town you do not know what the countryside is. It is a desert. The sheep die because we cannot buy winter foodstuff we are bankrupt. We cannot sell the animals. There is no life. Green things grow but it may as well be sand. Funny how you see cars on the road but it may as well be the middle ages or worse. So I and my Martha have left the land and Mr Taxes you will not find us, we are gone. We loved the land I and Martha but it drove us away. Edward Breckin, Farmer.'

> *A pause.*

BILLY. The place is free.

JANICE. Let's go in the house and get warm.

LIZ. For godsake, yes.

JANICE. Is there wood?

KEN. Round the back.

JANICE. Maybe there're tins a something somewhere in the house

> KEN *and* STACKY *go off.*

BILLY. Live off the land eh? We could make a country of our own, eh? Declare independence? From the whole world eh?

LIZ. I'm going a rummage round that house. May find a hairdryer for all I know. And a bus timetable, eh Janice?

JANICE. Why not?

> LIZ *goes off.* BILLY *puts his arm round* JANICE, *she puts her arm round him.*

JANICE. The farmer and his wife couldn't run the farm, Billy.

BILLY. No . . .

JANICE. So why can we?

BILLY. Don't know.

JANICE. Have to go back to the city.

BILLY. Not London . . .

JANICE. Manchester, I thought.

> BILLY *shrugs.*

It's the city we know.

BILLY. Yeah? 'Ere Jan, that old man. Old Joey. You really got funny for him didn't you?

JANICE shrugs. She and BILLY begin to walk off, their arms round each other.

JANICE. So?

BILLY. What was he?

JANICE. He was a Communist.

EPSOM DOWNS

To Harry

On Epsom Downs I met my love
An iron fist in a satin glove

Author's Note

JOINT STOCK has a distinctive way of working with a playwright. The final text is the writer's alone, but it is written in
full view of the company's constant, questioning gaze. I am
indebted to them for their painstaking research, their
encouragement and stamina, their endless but always creative
criticism, their flair and invention in workshops and rehearsals,
and for the many happy hours we spent together on race-courses
during the flat-racing season of 1977.

Howard Brenton
1977

Characters

BOBBY, seven years old
PRIMROSE, a traveller
SANDY, a father
CHARLES PEARCE, a horse
  trainer
SUPERINTENDENT BLUE
SAWBONES, a horse
POLICE HORSE
KERMIT FROG TRADER
MARGARET, a mother
SHARON, three years old
MAN DOWN ON HIS LUCK
LORD RACK, a racing man
HUGH, a stable lad
JOCKS, a stable lad
MINTY, a traveller
MR TILLOTSON, an
  evangelist
MISS MOTROM, an
  evangelist
MACK, a busker
BUD, a busker
GRANDPA
GHOST, of Emily Davison
BUNNY GIRL
DOROTHY DELAUNE, a
  society woman

ROGER COYLE, a society
  man
THE AGA KHAN
AGA KHAN'S BODYGUARD
LES BACKSHAKER, a
  bookmaker
MORRY BURROWS, a
  bookmaker
MRS BACKSHAKER
JUBILEE CHICKEN VENDOR
LOUIS, a bookmaker
JUBILEE DRUNK
POLICEMAN
STABLE LAD
HORSE, running in The Derby
FOUR OWNERS
JOCKEY
WOMAN, at the beer tent
1ST BEER TENT DRUNK
2ND BEER TENT DRUNK
THE DERBY
THE COURSE
Lester Piggot fans, drunks,
  crowds, jockeys, lovers,
  asylum inmates

EPSOM DOWNS was commissioned and first performed by the Joint Stock Theatre Company at the Round House, Chalk Farm, London on 8 August 1977. The cast as follows:

Miss Motrom	Gillian Barge
Sharon	
Horse Owner	
Woman at the Beer Tent	
Sandy	Simon Callow
The Aga Khan	
Les Backshaker	
Horse Owner	
Beer Tent Drunk	
Lord Rack	Paul Freeman
Roger Coyle	
Jubilee Drunk	
Stable Lad	
Sawbones	
Bud	
Charles Pearce	Tony Rohr
Mack	
Morry	
Horse Running in the Derby	
The Course	
Superintendent Blue	Bob Hamilton
Man Down on his Luck	
Grandpa	
Louis	
Beer Tent Drunk	
Margaret	Cecily Hobbs
Minty	
Bunny Girl	
Horse Owner	
Mr Tillotson	Will Knightley
Hugh	
Jockey	
Policeman	
Kermit Frog Trader	
Bobby	David Rintoul
Police Horse	
Jocks	
Jubilee Chicken Trader	
The Derby	

Primrose	Jane Wood
Ghost	
Dorothy Delaune	
Mrs Backshaker	
Lester Piggot Fans, Drunks, Crowds,	All the cast
Jockeys, Lovers, Asylum Inmates	

Directed by: Max Stafford-Clark
Designed by: Peter Hartwell
Lighting by: Gareth Jones
Company and Stage Manager: Alison Ritchie
Deputy Stage Manager: Donna Rolfe
Assistant Stage Manager: Alastair Palmer

Act One

BOBBY, *a seven year old, runs over the Downs flying a kite. He wears an indian headress of plastic feathers and has a plastic space-ray machine-gun hung on his back. BOBBY goes off. The kite remains in the sky.*

The Downs deserted.

PRIMROSE *a traveller, aged fifteen, comes on. She is dressed in a floral skirt, day-glow bright blue slacks beneath, a white blouse and a small frilly apron. She carries a basket full of twigs of heather and pieces of silver-paper. She also holds a David Soul magazine. She sits down on the slope of the hill. She lies back, sunbathing, the magazine over her face.*

The Downs, PRIMROSE *sunbathing, the kite above.*

SANDY, *aged thirty-four, with long hair on a receding pate, comes on dribbling a football. He has a cigarette in his mouth and carries an opened can of lager. He performs a few tricks with the ball. He stops, out of breath. He stretches his arms above his head. He attempts a press-up with the cigarette in his mouth. He gives up. He looks up into the sky. He whistles like a lark. He shades his eyes, squinting. He shrugs. He stands messily. He dribbles the ball off, over the skyline.*

The Downs, still. PRIMROSE *sunbathing. Above, the kite flutters.*

SUPERINTENDENT BLUE *and* CHARLES PEARCE *appear on the skyline, on horseback. The horses are played by naked actors.*

PEARCE. A lark. Up by that kite.

    PEARCE *and* BLUE *look up whistling.*

BLUE. The great day. It looks beautiful, does it not?

PEARCE. What?

BLUE. The South of England on the great day. Like a fat mattress on a fat bed.

    PEARCE *snorts.*

PEARCE. A bed soon to be trampled on by the common herd.

BLUE. It will be a very tough day. But we do love it so, do we not?

PEARCE. Do we?

PEARCE's *horse starts.*

Don't you, Mr. Bones.

BLUE. Good God, that Sawbones?

PEARCE. Blaze like a sickle. It is he.

BLUE. Your first first-class winner.

PEARCE. And you still smell it, don't you old man. The whiff of a great racecourse. The ozone of a competitive life. Probably fear.

PEARCE *pats the* HORSE.

Failed at stud though, didn't you. Silly old bugger. So I hack him for the memory.

BLUE. Sentimental of you, Charles.

PEARCE. The racing world is full of sentimental pigs. Sitting on horses.

They laugh.

BLUE. Derby Day. The Cockney's holiday. Half a million cheeky chappies on the grass stuffing 'emselves with Brown Ale and ham sandwiches. It has a lot of old world charm.

PEARCE. Always makes me shudder. When you look at half a million punters laid out on a hill – you think 'Democracy could go mad'.

BLUE. Never.

PEARCE. I'm glad the crowd control overlord is calm.

BLUE. I am shitting hot bricks. But that is my job.

PEARCE. That is your job.

BLUE. No no, come on. We are both Epsom boys. And both come far. You a trainer of two runners in the Derby, Charles?

PEARCE. And you the trainer of the Derby crowd, Alan?

BLUE. On horses since we were children, school satchels on our backs.

PEARCE. Now on horses with ulcers in our stomachs.

BLUE. There is a pride, Charles. Local boys made good.

PEARCE. Yes, I give you that. There is a pride. Funny to
think — I have done business with the Queen Mother.

BLUE. There is a lot to be said for a Grammar School education.

PEARCE. We have come far. But I sometimes think we could
find ourselves going all the way back again. I think that when
I see a crowd.

BLUE. The Derby crowd is the fruit displayed. The odd rotten
pineapple, but that is all.

A TRADER *appears carrying a big bundle of violent green
soft toys, 'Kermit Frogs'. They are large — about three feet
long.* PEARCE *and* BLUE *eye the* TRADER.

Morning.

TRADER. Morning.

BLUE. Frogs?

TRADER. Right first time.

BLUE. Will mankind buy anything?

TRADER. Right again.

BLUE. They did not hop off a lorry, did they? Those frogs?
Onto your honest shoulder?

TRADER. Me, the wife and kids — have been slaving over these
frogs since Easter, to flog to the punters today.

BLUE. How very moving.

TRADER. What, want to see my licence to trade?

BLUE. Too early in the morning, Lad.

TRADER. Right.

THE TRADER, *going. He turns back.*

You Mr Pearce? The Trainer? I follow your horses.

PEARCE. I am charmed.

TRADER. Not today though.

PEARCE. I am uncharmed.

TRADER. What do you think of the Groom?

PEARCE. French brothel-creeper of an animal.

TRADER. Won't stay?

PEARCE. Let me put it like this. If Blushing Groom wins The Derby today, I will eat the Pope.

TRADER. Oh. And I was going to put my frogs on it. Took it as a sign. French horse? Frogs? No?

PEARCE. No.

TRADER. No. Nice talking to you. Hope we all have a good day. All in the same boat, are we not?

BLUE. You reckon?

TRADER. Service industries to the mugs upon the Downs. The horseflesh, the law and order, the Kermit Frogs.

BLUE. Don't be fresh.

TRADER. Let's hope we all clean up, anyway.

The TRADER *goes off over the skyline.*

PEARCE. Phew.

BLUE. Phew.

PEARCE. All kinds.

BLUE. Well. Better get back. Bite a few necks.

PEARCE. Me too.

They walk their horses.

BLUE. If Blushing Groom blows up, what do you fancy? Piggot?

PEARCE. If Lester Piggott wins The Derby today, I will marry the Pope. Race you?

BLUE. To the Gyppo Evangelical tent?

PEARCE. You're on. Hup!

BLUE. Hup!

They gallop their horses off. The Downs deserted. The kite flutters above.

MARGARET *pushes* SHARON, *aged three years, over the grass in a baby buggy.*

SHARON. My want a ginger biscuit.

    MARGARET *zigzags down the slope with the baby buggy.*

SHARON. My want a ginger biscuit.

MARGARET. You cannot have a ginger biscuit. You have just had your porridge. Let's go fast and fly! Right up to the kite!

SHARON. My not want to fly — up the kite — my want a ginger biscuit!

MARGARET. You cannot have a ginger biscuit. You have just had your porridge.

SHARON. My want to see the horses.

MARGARET. You will see horses later.

SHARON. My want to see horses now!

MARGARET. Oh God, I have given birth to a female Ghengis Khan. It is early in the morning now, sweetheart. You have just got us all up, sweetheart. You'll see the horses later. Look at the kite. It's like a bird.

SHARON. NOT like a bird. My NOT look at the kite. MY want a ginger biscuit.

MARGARET. You cannot have a ginger biscuit. You have just had your porridge — come on, let's go fast —

    She runs the baby buggy in a figure eight.

SHARON. WHY MY just had my porridge?

MARGARET. Don't be a little bugger or I'll tickle you.

SHARON. MY WANT — set that kite on fire.

    MARGARET *stops and tickles* SHARON.

No no! NOT tickle me! NOT.

    SHARON *yells but ends up giggling.*

NOT do that.

    MARGARET *pushes the baby buggy again up the slope.*

MARGARET. Freedom. The open spaces. The land at peace and high summer come. Hey ho my little loved one.

SHARON. My want an orange.

They go over the skyline. The Downs deserted. The kite
flutters above.

MAN DOWN ON HIS LUCK *comes on. He takes a bottle of Brown*
Ale from his coat. It is empty. He looks at it. His legs splay.
He circles, rubbing the top of the bottle, he drinks as if rubbing
the top had restored the contents. He looks at the bottle
dismayed. He puts the bottle down on the grass. Above, the
kite flutters. He looks up at the kite. He waves at it angrily.

MAN DOWN ON HIS LUCK. Na. Na.

He pulls the lapels of his jacket up around his ears and, as if
ducking from an assault from the air, he runs off. The Downs
deserted. The kite above is still.

LORD RACK *comes on. He wears a fine but bulbous tweed coat,*
a homburg hat, ostentatiously large binoculars hanging around
his neck beside their case. On his back there is an old army
haversack. The neck of an unopened bottle of champagne pokes
out of it. He carries another bottle of champagne which is nearly
empty. He stands in the centre. His movements have parallels
with those of the MAN DOWN ON HIS LUCK. *He feels in his*
pocket for something. He looks up. He whistles huskily at the
lark. He returns to fumbling in his pocket. He takes out a
champagne glass. He pours himself a drink. He raises the glass in
a toast.

LORD RACK. Derby Day.

He drinks.

Eight a.m. Been up all night. Slept in the car. Picnic breakfast.
Tummy churning already. It's a gut thing for me. The Common
Man's race. They put me in 'House of Lords, but this is where
I belong.

He takes a deep breath and coughs horribly. He sucks back
phlegm and spittle. He scans the landscape through binoculars.
He sees, in the distance, PRIMROSE, *a traveller girl, come on.*
She carries a basket in which lie twigs of heather and pieces
of silver-paper. She squats and puts the basket on the ground.
She presses the pieces of silver-paper around the twigs of
heather.

Ah. Life at one with Nature.

He strides and stumbles down the slope.

Good morning young lady. Don't take fright now. Just an old horse, out for a canter. Bit of a crib biter in my day, eh?

PRIMROSE *stares at him.*

Traveller are you? Or show people? Hard life. The concrete and the mud. I was on a House of Commons Select Committee for your folk. Aye. Did bugger all. Here, look here.

He fumbles in his clothing, takes out a wallet and takes from it a ten pound note.

Now don't shy and run off. Sell us a bit of lucky heather.

PRIMROSE *gives him a piece of heather. She reaches to take the note but he holds it back.*

Give us a bit of a cuddle. French kiss? Odds on you're not a girl who brushes her teeth, eh? Hey hey.

PRIMROSE *judges her moment then grabs the ten pound note, gives LORD RACK a rude sign — a suck of a finger, the finger held up — and runs off.*

Lust. It went in like a knife, many years ago, never to come out. Eh oh, get it over with, you silly old man. Get out 'press cuttings of your court case.

He takes out a wodge of dilapidated newspaper cuttings. He rustles them.

Grubby wreathes and flowers — on the grave of a political career. Hey ho, read 'em. Promised your wife and 'Leader Of The Party in the House of Lords you would. Still. When you're caught with your trousers down and your cock in the till, that's all you've got left.

He turns the cuttings.

Oh the pain.

He turns the cuttings.

Down among the dirty vicars. On the page opposite the Leader in The Daily Telegraph. 'Labour Peer Found Naked In Curzon Street.' *(To himself.)* A trail of slime leads to back door of 'Bunny Club.

He looks up.

Mr Kite. When I was young, Mr Kite. I had ideals.

He sobs. He laughs. He controls himself.

I was kissed by Aneurin Bevan. In 1949. Great Welsh, slobby kiss. Ay. I was his brother in socialism. And I fought 'Ruling Class, I got my boot in in my day! I gave as good as I got! Ay well.

He stuffs the cuttings away and claps his hands.

That's the guilt back in the drawer for today.

He drains the bottle into the glass. He drinks. He takes a handkerchief from his sleeve and cleans the glass. He returns the glass to his coat pocket and the handkerchief to his sleeve. He looks about furtively. He places the champagne bottle next to the Brown Ale bottle.

The first breakfast done, of a glorious day.

He strides and stumbles off. The champagne bottle and the Brown Ale bottle on the Downs. The kite above flutters.

PEARCE *comes on with* JOCKS *and* HUGH, *two stable lads. Both carry their shirts, stripped to their waists, and wear boxing gloves.* JOCKS *carries a bucket of water.*

PEARCE. I won't pretend. I do have better things to do. But I will not have personal gripe between my stable lads. In the end it is the horses that suffer. And if the horses suffer, we all suffer. Is that staring you both up the arse as crystal fucking obvious?

HUGH. Yes Mr. Pearce.

PEARCE. Jocks?

JOCKS. What?

PEARCE. Is that staring oh never mind. Jocks, what is the matter with you? Family? Sick mother or something?

HUGH. He is a Red, Mr. Pearce.

PEARCE. He is a what?

HUGH. That is why he is so unpopular with the other lads, Mr. Pearce. Wants all the horses to go on strike, don't you Jocks.

PEARCE. Hughie, you really are a nasty little shit.

HUGH. Yes Mr. Pearce.

PEARCE. Are you a Red, Jocks?

JOCKS. What?

PEARCE. Dear God. Why does a sensitive creature like a horse get on with you so well.

HUGH. Sneaks out the cottage at night and licks their cocks. Don't you, Jocks.

PEARCE. All right!

HUGH. Can't have Reds in the Yard, Mr. Pearce!

PEARCE. Shut up! Right. Boxing match. My rules, every lad I employ knows 'em.

HUGH leers.

HUGH. Yes Mr. Pearce.

PEARCE. The two antagonists — in the open air — private place — bucket of water. Beat each other — one acknowledges defeat, pours bucket of water over himself — you come back, shake hands before me — then the three of us have a whiskey. I'll be on the 'phone in the Land Rover.

He backs away. He comes forward again close to JOCKS *and peers at him.*

I do hope you are as thick as you say you are, Jocks. I do hope so, very much indeed.

He backs away.

Well! Get on with it.

PEARCE *goes off, over the hill.* PRIMROSE, *with her basket and David Soul magazine, passes him. She sees* JOCKS *and* HUGH. *She sits down, a good distance away, and watches them. They do not notice her.*

HUGH. Hit me then. Go on.

Nothing from JOCKS.

I better hit you then.

JOCKS. If Pearce wants me bashed up, let him do it himself.

HUGH. What?

Nothing from JOCKS.

You give me the creeps. Ur, you're all sort of animally. The way you dribble. No, you're not even like an animal, you're like a fish. What you doing up here, on land with people? You ought to be in the sea, going glob glob with your fishy lips.

JOCKS. No point. Us hitting each other. And if we don't, who's to know?

HUGH. What a fishy thought.

JOCKS. Stupid.

HUGH. That's the way it is. That's the rules.

JOCKS. Stupid.

HUGH. And I've been really burning, you know? To have you swallowing your teeth in a pinky froth. It has been a real, burning ideal for me. A pleasure drooled over. Now one poke and I'm in heaven — and it's all a bit pissy.

JOCKS. Don't hit me then and I won't hit you.

HUGH. It's the rules.

JOCKS. Make our rules. Rules Pearce don't know about.

HUGH. You really are a little Red, in't you.

JOCKS. Don't know about that.

HUGH. Come naturally does it? Like B.O.?

JOCKS. Don't know about any of that.

HUGH. Oh brother, I've seen people go like you. And they go one way — straight out of racing. We don't fight — we get kicked out of Pearce's Yard — Pearce's Yard, one of the best — Pearce's mouth, very big — say you bad little indian, be lucky to muck out some old lady's nag at a Point-to-Point — savvy Kemo Sabay? So. What do you suggest?

JOCKS *picks up the bucket and empties the water over himself.*

Oh. Well. Fuck you. I mean, I know what you mean, but fuck you.

HUGH *gives him a 'V' sign and runs off.* JOCKS *looks up at the lark and whistles. He sighs. He sucks his teeth.*

JOCKS. It's hard. It's hard. And I like the horses.

PEARCE *appears over the skyline watching* JOCKS *through binoculars. He has a battered suitcase with him.*

PEARCE. Little fool. And he likes the horses, too.

PEARCE *strides down the slope to* JOCKS.

There is your card. There is your P.45. There are your belongings. There is one week's wages. Now get off.

JOCKS *stands there.*

Are you crying?

JOCKS. I'm wet all over aren't I.

JOCKS *kicks the bucket.*

PEARCE. That is highly unnecessary.

JOCKS *tears off the boxing gloves and throws them on the ground. He picks up his shirt and suitcase and walks away.* PEARCE *shouts after him.*

We are all on a billiard table Lad. Plink plink plonk. And we all end up — exactly where we are.

JOCKS. And who's putting the chalk on the end of the cue and going poke, eh?

JOCKS, *going over the skyline.*

PEARCE. You leave me cold Lad.

JOCKS *has gone.*

You can muck out sheep. All you're good for now.

He whistles at the lark.

Still there, birdy?

He picks up the bucket and the boxing gloves and goes off.

PRIMROSE *looks at her arms, then lies back covering her face with the David Soul magazine.* MINTY *comes on, dragging a car battery on the sack.*

MINTY. You'se old battery. Going to crack you like a nut. Get at that tasty lead in you.

PRIMROSE *snatches the magazine away.*

PRIMROSE. Oh Ma'am, what you doing?

MINTY. I bain't talking to you girl. You don't know how

dangerous that is, to go lying there shameless, all arms. When your Pa gets out the nick, won't he give you a wallop.

PRIMROSE. Oh Ma'am, let me lug that battery for you.

MINTY. Your Pa's tooken away, so I'll be the man. You sell that heather. And don't go getting green sludge off that grass on your new pants. And you go round with your sisters, when them crowds get up here. And I don't want you wearing that good apron. And I bain't talking to you.

PRIMROSE. Oh Ma'am —

MINTY. Nothing don't get me down. Not you, battery. Not a husband starry in Lowestoft nick. Not a girl acting the loobany in the grass. None of you get me down.

PRIMROSE. Don't go barmy Ma'am —

MINTY. We's the Gypsy Nation. You'se got to know that, ghl. For you's own good. You don't know that, you'll end up some hedgecrawler nothing. So you get that silver-paper round that heather. We'se on these Downs to make a living and don't you forget it.

PRIMROSE. Barmy all day.

MINTY goes out of sight over the skyline.

Oh. Oh. Oh.

She calls after MINTY.

Ma'am! Don't you go breaking those batteries! Sell them to the dealer as they are! Just the men, showing off, when they break the batteries. To see the acid squirt on their boots. Ma'am? Oh. Oh. Oh.

My Ma'am always goes barmy. That's why she keeps on getting her teeth knocked out by men from the Council. When they come round and do things to us. Like pile earth up round the trailers with bulldozers, so Pa can't get the scrap out. Like get the Police to take Pa away. Break sewage pipes near-to so we all get the squits. Get boys off the estates to chuck stones. Set dogs on us. Burn us out. She goes barmy too when I say I want to marry David Soul. I've got all David's records. We've got hi-fi speakers in the trailer. But they don't work. But Pa said he'll meet a man at Epsom who'll sell him a transformer. But Pa's got tooken away. But he'll get out and it's not bad at Epsom. I may get married and all. But not to David Soul, 'cos he's not one of us. Which is my hard luck. And his.

She lies back with the magazine over her face. JOCKS *comes on carrying his suitcase, his shirt held over his shoulder. He looks at* PRIMROSE *from a distance.*

JOCKS. Little darling. Would I like to tear you to pieces. Ah ah, don't touch the gypsy my old Grandma said. Eight uncles'll jump out on your head.

MINTY *comes back on, over the skyline. She rushes down at* PRIMROSE *and slaps her.*

PRIMROSE. Ow!

MINTY. I'll not tell you again. Get up off that grass, get that heather done!

PRIMROSE. Ow Ma'am!

MINTY. I'll wallop you myself.

MINTY *slaps her again.*

PRIMROSE. Barmy old cow!

MINTY *slaps her again.*

MINTY. Don't you talk to your mother like that. And I'll have that. Getting ways out of magazines.

MINTY *grabs the magazine.*

PRIMROSE. My pictures of David —

MINTY. That'll go on the fire. Pictures of men off the television. You don't know where those ways'll lead you girl. You don't know the dangers. The Gypsy got no friends in this world. You just sell the heather and stay clear of men. And I don't mean just in books. Now get to.

MINTY *strides up the hill.*

You'll not get me down, none of you. If I have to run from one end to the other all day, you'll not get me down. Batteries. Daughters.

She goes off over the skyline.

PRIMROSE. Barmy.

She rubs herself. She sees JOCKS. *She stiffens.*

What you gawping at?

JOCKS. Fancy a bit of heather don't I.

PRIMROSE. Oh yeah?

They stare at each other.

JOCKS. Come on the Fair with me?

PRIMROSE. You've got a hope.

JOCKS. See as far as Croydon off the top of the big wheel.

PRIMROSE. I said — you've got a hope.

JOCKS. Where's my heather anyway?

PRIMROSE hesitates, then takes out a twig of heather from the basket and walks to him.

PRIMROSE. Fifty p.

JOCKS. You're joking.

PRIMROSE. Take the Gypsy's luck or leave it.

She turns to go.

JOCKS. Here you are.

He fishes in his pay-packet and gives her a fifty pence piece. She gives him the heather.

Tell my fortune, I badly need to know my fortune.

PRIMROSE. Cross my palm with a five pound note —

JOCKS. Oh come on darling —

PRIMROSE. Pound then.

They stare at each other. JOCKS takes out a pound note from his pocket. She closes his hand round the pound note.

Have a wish.

JOCKS. You and me on the ghost train.

PRIMROSE. Don't tell me the wish. And don't make a stupid wish like that.

JOCKS smirks.

Wish then!

JOCKS smirks again. PRIMROSE pulls at his hand, takes the pound note and opens his palm.

You just got fired from your job.

JOCKS *takes her palm.*

JOCKS. You just got hit by your Mum —

PRIMROSE. You hate your boss —

JOCKS. You're none too pleased with your Mum, either —

PRIMROSE. You think you can go round do anything with anyone —

JOCKS. You want to go on the Fair.

PRIMROSE. You're going to end up with your teeth knocked out —

JOCKS. And you're going to end up going to the Fair.

PRIMROSE *pulls her hands away.*

PRIMROSE. You don't know about us! You'se ignorant!

JOCKS. Gypsy, in't you. Steal washing off lines, don't you. Drink milk bottles on doorsteps and piss in the empties. Steal babies and eat 'em. Coming?

PRIMROSE. My Ma'am'll kill me.

JOCKS *shrugs and begins to walk away.*

(*To herself*) Oh. Oh. Oh. (*To* JOCKS.) Mister.

JOCKS *turns.*

We'll go separate to the Fair. Don't want my Ma'am seeing us from the camp, on the skyline. Find me by the big Wurlitzer.

PRIMROSE *goes off quickly, not looking at* JOCKS.

JOCKS. What d'you know? Lose my job. Pull a Gypsy girl. The ups and downs, the swings of life —

He goes off.

MR TILLOTSON *and* MISS MOTROM *come on. He is dressed rather shabbily in a sports jacket, open-necked shirt and flannels and scruffy brown shoes. She is dressed neatly in a cheap coat, black stockings and black shoes and wears a little hat. He carries a placard which reads 'NONE IN HELL.'*

MR TILLOTSON. If you do not like the text, Miss Motrom, you must say.

MISS MOTROM. I will, Mr. Tillotson.

MR TILLOTSON. In all honesty. As a fellow in Christ.

MISS MOTROM. I do not like the text.

MR TILLOTSON. But what's the matter with it? I was up all night, stopping the edges of the paint going furry.

MISS MOTROM. It is not that I do not like the text, Mr. Tillotson. It is more that it is not a text at all. It's more a saying.

MR TILLOTSON. It's the text of a saying.

MISS MOTROM. But not said by Jesus or Jehovah. Or the Apostles. Or anyone in the Bible. Actually, it was said by you.

MR TILLOTSON. 'None in Hell'. I think it's very much on the nail. Go down a bomb.

MISS MOTROM. Don't let's argue. It's a beautiful morning. Look at God's grass. God's air. And there's a lark.

They look up.

They could have builded a New Jerusalem here.

MR TILLOTSON. Yeah. 'Stead they builded a race track. I am not happy in my mind, Miss Motrom.

MISS MOTROM. But why not, Mr. Tillotson.

MR TILLOTSON. They bitching me, down the Mission? Putting the knife in, behind my back?

MISS MOTROM. They are good souls --

MR TILLOTSON. Prissy old dears. Who don't know sin from the back end of a bus. I know about Sin, Miss Motrom. I have seen it. I have done it.

MISS MOTROM. The congregation at the Mission are all with us, in Christ.

MR TILLOTSON. Yeah? Where are they then? Other Missions'll be here. Come lunchtime the punters won't be able to move for missions. Thick, the praises to the Lord will be.

MISS MOTROM. It was felt --

MR TILLOTSON. It was felt it was Jim Tillotson's idea. Come down here. Bear witness at The Derby. So it was given the holier-than-thou cold shoulder. And none of 'em turned up. Fucking about --

MISS MOTROM. Mr. Tillotson!

MR TILLOTSON. Sorry I'm terribly sorry.

MISS MOTROM. Mr. Till —

He lowers his placard.

MR TILLOTSON. See, I met my low here. At Epsom. For thousands it is a good day out, but for me — it is the grimy edge of the pit of hell, covered with ash. See, the root of my evil — the root of my evil —

MISS MOTROM. Jim, you don't have to talk about it.

MR TILLOTSON. I want to talk about it. *(He takes a long breath, lets it out.)* I was a gambler. I mean I really was a gambler. Some take it or leave it. But I had compulsion. Compulsive gambler, me. Have you any idea what that means? To get gambling money in my hands, I would have sold my children. I did sell my children. Where are they now? Twenty-four hour gambling! Ten-thirty, betting shop. The manager'ld keep my stool free. Bring me a cup of tea halfway through the afternoon, for I did not eat! Money was not for food! Never break a note, gambling money! Five-thirty, out the betting shop. Casino! 'Til four in the morning. Then — illegal casino! I have left a betting shop with twelve thousand pound in my hand! On to Soho, Windmill Street! Come the dawn, not a bus-fare. Oh, I was action man.

He takes a long breath, lets it out.

The end came at Epsom. Roberto's Derby. I motored down with this investment broker in his Rolls-Royce. Heavy gambling is a great leveller, a real brotherhood of ghosts. The second race gone, I'd done my money in. He nipped off for a pee. Know what I did? I sold his Rolls-Royce. To a bookie for ten thousand pounds. Come the last race I'd done that in too. Everyone was looking for me, wanting my blood. Investment brokers, bookies' runners. And I was marooned on the Downs all night. And caught pneumonia. And had my nervous breakdown. And came to Jesus. You don't know what I'm talking about, do you.

MISS MOTROM *(hard voiced).* My father had it.

MR TILLOTSON. Yeah but not the — real thing?

He looks at her.

MISS MOTROM. I was my father's mascot. He took me everywhere. I was seven the night he cleaned out six bookies at White City dogs. The runners were looking everywhere for us. We ran away from the stadium. My little blouse was full of five pound notes, the old white paper five pound notes? We got on a train to Brighton.

MR TILLOTSON. Casino.

MISS MOTROM. Casino. We booked into a lovely hotel. He had a heart attack in the bathroom. I stayed in the bathroom with him all night. He was dead. There were five pound notes all over the floor, like snow.

MR TILLOTSON. What did you do?

MISS MOTROM. Became an alcoholic. Until I was thirty. Then I came to Jesus.

MR TILLOTSON. Oh.

He nods.

MISS MOTROM. We're strong now. With Jesus.

MR TILLOTSON. Yeah. (*He raises the placard and looks at the text.*) Maybe 'None in Hell' is a bit — quirky.

MISS MOTROM. It will make a talking point.

MR TILLOTSON. Yeah that's the idea!

MISS MOTROM. Shall we go and have a cup of tea?

MR TILLOTSON. Yeah. And we'll leave some of the leaflets on the stall.

He takes her hand. She withdraws it at once, as if hurt. They walk away.

I don't know what we're going to do about hymns.

MISS MOTROM. We'll make do.

MR TILLOTSON. Bit difficult with two of us, to whip up a hymn.

MISS MOTROM. We'll make do.

They go off.

The Downs deserted. LORD RACK *comes on. He is eating half a chicken.*

RACK. The morning going wonderfully. Walked the course. Found a hamburger stall already serving. Had a couple and a hot dog. I'm up to breakfast number four and it's not yet half-past nine. Aaah. Always stuff myself on Derby Day. And if you sick up, why there's room for more. They don't understand that in Labour Party. Labour Party. Always thought of myself as a gentle, kindly man. Soft and sunny. But in politics they always called me a butcher. And I was! I have turned Division Lobbies into abattoirs. No no, I must not become sentimental, not upon the Holy Turf.

PEARCE *appears at the top of the slope, carrying the boxing gloves and bucket of water.*

Oh no. Not him.

PEARCE. Oh no. Not him.

RACK. Trainer Pearce, on the Downs.

PEARCE. Lord Rack, on the Downs. The red punter.

RACK. You crave the anonymity of a good day out — and that comes over the horizon.

PEARCE. Look the other way.

RACK. Look 'other way.

PEARCE. Scan the tree tops.

RACK. Let him see what a good time I'm having, and bleed.

PEARCE. A man who stands for everything I can't stand. Socialism and racing? Like an elephant trying to get up a nanny goat.

RACK. Managerial whizz kid. Selling his skills, not realizing how he is used. With his mod cons — horses stuffed with vitamin pills, poor animals badgered by swarms of accountants. Perverting 'sport of the common man.

PEARCE. Threatening my livelihood with 'tax the winnings' and lefty parrot cries. Without winnings how the hell are you going to improve the bloodstock?

RACK. Entertainment!

PEARCE. The bloodstock! I'm getting too angry. If I have to meet him now I'll make a fool of him.

RACK. He's going away.

PEARCE. No, what's the matter with you? We are on common land. Angels and worms, both have a right to the grass.

PEARCE begins to walk down towards LORD RACK.

RACK. No he's coming up. Bugger'll smell drink on me breath. I don't mind being a leper to the Racing Hierarchy, but why do they have to keep on coming up and ringing me bell?

LORD RACK hides his half chicken behind his back. They stare at each other.

PEARCE. Morning.

RACK. Morning.

They stare at each other. Then LORD RACK *takes a step back and* PEARCE *walks away.*

PEARCE. That went off all right.

RACK. That weren't too bad.

PEARCE. 'Spose the man is human.

RACK. You've got to be civil.

PEARCE. It's just a fact of life you live with − that the shits are always with us, like the poor.

RACK. Civil. While you store up your spit.

PEARCE goes off.

Hey hey. And now, I think − a visit to a bookie, a beer tent, bookie, another bookie, beer tent, beer tent bookie, bookie beer tent and bookie in that order.

LORD RACK goes off. The Downs deserted.

The kite flutters three times and falls to the ground. BOBBY *comes on and picks up the kite. He tests its tautness.* SANDY *appears at the top of the slope. He still smokes and carries a can of lager. He dribbles the football.*

SANDY. Football, Bobby.

BOBBY. I'm doing my kite, Dad.

SANDY. He is like a ghost in the midfield. And then from the deep it comes. The Trevor Brooking cross.

He passes the ball to BOBBY. BOBBY *ignores it.*

BOBBY. I'm doing my kite, Dad.

SANDY. Come on, the old one two. Set me up an overhead kick.

BOBBY. I'm doing my kite.

SANDY. Here. What's the matter with it.

BOBBY. It fell down.

SANDY. Let's have a look.

BOBBY *pulls the kite away protectively.*

BOBBY. It's a Kung-Fu kite, Dad.

SANDY. Four pound ninety-nine p. Bit of plastic and four sticks.

BOBBY. It's a Kung-Fu kite. In China they put bits of glass on the strings and cut down birds.

SANDY. Why?

BOBBY. 'Cos it's Kung-Fu.

SANDY *sighs.*

SANDY. Where's your mother?

BOBBY. Wheeling Sharon about.

SANDY. And where's your Grandpa?

BOBBY. Gone betting.

SANDY. At ten o'clock in the morning?

BOBBY. He said he knew a bookie.

SANDY. God almighty.

BOBBY. What's a gelding, Dad?

SANDY. What?

BOBBY. Grandpa says a gelding's a horse that's got its balls cut off.

SANDY. I must tell you about your Grandpa one day.

BOBBY. What's a prostitute?

SANDY. Well —

BOBBY. Grandpa says a prostitute is a woman who paints her nipples —

SANDY. Right! I am West Ham and you are the Arsenal.

BOBBY. Grandpa says you stuffed him in the Old People's Home. And you just get him out once a year to go to the Derby. 'Cos you and Mum have got a bad conscience.

SANDY. That's about it.

BOBBY. Why don't Grandpa live with us, Dad?

SANDY. Guess.

   SANDY, *clapping his hands.*

BOBBY. Cos we haven't got anywhere to live! Cos we're living in the dormobile! In Mum's friend's garage!

SANDY. Ten out of ten.

BOBBY. How long we going to live in the dormobile, in Mike and Patricia's garage, Dad? Dad? Dad?

SANDY. Give it a rest, Bobby. We only been there eight weeks. While we look for something else. Do you mind living in the dormobile, Bobby?

BOBBY. It's great!

   BOBBY *runs round in a circle, pretending the kite is an aeroplane.*

SANDY. You're great too. But why won't you play football with me?

   SANDY *runs round dribbling the ball in a circle, the opposite direction to* BOBBY.

   Oh control, oh grace —

BOBBY. Death in the sky —

SANDY. Utterly fit, utterly in tune —

BOBBY. Cut off their wings, down they fall —

SANDY. Harmony sings —

BOBBY. Death strikes —

   MARGARET *appears on the skyline pushing* SHARON *in the baby buggy.* SHARON *now clutches a green Kermit Frog.*

MARGARET. Your sainted father, Sharon. We have found him.

SHARON. My want an orange.

MARGARET. You cannot have an orange, lady-one-note. We'll play football with your Dad.

SHARON. NOT play football.

MARGARET and SANDY kick and pull each other over the football, laughing. They grab each other, fall and roll on the ground laughing.

BOBBY. She's got a Kermit Frog!

SHARON. MY WANT AN ORANGE.

MARGARET. Ask your father.

SHARON. My want an orange, Daddy.

SANDY. You cannot have an orange.

MARGARET. Because we have only got one left.

SANDY. Because we have only got one left.

SHARON cries. MARGARET and SANDY stop rolling and kiss.

Bobby — cheer your sister up.

At once BOBBY goes to SHARON and tickles her. SHARON tries to keep crying but cracks and begins to giggle. BOBBY pulls the Kermit Frog. SHARON resists. BOBBY stops. Then makes another pull. SHARON resists.

SANDY. Hang about, hang about. What's that thing?

MARGARET. A Kermit Frog.

BOBBY. I want a Kermit Frog.

MARGARET. It's for both of you Bobby. It's for both of you Sharon.

SANDY. How much did they knock us for that?

MARGARET. Three pound fifty.

SANDY. Bloody hell.

MARGARET. Derby Day?

SANDY. Oh yeah. Let's all go mad.

MARGARET. Let us do that.

They kiss and roll. Two buskers, BUD and MACK appear

on the skyline. MACK *carries an accordion.* BUD *carries a paper bag.*

BOBBY. I want to fly the frog on my kite.

SHARON. NOT fly my frog.

BOBBY. It's my frog too. They said. Be like an astronaut up on the moon.

SHARON. NOT fly my frog on the moon.

BOBBY *pulling the frog intermittently,* SHARON *resisting.*

MACK. Customers, Bud.

BUD. Right, Mack.

BUD *takes out a pair of dark glasses. Then a telescopic blind person's cane which he extends. Then a notice which he bangs round a little canvas bag on a wire hoop. Then a notice which he bangs round his neck. It is on a piece of black board, the letters are screwed-on garden gate letters. They read 'EX-JOCKEY ALMOST BLIND'.* MACK *strikes up 'When Irish eyes are smiling'. They advance confidently.*

They reach the family, who stare at them. MACK *stops playing.*

BUD. Ah — any musical requests?

SANDY. You've got to be joking.

BUD. Thank you thank you.

BOBBY. Play The Rolling Stones.

MACK. The Rolling Stones. Play The Rolling Stones.

BOBBY. Dad's always playing The Rolling Stones, in't you Dad.

SANDY. Shut up Bobby.

SANDY *puts ten pence in* BUD's *bag.*

BUD. Good luck. Follow The Minstrel today. Lester on The Minstrel. Look at the trainer's name. O'Brien! Follow the Irish today. Me old father were a tipster. I'll give you that one for free.

SANDY. Thank you very much.

BUD. Follow the Irish today.

The buskers shamble away, BUD *on* MACK's *arm.* BOBBY *follows them, suspicious.*

MARGARET. How much did you give them?

SANDY. Ten p.

MARGARET. Sentimental pig.

SANDY. Store up pennies in heaven.

MARGARET. The amateur gambler speaks.

SANDY. He does.

MARGARET. Three to one — that cloud will go over the sun.

SANDY. Mm — give you five to two.

MARGARET. Mm, five to two — subtle.

SANDY. Give you eight to one — there are ants crawling up — your left thigh.

MARGARET. Ah.

SANDY. Ah.

They kneel facing each other.

Maggy. Mike and Patricia wrote me a letter. It's getting bad, Maggy. I mean, they could come and talk to us. We are living in their garage.

MARGARET. Don't want to talk about it.

SANDY. And the dormobile's going to start smelling any day now. There's a limit to what half a dozen airwicks can do.

MARGARET. Not talk about it.

SANDY. They want to know when we're going to get a house.

MARGARET. We want to know when we're going to get a house.

SANDY. I don't blame 'em. They don't know about kids. And the scene in their bathroom does get pretty torrid. What with Bobby's theory about water going uphill. Jesus! If only I could get a set of aluminium ladders. I could set up and do roofing on my own. 'Stead of working off and on for any Dick and Harry. Ladders, light enough for one man.

MARGARET looks up into the sky and closes her eyes.

MARGARET. The airwicks. The bathroom. The ladders.

BOBBY. My Grandpa says buskers make a hundred pound a day. Are you really blind? My Grandpa says you live in big houses in Hampstead, surrounded by Alsatian dogs. My Grandpa says you keep your dirty clothes in the boot of a Rolls-Royce.

BUD. On your bike, sonny.

The BUSKERS *go off over the skyline.*

MARGARET. Buy ladders with the money in the Halifax.

SANDY. That four hundred pound's for a deposit Maggy. Hit that and.

MARGARET. And.

SANDY. Yeah, and.

MARGARET. Not be serious today. Frogs and kites and oranges today.

SANDY. Frogs and kites and oranges.

SHARON. MY want an orange.

SANDY. Have the orange my love! The last orange on earth! Why not?

MARGARET. Why not?

BOBBY. I want a Kermit Frog to fly from my kite.

MARGARET. Yes!

SANDY. Yes!

SHARON. My want a ginger biscuit with my orange!

MARGARET. Yes!

SANDY. Yes!

BOBBY. Dad, can I sit in the driver's seat in the dormobile?

SANDY. Yes!

BOBBY. With the, with the engine on?

SANDY. Yes!

BOBBY *dances in a circle, hop style, round* MARGARET, SANDY *and* SHARON.

MARGARET. We could — we could — put the money in the Halifax on The Minstrel.

MARGARET *and* SANDY *stare at each other.*

SANDY. You're a wonderful mother, Maggy.

MARGARET. It's eight to one — some gave nine —

SANDY. Ante post. It will shorten —

MARGARET. Four hundred pounds —

SANDY. A win, that would be —

MARGARET. Three thousand, six hundred pounds —

SANDY. Less tax —

MARGARET. Thirty-six times four p in the pound — hundred and forty so we would win — three thousand, four hundred and six pounds.

SANDY. If The Minstrel wins. It's mad.

MARGARET. Where have we got being sane?

SANDY. The deposit.

MARGARET. A garden.

SANDY. Aluminium ladders.

MARGARET. There'll be a Halifax in Epsom Town.

They stare at each other.

The trouble is — is The Minstrel going to win?

BOBBY. What you going to do, Dad? Dad, what you and Mum going to do?

MARGARET. Throw our lives away!

SANDY. Before the flashing hooves of a horse, going at forty miles an hour!

MARGARET. The right horse.

BOBBY. Great! Can I come?

GRANDPA WILLIAM *comes over the skyline talking. He wears a cloth cap and carries a tin lunch box and a small collapsible canvas stool.*

GRANDPA. Fifty-third Derby I have seen in my life. 'Cept in the last World War, when they ran it at Newmarket, on account of the Zeppelins. Or was that the First World War?

BOBBY. Grandpa! Grandpa!

SHARON. Grandpa! Grandpa!

SANDY. Oh dear. Here comes England's walking racial memory.

GRANDPA. The Derby's gone to the dogs. May as well be a dog race. I put it all down to that man on the telly, with the hat. He is in on the conspiracy to cheat the working man of his gambling rights.

BOBBY dances around GRANDPA WILLIAM.

BOBBY. We're going to throw ourselves in front of a horse and win a lot of money —

SHARON. Grandpa! Grandpa!

GRANDPA. They don't wear hats now, do they! You look in vain at the Derby crowd for a hat. Only the toffs wear the odd hat. And they do it to make the rest of us feel bad.

SANDY. Come on. Let's get down to our pitch. The two furlong marker.

MARGARET *and* SANDY *touch each other's hair.* SANDY *stands. He wheels* SHARON, *kicking the ball with* BOBBY *up the slope.*

BOBBY. Can I have an ice-cream?

SHARON. MY WANT ONE.

BOBBY. Can she have an ice-cream too?

SANDY. We will go down by the rail. By the magic strip of the grass. And you will eat ice-creams and your parents will consume many cans. It will be — like the beach!

SANDY *kicks the ball over the hill.* GRANDPA *follows them over the skyline.*

GRANDPA. In my day we all wore hats. If you saw a man walking down the street without a hat on, you'ld all shout at him and say — oy! Look at him! He's got no hat on.

MARGARET *is momentarily left behind, picking up a child's clothing. The* GHOST *of Emily Davison comes on.* MARGARET *and the* GHOST *stare at each other.* MARGARET *goes off.*

GHOST. On the first day of June, nineteen-thirteen, Emily Wilding Davison got off the Derby Day train at Tattenham Corner Station. She held her coat around her. I held my coat tight around me. Beneath, around me, I had two flags, the green purple and white of the Movement. I had learnt the colours of the jockey who would ride the King's horse.

Purple and gold. Through the morning, through the crowd,
Emily Wilding Davison steeled herself.

The GHOST *goes off.*

*The Downs deserted. In the centre stand the bottle of Brown
Ale, the champagne bottle and* SANDY'*s lager can.*

FOUR YOUNG MEN *and* TWO YOUNG WOMEN *appear on
the skyline. They are bedecked in Jubilee Regalia. They carry
carrier bags of beer bottles, drink from bottles. They hold the
edge of a large Union Jack. They run down the slope.*

ALL *(sing).* God Save our gracious LESTER
Long Live our noble LESTER
God Save our LESTER.
Happy and glorious long to reign over us
God save our gracious LESTER
God save our LESTER.

They go off.

SUPERINTENDENT BLUE *comes over the skyline, walking
across the Downs, talking into a walky-talky radio.*

BLUE. Everybody chop chop over.

The radio crackles a short burst.

If there is a tailback on the A24 because of some Gyppo
lorry stuck out of a B Road I do not want to know about it.
What the hell is he doing with a load of gas stoves on the
Downs on Derby Day anyway. Get him up on the verge, check
his brakes and book him. What about the A217 junction over.

The radio crackles.

If we do not move those vehicles we will have bookies going
down the white lines. What about that drunk who got off the
ten twenty-eight train with a heart attack, over.

The radio crackles.

He wants what?

The radio crackles.

No we cannot send a panda car for a roman catholic priest. What is our petty theft tally so far?

The radio crackles.

When will they learn. And there are three card tricks round the back of the toilets near the Rosebery Stand. Send a PC up to scatter 'em. And anyone seen the Chief Constable yet?

The radio crackles.

Well keep an eye peeled on the bushes.

BLUE *goes off.*

A BUNNY GIRL *comes on, with net tights and ears.* CHARLES PEARCE *comes on, nervous, looking at his watch.*

PEARCE. Come on come on.

The BUNNY GIRL *smiles at him.*

Did you say something?

BUNNY GIRL. Sir.

PEARCE *(to himself.)* Where are you, where are you? I'm a trainer of horses. Not a bloody butler.

PEARCE *looks at his watch.*

Your tail's on fire. There's a fish in your net stockings. Your ears are wilting.

BUNNY GIRL *(without changing her smile.)* I just stand here like this for the money. So don't give me a bad time you bastard.

PEARCE *stares at her.*

Here comes the helicopter now, Sir.

PEARCE. About time.

A MAN WITH BATONS — *like two orange table tennis bats – backs on to the stage. A whoosh of air and litter as a helicopter lands.* ROGER COYLE *and* DOROTHY DELAUNE *run on, crouching from the blades, their hats held to their fronts. They straighten, putting their hats on.*

DOROTHY. Charles.

PEARCE. Mrs Delaune.

DOROTHY. Do you know Roger Coyle? Charles Pearce my trainer, Roger.

PEARCE. How do you do.

ROGER. How do you do.

PEARCE. I knew your father.

ROGER. Did he know you?

DOROTHY. Roger!

BUNNY GIRL. Brochure, Sir?

ROGER. What?

BUNNY GIRL. Brochure, Sir.

ROGER. Your ears are wilting.

BUNNY GIRL. Thank you Sir.

DOROTHY. How is my darling, Mr. Pearce?

PEARCE. Frisky in his box, I am afraid.

ROGER (to the BUNNY GIRL.) There are fish in your net stockings.

DOROTHY. Roger! Forgive us, Charles. We are a bit merry.

ROGER. Quite. Breakfast was a trial.

BUNNY GIRL. Your car is waiting, Sir. Madam.

ROGER. Take it away. We will walk across the Downs. Bathe in the local colour.

PEARCE. I don't think —

DOROTHY. Roger, I've got you on a tight string. Don't forget it.

BUNNY. Your car is waiting.

PEARCE. It's getting a bit crushed down there in the dip —

DOROTHY. We will go by car.

ROGER. She is afraid she will get raped by the London poor.

DOROTHY. Don't play up Darling. No doubt the Daily Express is lurking in the bushes.

SUPERINTENDENT BLUE *comes on.*

BLUE Madam, your car is waiting.

DOROTHY. Thank you, Superintendent.

ROGER. All right! Roger Poodles will be a good poodle.

DOROTHY. I do hope we're going to have a good day, Charles.

PEARCE. Do you, cr, want to look him over? Your horse?

ROGER. Later old man. Shampoo first.

> DOROTHY *and* ROGER *go off.*

BLUE. Thighs worth two hundred thousand a year, stretching out of a helicopter onto the grass. Very arousing.

PEARCE. Huh.

BUNNY GIRL. Will her horse win?

PEARCE. A donkey versus the Concorde. Not that that woman cares. The owner of a Derby Runner. But to her just another handbag to chuck in the cupboard. (*To the* BUNNY GIRL). Look the other way, love.

> *The* BUNNY GIRL *turns away.* PEARCE *takes out a hip flask.*

PEARCE. Alan?

BLUE. Not just now, Charles. One of the bigger moments of the day coming up. There is his chopper.

PEARCE. Who?

BLUE. The owner of Blushing Groom. The owner of the Derby favourite.

PEARCE. Not —

BLUE. The Aga Khan.

PEARCE. The Aga Khan. Oh my God.

> *The noise of the helicopter coming down is heard.* THE BUNNY GIRL, PEARCE *and* BLUE *brace themselves, touching items of their clothing. The rush of air and litter rises and dies. The* AGA KHAN *comes on followed by his* DETECTIVE. *The* AGA KHAN *is dressed in black morning suit and hat and large, impenetrable dark glasses. The* DETECTIVE *wears dark glasses behind him, circling, a gun hand held to the button of his jacket.*

BLUE. Votre excellence. Je suis le Chef de Police du champ du course. Permettez-moi de vous accompagner à votre voiture.

AGA KHAN. Merci bien, monsieur le Chef de Police.

The AGA KHAN *surveys the scene.*

Pourquoi tout le monde agite-t-il le Union Jack?

BLUE. Ah. Ce sont les celebrations Silver Jubilee de notre Reine, votre excellence.

AGA KHAN. Un spectacle extraordinaire.

BLUE. C'est pour la gloire de la Patrie, votre excellence.

BLUE, *pleased with that.*

AGA KHAN. Tres jolie. Une image piquante de l'économie anglaise. Eh bien! Nous avons vu la scène, et maintenant – la victoire.

The AGA KHAN *and his* DETECTIVE *walk away.* BLUE *follows.*

BLUE. La voiture est là –

The BUNNY GIRL *curtseys as the* AGA KHAN *passes. The* AGA KHAN, *his* DETECTIVE *and* BLUE *go off.*

BUNNY GIRL. Every year they weigh him in diamonds.

PEARCE. Yes, he is a wonderful man. But for British Racing an Angel of Death.

BLUE *comes back on.*

BLUE. I'll have that nip now.

PEARCE (*handing* BLUE *the hip flask.*) He spends the money on the bloodstock. Why can't the Government learn that lesson?

BLUE (*to the* BUNNY GIRL.) Look the other way, love.

The BUNNY GIRL *looks away.* BLUE *drinks.*

PEARCE. Big winnings. The secret of success in racing.

BLUE. And in life.

BLUE *burps and hands the flask back.*

PEARCE. Forty-five million pounds of Government Subsidy a year to poofdahs poncing about in ballets and theatres. But to a mass entertainment, beloved by all sections of the Community? Ten million. No wonder foreigners win all our races.

BLUE. Still. British horses are still born with four legs.

PEARCE. But for how long?

BLUE. Well! That's our bowing and scraping done. Drop you both near a place of refreshment?

BUNNY GIRL. Ta.

They go off.

LES BACKSHAKER, *bookmaker, comes on with his wife* CYNTHIA BACKSHAKER *and his settler* MORRY BURROWS. *They carry their stand, boxes to stand on, big black bags with chains and padlocks on them.* CYNTHIA BACKSHAKER *lays out a blanket, on the blanket a fine table cloth, on the table cloth an elaborate meal of cold lamb, chicken, salads, pâté, cheese, with a champagne bottle in a silver bucket. She makes sandwiches.* LES *and* MORRY *stand on their boxes.* CYNTHIA BACKSHAKER *completes a sandwich and holds it up to* LES BACKSHAKER. *He takes it, not looking at her. He chews. This takes place during the* PUBLIC ADDRESS SYSTEM's *announcements.*

PUBLIC ADDRESS SYSTEM. Here is an announcement about crossing the course. Please do not cross the course.

The PUBLIC ADDRESS SYSTEM *plays 'The Sound Of Music', played by a military band. The music stops.*

Do not drop bottles on the open Downs. Later on in the day the Downs will be used by horses and children. After the Meeting the Downs become an open space for the enjoyment of the public. It is impossible to find glass.

The PUBLIC ADDRESS SYSTEM *plays 'The Sound Of Music' for a brief burst.*

Please remember you can assist the organizers by not paying more than twenty-five pence for an official race-card. There are plenty of race-cards so please, insist.

THE PUBLIC ADDRESS SYSTEM *continues with 'The Sound of Music'. The music stops.*

Do not place bets with bookies unless they are displaying
the official colours, the colours today are blue and white.

The PUBLIC ADDRESS SYSTEM *is silent.* MR TILLOTSON
comes on with his placard 'None in Hell'. MISS MOTROM
is with him. She carries a sheaf of leaflets. MR TILLOTSON
preaches, with halting and bizarre rhythms.

MR TILLOTSON. 'Gospel tracts everywhere.' Said a Youth.
With a sneer. As a young Christian Lad handed him a Gospel
tract. 'No not everywhere,' said the Christian Lad. 'There
will be None in Hell.'

MISS MOTROM. None in Hell.

MR TILLOTSON. God fastened that single sentence in the
Sneering Lad's brain. And ultimately he was converted.
There will be no tracts. No preaching. No second chance. No
Salvation. Not in Hell. I know. I've been there and looked.
And come all the way back. So. So.

The bookmakers have ignored them completely.

I think that went down very well.

MISS MOTROM. Very imaginative, Mr. Tillotson.

MR TILLOTSON. I'm not in the swing of it yet.

MISS MOTROM. More like this.

She is very aggressive and practised.
Meanwhile the bookmakers look one way, then the other,
chewing food impassively.

Lester Piggott? What horse does he ride? The Minstrel. Minstrel
means singer. But what song does he sing? Not the Lord's.
Not the Lord's song. Blushing Groom is the favourite today.
But what does he blush for? Right — sin. Not for happiness.
Hot Grove is the third horse fancied here today. But is that
a grove of trees in the garden of Gethsemane? No, it is a hot
grove of flames in Hell. There is only one race being run here
today, brothers and sisters. The Race Of Life. And only one
winning post. The cross of Jesus Christ.

MR TILLOTSON. Very good.

MISS MOTROM. Shall we go and have a hot dog?

MR TILLOTSON. I will buy it for you.

MR TILLOTSON and MISS MOTROM go off. LES BACKSHAKER belches loudly. MORRY BURROWS belches loudly. A VENDOR comes on selling paper cups with a string hanging from the bottom and a polyester, crudely cut chicken stuck on top. Rosin applied to the fingers resonates the cup in a loud, chicken-like noise. He makes the noise.

VENDOR. Jubilee chicken! Get your Jubilee chicken! Get your Jubilee chicken here! Buy it and cherish it for years! Your Jubilee chicken!

The VENDOR goes off. LOUIS, another bookmaker, comes on carrying a bookmaker's bag.

LES. Oh no. That's my day ruined.

MORRY. Bottle it up, Les.

LES. That bastard.

MORRY. Just carry it off. Bottled up.

LES. I will bottle it up. It may come out of my ears, but I will bottle it up.

MORRY. And we'll get him later in the day.

All smile.

LES. Hello Louis!

LOUIS. Hello Leslie!

LES. You know Morry Burrows. The Morry Burrows.

LOUIS. Hello Morry, how's the lung?

MORRY. The fucking bastard's knife, third and fourth rib —

LES. Now now, bottle Morry. He's very good about his wound. He's practising yoga. Mental control. Sucks the cigar smoke in one lung and not the other. How's the family, Louis?

LOUIS. You know how it is, Leslie. The worm in the bud.

LES. Making money?

LOUIS. A drizzle of pennies.

They laugh. Frost. LES and LOUIS take out cigar cases.

Cigar, Leslie?

LES. Have one of mine Louis!

LOUIS. No you go ahead.

LES. No you go ahead.

LOUIS. I insist.

LES. That is very tough, Louis. So do I.

LOUIS. Smoke our own.

LES. All right.

LOUIS. No. Have we not known each other long enough?

They simultaneously take a cigar from each other's case and light up.

LES. So. You have left the big boys in Tattersalls. Come down here amongst we small fry.

LOUIS. My son-in-law is holding the fort in Tattersalls. I thought a day on the Downs would do me good, with the little punters. Don't want to lose the common touch.

LES. It's God's grass —

LOUIS. God's air —

LES. God's money —

They laugh. They pat each other. They suddenly grip each other's arm. LES *nearly topples from his box.*

LOUIS. We got to end the feud between our families, Les.

LES. Oh really?

LOUIS. The tide comes in on us all.

LES. Does it?

LOUIS. I know I've done a bit better than you, over the years. And I don't mind a niggle. But not all this blood.

LES. What blood?

MORRY. Blood from the tyres on his Rolls-Royce he means.

LOUIS. That was you at Sandown, then. Leslie Leslie. This is the era of the Horserace Betting Levy Board. V.A.T. All the Romeo and Juliet stuff — rumbles on Brighton beach, that is obsolete.

PUBLIC ADDRESS SYSTEM. Please, if you must cross the course, please use the tunnel opposite the Rosebery Stand or the official crossing at Tattenham Corner. The police will help you. Thank you.

LOUIS. Can you even remember why we hate each other? Eh?

LES *and* MORRY *look one way then the other.*

Good luck to you then. Brother. Morry. (*To* MRS BACKSHAKER.) Cynthia.

MRS BACKSHAKER *does not look up, continuing to prepare food.* LOUIS *goes off.*

MORRY. Incredible.

LES. God Almighty.

MORRY. The pip.

LES. Almighty God.

LES *and* MORRY *look one way then the other.*

MORRY. Why do you hate his guts?

LES. I can't remember.

LES *and* MORRY *burst into laughter.* LORD RACK *comes on. He looks through his binoculars at the bookmakers.*

LORD RACK. Two big bookmaker crows on the gate. Hey hey, lunch underway. Time to make a bet on The Derby.

LORD RACK *pats his clothing.*

Lucky rabbit — little Indian God — bit of Newmarket turf tucked in me knickers — right -- just get at one with 'universe.

LORD RACK *kisses his hand and touches the earth, then paces about with strange, erratic steps.*

Before betting on a classic race — I always try for two days — never to step on a crack in 'pavement — and when I approach 'bookmakers — to never stand on a patch of bare earth — and never to speak to a woman wearing red —

LES (*to* MORRY). Oh my God, look at that. (*Aloud.*) Watch it Lads! Here comes a betting man! It'll be the workhouse for us all! (*To* MORRY.) Telephone the bank manager — get him to clear out a few cupboards.

LES *and* MORRY *giggle.*

LES. Good morning my Lord.

RACK. Gentlemen — I come to lay myself upon that bed of nails — the on course odds.

LES. What does he take us for, Morry?

MORRY. Bookmakers, Leslie.

LES. How do these slanders get about?

RACK. I have observed a close correlation between the pulpit
and the bookies stand —

LES, RACK and MORRY. Men kneel before both.

RACK. What do you fancy for The Derby then, Leslie?

LES. Ah. Now. There's a curly one.

RACK. Never will say will you, bookies. The only true professional gambler is a bookmaker. And he never loses.

LES. I run a public service. We are the dream-weavers are we not,
Morry?

MORRY. Like fuck.

LES. Quite right. We're just here to make a bundle. A bet on
The Derby, My Lord?

RACK. Forty quid on Blushing Groom.

LORD RACK *gives* LES *four ten pound notes.*

LES (*to* MORRY). Ticket number sixty-seven. Forty pound to
one hundred pound, The Groom.

RACK. What will you give for Milliondollarman?

LES. Milliondollarman, sixty-six to one.

RACK. I'll go twenty quid, each way.

LORD RACK *gives* LES *four pound notes.*

LES (*to* MORRY.) Same ticket. Twenty pounds to one
thousand, three hundred and twenty pounds to win, and for
a place — one fifth of the odds —

MORRY (*with no hesitation.*) Two hundred and sixty-four
pounds.

RACK. That's all.

LORD RACK *steps away. He thinks again and returns with
a zig-zag manoeuvre.*

Look, er — I'll have thirty quid each way on Lucky
Sovereign. You know, flags everywhere. And Liz motoring
up 'course later on. Be a shame not to.

LES. Patriotic. And the horse may win. Lucky Sovereign, twelve to one. (*To* MORRY.) Ticket number sixty-eight. Thirty pounds to three hundred and sixty pounds to win, and for a place —

MORRY (*with no hesitation.*) Sixty-two pounds.

RACK. That's me, gentlemen.

LES. My Lord.

> LORD RACK *strides away with his superstitious step.*

> Amusing little bet.

MORRY. Hundred and eighty quid. Better lay it off, Les.

LES. Let's see. Blushing Groom? It's not going to stay. No matter what they say. First three, maybe. But he bet to win. Milliondollarman? Be the marker, won't it. Front runner down the hill, busting its bollocks to exhaust The Groom. Lucky Sovereign? Three legged guinea pig. Still, we'll lay it off.

MORRY. On the safe side.

LES. What other side is there?

MORRY. Bloody socialist. He should get back to Russia. What's he doing, sitting in the House of Lords anyway? Bloody insult to the Queen.

LES. What a man of parts and passions you are, Morry.

MORRY. Don't know why you take his bet.

LES. A bet is a bet.

MORRY. Oh yeah, you must have your pound of flesh. You don't need a bank account, you need a deep freeze.

LES. Thank you, Morry. Thank you. I needed that.

MORRY. There is a code.

LES. There is no code.

MORRY. There is a code.

LES. There is no code. There is only the punters — twenty-five p. or a hundred and eighty quid. And there is the strength of locks upon my bag. And there is the threat of powerful friends with knuckles.

MORRY. All right, all right!

LES. It gets to me! Talk of codes. We all want the same thing, right? Us. The mugs. The boss in the Club Stand, glass of champers in his hand. The working man on the Downs, in his hand a doctor's sick-note. And what do we want? Why, just a big front room. Cocktail cabinet in the shape of the World. Malt whiskey and pearly telephones. And all the rest — codes — is a bit of a mashed turd.

LES *eats.*

Five to two the field. Five to two the field.

GRANDPA *comes on. He sets his little stool by the two-furlong marker and sits upon it.*

GRANDPA. Queen Victoria. Silly old bugger. Silly old cow. Thought the world owed her a living. I tell you what was really weird about Queen Victoria. She couldn't bear to look at a gardener. Buckingham Palace gardens of a morning, when she came out after breakfast, for a smoke, all the gardeners had to duck down behind the rhododendron bushes. She could not bear to see a gardener working. If she saw a gardener working, she fired him.

MARGARET *wheels* SHARON *on in her baby buggy with* BOBBY. MARGARET *carries a rug and plastic bags containing food. She begins to lay out the rug and food.*

BOBBY. We going to have the picnic now?

MARGARET. When the Queen's gone by.

BOBBY. She gone by now?

MARGARET. No Bobby, she has not gone by now.

A POLICEMAN *takes up his position standing on the course.*

GRANDPA. 'Nother funny thing about Queen Victoria, she had the Royal chinese laundry wash her black widow's weeds two times a day.

MARGARET *stares at* GRANDPA.

MARGARET. What?

SHARON. Mummy? What is the grass?

MARGARET *stares at* SHARON.

MARGARET. What?

SHARON. What is the grass, Mummy?

A young man, a JUBILEE DRUNK, *bedecked in Union Jacks and wearing a Union Jack cardboard top hat comes on. He carries bottles of Guinness.*

MARGARET. Make your frog jump up and down, Sharon. See, he's all flobbily.

SHARON. Flobbily.

JUBILEE DRUNK (*to* MARGARET). Alone with all your brood, darling?

MARGARET. Go away.

JUBILEE DRUNK. Don't give me a hard time.

LES. You heard the lady. Waddle away.

JUBILEE DRUNK (*backing away*.) No offence. It's just me. That's all.

He goes a distance away and stands drinking.

LES. It was a plague of ladybirds last year. This year it's Jubilee Drunks.

MARGARET (*to* LES). What are you giving for The Minstrel?

LES *taps his board.*

LES. Lester seven to one darling.

MARGARET. Will that price get any shorter?

LES. That depends upon the market. Before market forces, we are but trees in the wind.

MARGARET. But very much shorter?

LES. You want to read minds, Gypsy Lee is in her caravan.

GRANDPA. Funny thing about coppers. They hate you calling 'em copper. (*To the* POLICEMAN.) Hello copper!

POLICEMAN (*relaxed and smiling*). Grandad. Lovely day for it.

LES. Thinking of a little bet on The Minstrel then darling?

MARGARET. My husband's gone into town. To get it out. Of the Building Society.

LES. Big time. You know where to come.

MARGARET. I do.

LES *eats.*

GRANDPA. You got flat feet, copper! Your whistle's bunged up, copper!

MARGARET. Grandpa!

GRANDPA. You got tramlines on your Y-fronts!

MARGARET. Grandpa!

POLICEMAN. You have a good day, Grandad. All of us have a good day.

BOBBY. He doesn't hate it, Grandpa. He likes it.

GRANDPA. That's because they've all been threatened by Scotland Yard. I saw 'em, over the other side of the coaches, in a little wood. All sitting on the grass, in ranks, having a cup of tea. Being threatened − like it or else.

MARGARET. Sorry. He's an old aged P.

POLICEMAN. Don't worry love. He earned it, let him enjoy it.

BOBBY. When's the Queen coming?

POLICEMAN. She'll be along.

BOBBY. Copper!

MARGARET *slaps* BOBBY's *leg.* BOBBY *yelps.*

MARGARET. And don't step on the rug, Bobby. Kneel on it.

BOBBY *glowers and flops to his knees.*

GRANDPA. It is a lie I've got it in for the Queen. It's just her forebears I've got it in for. Because their hands are stained with English blood.

BOBBY *is fishing in a bag.*

MARGARET. Bobby don't poke in the food!

MARGARET *hits* BOBBY *again. He yelps.*

JUBILEE DRUNK. Showing a nice bit of leg there darling!

BOBBY. I want to go on the Fair!

SHARON. Mummy, what is green? Mummy, what is green? What is green, Mummy?

MARGARET. Green is green!

BOBBY. You and Dad never let me go on the Fair!

SHARON. Why is green green!

GRANDPA. I'll say this for the Queen. At least they nationalised this one.

MARGARET, *a knife covered with butter, looks up to the sky.*

You can tell that by the arm she waves with. And here I am letting all and sundry into a bit of privileged information. That arm is a mechanical arm, operated by the Central Electricity Generating Board, a nationalised industry. Therefore that arm is an advance for Socialism, of a kind.

LES. Five to two the field.

GRANDPA. Though I still say chop it off.

JUBILEE DRUNK. No offence darling?

He toasts MARGARET with a Guinness bottle.

BOBBY. I'm kneeling on the rug Mum. I'm not poking in the food Mum. So can I go on the Fair?

SHARON *throws the Kermit Frog onto the course.*

LES. Oy! Behave yourself!

JUBILEE DRUNK. Oy oy!

MARGARET *ignores the incident. The* POLICEMAN *picks up the Kermit Frog.*

POLICEMAN. Now now Kermit. What's a frog doing in The Derby?

The POLICEMAN *throws the frog back.*

Don't let the kids throw things over the rail, love. Bit of sense.

JUBILEE DRUNK. Here comes Liz to see The Derby.

MORRY *stands, he and* LES BACKSHAKER *raising binoculars. The* POLICEMAN *comes to attention.* BOBBY *strains to see.*

BOBBY. That's not the Queen that's a car.

GRANDPA. They put her in a car.

LES. A Daimler.

MORRY. She is wearing blue with white accessories.

JUBILEE DRUNK. The Loyal Toast.

A tableau of these figures as the Queen's car approaches down the course – unseen in the play. MARGARET still kneels on the rug, the buttery knife in her hand. The MRS BACKSHAKER actress has become the GHOST of Emily Davison.

GHOST. It's only a white rail. You could jump. Push the copper over. Crack the windscreen with your knife.

MARGARET. It's got butter on. Be blood and Anchor butter, all over the place.

GHOST. England at peace on Derby day. It is just a picture, thin as paint. Slash it.

MARGARET. What's the point? They're bound to have a spare Queen in the boot.

GHOST. See the dirty wall behind.

MARGARET. I don't mind making the food. Bobby likes coleslaw sandwiches. Coleslaw is twenty-seven p. a tub, in Sainsbury's.

GHOST. I saw the wall. In a flash. A second before the king's horse smashed my skull. Did I do that for you to sit on the grass and make sandwiches?

MARGARET. There is nothing wrong with being a mother, there is nothing wrong with making the food, there is nothing wrong with sitting on the grass.

GHOST. No. Everything is wrong.

In silence – the figures in the tableau raising their arms and opening their mouths to cheer. A blackout.

Act Two

The parade ring. A HORSE *is being led around by a* STABLE LAD.

HORSE. I am a Derby outside chance.

They parade.

The mentality of a race horse can be compared to the mentality of a bird. Nervous, quick, shy and rather stupid.

The HORSE *flashes his teeth at the spectators. The* STABLE LAD *restrains him.*

STABLE LAD. Don't give me a bad time.

HORSE. Many a racehorse has a fixed idea. Chewing blankets. Kicking buckets over. Biting blacksmiths.

They parade.

My fixed idea is that I must have a goat tied up with me, in my box. And there, tied to a stick in the Yard, when I come back from the gallops. I will kick the place down, if I don't have my goat.

They parade.

Where is my goat?

They parade.

I want my goat!

STABLE LAD. Stop thinking about your bloody goat!

Owners walk gracefully into the parade ring — a SVELTE VOICED MAN, a HARSH VOICED MAN, a SMOOTH VOICED WOMAN and a SWEET VOICED WOMAN. The men are dressed in grey morning suits and top hats, the women in fine clothes and fashion hats.

SWEET WOMAN. It is so difficult, when you go small, to find any rooms to lock things up.

SMOOTH WOMAN. But we must meet before Ascot. If only for tea and cakes?

SWEET WOMAN. Not before Ascot. Perhaps in September? My diary is a traffic jam.

SMOOTH WOMAN. One's life does flow over. (*She looks at the HORSE.*) When I look at a race horse, I always think of footballers' legs. So lean and tight.

SWEET WOMAN. Mm.

HORSE. Goat?

SVELTE MAN. Nervous?

HARSH MAN. Can't stop going to the bog.

SVELTE MAN. What owning a race horse in The Derby is all about.

HARSH MAN. Bowels like ice-cream and hot chocolate sauce.

SVELTE MAN. Owner's tummy. Get sloshed.

HARSH MAN. I am sloshed. It never shows in my family.

He gives a little stamp of his foot.

God! I want to win this race. On this fat, lazy afternoon.

SVELTE MAN. I'm just here for the fat, lazy tax loss.

HARSH MAN. I do love the sport too, you know.

SVELTE MAN. Oh we all love the sport.

SWEET WOMAN. Here comes our jockey. Doesn't he look a little pea on a drum?

The owners turn toward a JOCKEY, who comes on dressed in silks, crash helmet and cap, riding boots and carrying a whip. The JOCKEY actor walks upon his knees.

JOCKEY. I walk out into the ring. A professional. Weighed on the scales. Ready. Sharp. All there. I have eaten one piece of toast since dawn. It lies now beneath my diaphragm. Which is taut and hard as leather. I feel the eyes of Lords and Ladies upon me. The owners and trainers. The Chairmen of Boards. The yellow eyes of the mug punters, the piss-pots and the know-alls, the down-and-out and the cracked. And I clench my arse for action.

The owners turn away. The JOCKEY *walks to them. He touches his cap.*

SVELTE MAN (*to the* JOCKEY.) Spruce and raring to go?

JOCKEY. It'll be a good long ride.

The HARSH VOICED MAN, *the* SVELTE VOICED MAN *and the* SWEET VOICED WOMAN *stand around the* JOCKEY. *The* SMOOTH VOICED WOMAN *looks away.*

SMOOTH WOMAN. One does feel contempt for the people who look at one, around the parade rings. From the quay-side at San Tropez. It is hard not to. People are such silly empty dustbins, gaping. And I could fly above them, if I wished. On that slicky feeling of a perfect day.

PUBLIC ADDRESS SYSTEM. Will the Jockeys please mount for the third race, the Epsom Derby Stakes. Will the Jockeys please mount.

The STABLE LAD *leads the* HORSE *to the group of owners. The* SMOOTH VOICED WOMAN *runs her hand down the* HORSE's *body.*

SMOOTH WOMAN. So elegant and within himself.

The two men help the JOCKEY *to mount the* HORSE.

SVELTE MAN. Just let him go naturally down the hill, old man.

JOCKEY. Sir.

HARSH MAN. That's right. Let his nature come out to the fore.

SWEET WOMAN (*sharply*). Stay away from a horse with blinkers. And if you are within shouting distance come the last two furlongs, let us not be over-confident because he naturally drifts to the right. The tilt of the ground may yet fool him. And you.

JOCKEY. Ma'am. (*Aside.*) You wade through the bullshit — then, at last, you get where you belong.

The HORSE *and his* JOCKEY *are led away by the* STABLE
LAD *to circle the parade ring again. The owners watch the*
HORSE, *turning in a group.* PRIMROSE *and* JOCKS *come
on. She carries a Kermit Frog in one hand and a stick of
candyfloss in the other.*

JOCKS. There you are. The parade ring at The Derby. Three
kinds of animal, and all bred for it. The horses, bred for it.
The little men to ride the horses, bred for it. The owners
of the horses, bred for it.

PRIMROSE. Don't look like they're having much of a good
time.

JOCKS. They're having a good time all right. They just button
it in.

He looks sideways at her.

Hold my hand then.

PRIMROSE. Not round here.

JOCKS. Trip on the big wheel? Kermit Frog, candyfloss, visit
to the parade ring? Ought to be a hold of a hand in that.

PRIMROSE. I said, not round here.

JOCKS. Show the bastards we don't care. And it's public, if you
pay your money.

PRIMROSE. A Romany girl does not hold hands. It's not decent.

JOCKS. All right, all right. Don't go up the wall.

They watch the parade ring scene for a while.

PRIMROSE. You can have a lick of my candyfloss.

JOCKS. Oh very sexy.

He tries to bite the candyfloss.

PRIMROSE. Not while I'm holding it!

JOCKS. Oh dear oh dear.

PRIMROSE *gives the candyfloss to* JOCKS *who takes a bite
out of it.*

The JOCKEY *rides the* HORSE *out of the parade ring.*

JOCKEY. Hup!

HORSE. Oh good! I'm going to see my goat!

The owners drift off slowly.

SVELTE MAN. Did you see that ridiculous little man, in the Club Stand, take his hat off late when the band played The Queen?

HARSH MAN. Yes. Did you hear what that other ridiculous little man said to him?

SVELTE MAN. No. What?

HARSH MAN. He said — you are a ridiculous little man, take your hat off. They both left, ashen in the face.

SVELTE MAN. Ridiculous.

The owners go off. JOCKS *and* PRIMROSE *alone.*

JOCKS. I'll never get back in. I look at them, the way they walk over the grass — and know I'll never get back in. Horses get on with me. It was the human beings kicked me in the face. Marry me.

PRIMROSE *takes a step back.*

PRIMROSE. You watch your lip.

JOCKS. Why?

PRIMROSE. You gone wrong in the head?

JOCKS. Not that bad an idea. I know horses. You're all off to Appleby Horse Fair next week. I'll come and live with you. Be a Gypsy.

PRIMROSE. We're travellers. We call us that, not you.

JOCKS. I'll talk to your father.

PRIMROSE. Pa's away —

JOCKS. Talk to your mother —

PRIMROSE. My Ma'am'll set the dogs on you. I will and all.

JOCKS. All right, I'm joking.

PRIMROSE. You don't know our life!

JOCKS. All right!

PRIMROSE. Gorgios, you're filthy!

JOCKS. All right I'm not joking! They chuck you and your trailers on dumps, right? And where am I? Six foot high would-be jockey, ex-stable lad — with the bad mouth on him? Chucked on a dump.

They stare at each other.

Both of us, shoved out the door aren't we?

They stare at each other.

If you won't marry me, least come out over the Downs. Show the bastards we don't care. Give us a lovely long fuck in the grass, eh?

PRIMROSE *throws the Kermit Frog at* JOCKS *with all her strength. He catches it, startled.*

PRIMROSE. You don't know anything of us. How we get by. What we do. My Ma'am were right. You're filthy.

JOCKS. Just hold hands —

PRIMROSE. You don't know what we do. You're filthy.

PRIMROSE *runs off.* JOCKS *looks at the candyfloss and the Kermit Frog. He circles, embarrassed.*

JOCKS. Asked for that. Me who has worked in stables? Try to pull a Gypsy girl on Derby Day? For that bigger men than I — have had their hearts and their kneecaps broken. Oh well.

He tosses the Kermit Frog and the candyfloss away. He takes out his paypacket.

Two pound, eighteen p. left. And I went and bought her a frog. I have got to get a grip on my affairs. Two pound, eighteen p. Maybe you'll stay dead still up there, sun. And The Derby'll go on forever. And I'll live on the grass. And a kind old — hamburger fairy godmother'll come and feed me And lovely Gypsy girls'll wash me all over. *(He looks at the money.)* I think I'll put a pound on Lester. And blow the rest in the beer tent. Then, just before the last race — the Revolution will break out. And there will be a mass distribution of the profits of William Hill Limited.

He clenches the money in his fist.

Oh God. What am I going to do?

He calms himself.

Lester. Beer tent.

Outside a beer tent. LORD RACK. He clutches bottles of light ale. Bottles of light ale are at his feet. A woman with a LOUD VOICE is ordering drinks, waving a ten pound note high in the air. Two DRUNKEN YOUNG MEN writhe around each other, unable to stand as they try to pull a crate of beer away.

RACK. The great race looms. A bright banner unfurled, among half a million punters.

LOUD VOICE. Who wanted a brandy? There was someone who wanted a brandy. What? There was no one who wanted a brandy.

1ST DRUNK. Just get this — down to the Lads on the rail.

2ND DRUNK. What we got to do — is get this down to the Lads on the rail.

1ST DRUNK. I've got an idea. Let's get this down to the Lads on the rail.

RACK. This is what I want. I suck back every moment.

JOCKS *approaches.*

I know you. Stable Lad. In Pearce's Yard.

JOCKS. Oh yeah.

RACK. Have a drink with me.

JOCKS. I'm all right.

RACK. Nay. Ten minutes to the great race. First wave of boozing at its height — ride the crest, Lad, while you can. What are you having?

JOCKS. Light ale.

LOUD VOICE. No. Four gin and tonics, not five. Don't bother to open the lagers. And a Coca-Cola for a kiddy.

1ST DRUNK. We've got a problem.

2ND DRUNK. There is no problem.

RACK. The betting and the boozing. Deep seated social habits. There is something magnificent in deep seated social habits. I do not accept there is anything evil.

The 1ST DRUNKEN YOUNG MAN *peers at* LORD RACK.

1ST DRUNK. Here. That's Robert Morley.

2ND DRUNK. That's not Robert Morley.

1ST DRUNK. It's Robert Morley.

2ND DRUNK. That's not Robert Morley. Robert Morley's a
teetotaller.

1ST DRUNK. Never. Is he?

RACK. Why, George Wigg himself said to me — George Wigg
with his sleeves rolled up, yanking the balls off the Jockey
Club — he said to me, what did he say to me?

JOCKS. I —

RACK. I do not accept there is any evil. That is what George
Wigg said to me. And he was right! The punter's got a lot to
thank George Wigg for. First man to take on the Jockey
Club. Tell the Duke of Norfolk what he could do with
Norfolk. George Wigg wrenched the Horserace Betting Levy
Board out of grip of 'English Aristocracy. Bought Epsom
Downs for 'Nation. Helped the Common Man have a bet on
street corner with dignity. Good on you George. We love
you Lad.

   LORD RACK *lurches*.

LOUD VOICE. Oh for godsake. People are drinking
in here.

RACK. Take British Leyland. You know what the lavatories
are in British Leyland? Betting shops. I don't tell a lie. The
lavatory attendant in there, he's a runner for William Hill's!
They should open a betting shop, middle of the shop floor.
Bingo, all problems solved. Lives brightened.

JOCKS. What about the Stable Lads' strike, in nineteen
seventy-five?

RACK. Don't heckle me Lad! Were you with that lot?

JOCKS. I was at the back of the crowd. When George Wigg
came down to Epsom, to talk them out of it.

RACK. Shouting?

JOCKS. Having a drink.

RACK. Ah yes, but — he were right. Don't think I don't feel
with you lad. You can't disrupt Derby. National Asset. The
damage to the image of Britain abroad — too horrible to
contemplate. Exports. What you don't realise is, a British
victory in The Derby, that's worth more internationally —
than gunboats up the Nile ever were. You've got to have

vision. And another thing. Derby belongs to everyone. See, ordinary men and women are cut off from decision making. Only time in their lives they make a decision — is having a bet on a race like The Derby, in local betting shop.

JOCKS puts the bottle of beer down, walks away and goes off. LORD RACK does not see he has gone.

If I had my way in betting shop. They'ld have carpets. Colour tellys. Nice lights. Little — bar at one end. Coffee, sandwiches, ale. Play-pen for the kiddiwinks.

The woman with a LOUD VOICE walks away, laden with drinks. The two DRUNKEN YOUNG MEN are making progress across the grass.

LOUD VOICE. They are always there. Every year. Labour life peers. Chewing through the canvas of the Tattenham Corner beer tent. I point them out to Japanese tourists, as part of the local colour.

The woman with a LOUD VOICE goes off.

RACK. Brighten their lives. All I wanted. I do not accept there is any evil.

1ST DRUNK. Get down to the Lads.

2ND DRUNK. Right. But we'll just get down there to the Lads.

PUBLIC ADDRESS SYSTEM. And now the runners for the one hundred and ninety-eighth Epsom Derby Stakes, the Jubilee Derby, are parading before the Grandstand — in the order in which — they appear on your race-card.

LORD RACK has slid to his knees.

RACK. Oh you gambling nation on the grass. Come to graze at Epsom Races. Dreaming things will look up. That gates of Paradise will open — on 'flash of an horse's hoof. I love you all — and I'm sorry I let you down.

1ST DRUNK. I'm going to bloom my cheeks.

2ND DRUNK. You're what?

1ST DRUNK. I'm going to flash my arse.

2ND DRUNK. Yeah, but we got to get down —

1ST DRUNK. I want to. It's The Derby.

2ND DRUNK. Yeah?

1ST DRUNK. Here we go!

2ND DRUNK. Oh dear oh dear.

The 1ST DRUNKEN YOUNG MAN *drops his trousers and flashes his behind in* LORD RACK's *direction. He waves an arm in recognition.*

1ST DRUNK. Eh up!

2ND DRUNK. Eh up!

RACK. Eh up and good luck!

The TWO DRUNKEN YOUNG MEN *and* LORD RACK *go off, leaving beer bottles behind.*

The JOCKEY *comes on, riding the* HORSE.

JOCKEY. You ride out, over the Downs. To the mile and a half start. Of the Epsom Derby Stakes.

HORSE. Where are you, goat?

JOCKEY. Don't you, you bastard.

HORSE. Goat.

The JOCKEY *smoothes his hand upon the* HORSE.

JOCKEY. And suddenly it is peace. Twenty-two professionals, twenty-two animals. In the countryside. For the first time for hours, you hear the birds. And over the hill there waits for you — a tunnel of your own fellow human beings. Out of their minds with joy.

The JOCKEY *rides the* HORSE *off over the skyline.*

The GHOST *of Emily Davison comes on.*

GHOST. Emily Davison pushed through the crowd at Tattenham Corner. Stood by the rail. She watched her thoughts — I watched my thoughts, like lights over a marsh, flaring on the grass. King George the Fifth's horse, Amner, was halfway down the field when they reached Tattenham Corner. Emily ducked under the rail onto the course. Stood with her coat open. Opened her arms. The horse hit me. My skull was cracked. The jockey broke a rib. I lay in a coma for five hours before I died. The Queen sent a telegram asking after Emily. The King refused to do so. He sent a telegram asking after the jockey. Stupid Emily. Rash Emily.

The GHOST *goes off.*

Two TICK TACK MEN *and two* BOOKMAKERS *appear above. The* 1ST TICK TACK MAN *whistles.*

2ND TICK TACK MAN. You what?

The 1ST TICK TACK MAN *whistles and signals again.*

You what? Oh got you.

The 2ND TICK TACK MAN *whistles to the* 1ST BOOKMAKER.

Alf! Alf!

1ST BOOKMAKER. Nine to four the field!

2ND BOOKMAKER. Nine to four the field!

1ST BOOKMAKER. Nine to four The Groom!

2ND BOOKMAKER. Lester, five to one!

1ST BOOKMAKER. Get your money on Lester, girls. Five to one The Minstrel!

Below MARGARET *pushes* SHARON *in her baby buggy. They are in a lavatory queue.* SHARON *holds her Kermit Frog.*

MARGARET (*to herself*). Come on queue.

SHARON *stares.*

SHARON. Mummy, why – the men waving money?

MARGARET (*to herself*). Ooh God.

SHARON *stares.*

SHARON. Mummy, why -- the man and the lady doing lying down?

SHARON *stares.*

MARGARET (*to herself*). A simple, common garden piss.

SHARON. Mummy, why -- man on the bus throwing beer? Mummy –

SHARON *stares about for something to stare at.*

Why that policeman running? Why that fat man laughing?

Why that man and that little girl doing dancing? Mum!
Do dancing with me!

MARGARET. Not now.

SHARON. Why?

MARGARET. Do dancing with your frog.

SHARON. Dance stupid frog.

SHARON, *making the frog dance manically.*

Dance dance dance.

MR TILLOTSON *comes on with his placard, 'None In Hell'.*

MR TILLOTSON. Miss Motrom. Got split up in the crowd. Miss
Motrom. Got lost. (*To* MARGARET.) 'Scuse me Mrs. You
seen a religious lady going in that toilet?

MARGARET *looks at him, then looks away.* MR TILLOTSON
stumbles a distance away.

I want a bet. The marrow in my bones wants a bet. The
action all around me. I can't breathe.

SHARON. What's that man want, Mum?

MARGARET. He just believes in God, Sharon.

MR TILLOTSON. I can go through the whole field.

He takes a deep breath.

Forty to one, Baudelaire. Sixteen to one, Be My Guest.
Eleven to four, Blushing Groom, favourite. Twenty to one,
Caporello. Twenty-eight to one, Gairloch. Ten to one, Hot
Grove. One hundred to one, In Haste. Twenty-eight to one,
Lordelaw. Eight to one, Lucky Sovereign. Thirty-three to
one, Milliondollarman. Thirty-three to one, Milverton.
Thirty-three to one, Monseigneur. Hundred to one, Mr Music
Man. Ten to one, Nebiollo. Fifty to one, Night Before. One
hundred to one, Noble Venture. Sixty-six to one, Pampapaul.
Twelve to one, Royal Plume. One hundred to one, St.
Petersburg. Hundred and fifty to one, Sultan's Ruby. Five
to one, The Minstrel. Eleven to one, Valinsky.

He rests on his placard stick, panting.

1ST BOOKMAKER. Eleven to four the field!

2ND BOOKMAKER. Eleven to four the field!

1ST BOOKMAKER. Get your money on The Derby!

2ND BOOKMAKER. Five to one Lester!

1ST BOOKMAKER. Comes but once a year!

2ND BOOKMAKER. Eleven to four the field!

MR TILLOTSON *rummages in his pockets.*

MR TILLOTSON. I'll just do The Minstrel. Fifty p. each way. And an outsider. Or two outsiders. And Blushing Groom on the nose. Oh —

He stops still.

I'm breathing again.

He rushes off.

2ND BOOKMAKER. Come on girls, get your money on Lester! Five to one!

1ST BOOKMAKER. Lester, the housewife's fancy!

2ND BOOKMAKER. Let Lester be your tipple, ladies!

The 1ST TICK TACK MAN *whistles.*

1ST BOOKMAKER. What? What?

1ST TICK TACK MAN. Alf! Alf!

1ST BOOKMAKER (*to himself*). What's he trying to say? Oh, Hot Grove's gone eleven to one. (*He shouts.*) Hot Grove, eleven to one! Willie Carson's horse, eleven to one! Willie Carson, another ladies' man!

SANDY *comes on.*

PUBLIC ADDRESS SYSTEM. Please keep pets, dogs, children and other animals under strict control. Thank you.

SANDY. I got the money out. Three hundred and ninety-nine pound. I left a pound in. Terrified I was going to miss the race. The Manager had to telephone London. Then the traffic back from the Town — like a squeeze box. Maggy? I got the money in my socks. Squelch squelch on our future.

He sits down, pulling at his socks.

PUBLIC ADDRESS SYSTEM. And now the riders are arriving behind the stalls.

SANDY. They'll be off. I've got to get our bet on.

MARGARET. Your bet.

SANDY. Maggy, what's the matter?

MARGARET. I've got a headache.

SANDY. Get down to our pitch on the rail, Maggy. Grandpa
  will be swamped down there. They go woomph, up to the
  rail when The Derby starts.

MARGARET. I'm queuing to go to the loo.

SANDY. Maggy —

MARGARET. I'm queuing to go to the Ladies' Lavatory.

SANDY. Don't bitch me! Not when we've had a good day.

  He takes two handfuls of bank notes out of his socks.

  I'll go and get the bet on. Yes? No? Tell me.

  *SHARON looks from her mother to her father to her mother
  and bursts into tears.*

  Get down to the rail, Maggy. I'll make the bet. Yeah? Go and
  piss in the grass. I feel like a worm.

  *SANDY goes off. SHARON continues to cry as
  MARGARET speaks.*

MARGARET. I love The Derby. I always have loved The Derby.
  But in this queue, with my child yelling, waiting for a
  common garden pee, I hate The Derby.

  She looks up to the sky and closes her eyes.

  I hate the fat, happy people on the grass, with their teeth
  stuck in chicken drums. Jubilee flags coming out of their
  hairy ears. Minds red with booze and bets. I hate the little
  men in pretty colours, who go by on the horses, with their
  mean, hard little heads and mean, hard little bums. I hate the
  penguins in the grandstand we gawk at through binoculars. I
  hate the race officials whizzing along the other side of the
  rail in their yellow car, chinless wonder masks behind the glass.
  I hate the jolly boys on the tops of the buses, roaring pissed,
  stripped to their navels, showing off their lovely tummies in
  the sun. I hate the coach party lovers. The totties that are
  pulled. The marriages that are made beneath the great wheel
  at the fair. Oooooh I begin to hate my fellow men and
  women, squeezing my insides, keeping my knees together

in this queue. Trying to think of something else. If I get a pee, will I join in? Have a good time again? Love my husband and my children again? Love the crowd by the rails again? Not feel choked by the gas, rising over the crowd, the gas of a good time had by all -- ooooch, come on Sharon. Let's go and have a piss in the grass.

MARGARET *runs off pushing* SHARON *who, still crying, waves her frog round her head.* MR TILLOTSON *comes on.*

PUBLIC ADDRESS SYSTEM. And the runners are going into the stalls — now.

1ST BOOKMAKER. The Derby comes but once a year!

2ND BOOKMAKER. One minute before they go!

1ST BOOKMAKER. Lester, still five to one!

MR TILLOTSON. Seven bets on. So sweet. Like warm blood. And easy. Like Our Lord, walking on water.

2ND BOOKMAKER. Blushing Groom, gone out to three to one now! Three to one the favourite!

MR TILLOTSON *hunts in his pockets.*

1ST BOOKMAKER. Ten to one, Hot Grove!

2ND BOOKMAKER. Ten to one, Lucky Sovereign!

MR TILLOTSON. Lucky Sovereign? Jubilee year? It can't fail. I got to get it on.

MR TILLOTSON *runs off.* MARGARET *wheels a happy* SHARON *on.* SANDY *comes on from the other side.*

PUBLIC ADDRESS SYSTEM. All the runners are in the stalls now.

MARGARET. The Derby, Sandy.

SANDY. The Derby, Margaret.

SANDY *and* MARGARET *embrace, he lifts her and swings her in an arc.*

SHARON. My want — see The Derby.

SANDY. Come on then!

They run off, MARGARET *pushing* SHARON. *The stage is deserted.*

PUBLIC ADDRESS SYSTEM. The flag is up. They are under
starter's orders — now.

The stage deserted. THE DERBY *played by one actor, comes
on over the hill. The actor is festooned with the regalia of the
race.*

THE DERBY. I am the Epsom Derby Stakes.

Being —

Twelve tons of twenty-two horses and twenty-two small
men —

Boots, bridles, crash helmets, weights and whips — silks and
light underwear —

Each horse carrying nine stone —

The lot worth twelve million pounds sterling plus —

A race for three year old horses, run over one and a half
miles —

Begun over a hill, behind trees, where no one can see a blind
thing that's going on.

THE DERBY *strides over the hill out of sight. The* DERBY
COURSE *comes on. He smokes a cigarette in a long holder,
wears a summer suit with two-toned shoes and carries a cut
turf in the palm of a hand.*

THE COURSE. I am the Derby Course. Don't be fooled by lush
green curves in the countryside. I am dangerous. I am a bad-
tempered bastard. I bite legs. On me the second-rate burst
blood vessels and heart valves. Only the fast, the brave and
the beautiful get anything out of me. First, I am a killer
gallop, up a long hill. Then I sweep down, curving to the left,
to the real ball-tearer, a vicious left-hand corner, Tattenham
Corner, turned at forty miles an hour. Then the straight run
to the finish, but down another hill. And at the last hundred
yards — the ground falls away from the Stand into the farside
rails. That's me. Switchback. Twisty. Feared by the hardened
man and animal. To win the Derby — out-think me. Then
kick my brains in. Or I'll break you apart.

The actor lays the turf in the centre of the stage. A CROWD,
rushing to the rails, comes on. Among the crowd is

MR TILLOTSON. *He carries his 'None In Hell' placard. The* DERBY COURSE *actor joins the crowd.*

FIRST CROWD

MAN IN THE CROWD. Get down on the rails now, don't take no for an answer, woomph!

THE DERBY *out of sight.*

2ND MAN. Where are they?

3RD MAN. Miles away, over behind us.

4TH MAN. Henri Samani, my dreams go with you!

MR TILLOTSON. I've got it. That trembling feeling. They're going to go, any moment now.

1ST WOMAN. I can't see anything. Just grass.

2ND WOMAN. You'll just see 'em when they go by.

3RD WOMAN. Where's Lester? Annie, where's Lester?

2ND WOMAN. He's not gone by yet! You'll know him, when he does. He's got an arse like a little cream bun.

4TH MAN. Henri Samani! My life is in your hands.

3RD MAN. How much you put on him then?

4TH MAN. Fifty p.

MR TILLOTSON. My tongue's gone furry! I'm going to be sick, I'm going to die, no I'm not! Oh Jesus Christ Our Lord forgive me I've bet on The Derby and I'm in Heaven!

PUBLIC ADDRESS SYSTEM. And they are off.

THE DERBY *actor begins his display of the race.*

THE DERBY. Clang go the gates!

Leap goes twelve tons of horse and men!

AND it's Baudelaire the first to show. Frankie Durr that tough little walnut on top. Then Lucky Sovereign, the no-hope offspring of the great Nijinsky, the Jubilee mug punters' tipple. Then Milliondollarman, then Nebiollo, the Two Thousand Guinea winner — is this horse a paper tiger?

AND now it's Milliondollarman on the farside, neck and neck with Baudelaire and Lucky Sovereign going up to join them.

Just in behind comes Nebiollo, then Caporello, then Be My Guest.

Who's going to blow it going up the hill? Who's going to take up the running? What the fuck is Lester Piggott doing?

The CROWD *runs to another position, as if six furlongs from the start at the top of Tattenbam Hill.* MR TILLOTSON *keeps bis position. The* CROWD *leaves litter behind.*

MR TILLOTSON. The action is what a gambler craves for. Two and a half minutes the race lasts, but I'll hold my breath and the action will go on forever.

MR TILLOTSON *takes a deep breath and bis cheeks puff out.*

SECOND CROWD.

1ST WOMAN. Why we got to stand on the hill?

2ND MAN. Always watched The Derby from here. You see 'em come up and you see 'em go down.

1ST WOMAN. Why can't we watch the finish?

2ND MAN. Cos you got to pay ten quid and dress up like a bloody penguin.

2ND WOMAN. I'm pregnant. I'm pregnant.

3RD WOMAN. Don't tell me, tell your husband.

2ND WOMAN. Ted — I'm pregnant.

3RD MAN. What?

2ND WOMAN. I wanted to tell you. When The Derby goes by.

3RD MAN. Great. If it's a boy we'll call it Lester.

2ND WOMAN. What if it's a girl?

3RD MAN. We'll call it Lesterine.

THE DERBY *coming into sight.*

THE DERBY. And suddenly all the jockeys know. Baudelaire is buggering himself up the hill, giving them all the ride.

AND as they race up to the top of the hill it's still Baudelaire — Gairloch makes a challenge but falls back, broken by the speed. And breaking the hearts of his owners, Mr Paul de Moussac and Miss V. Hermann-Hodge.

Baudelaire continues the ball-breaking gallop on the inside, Royal Plume comes to challenge but being driven hard by Joe Mercer.

AND it's Royal Plume from Valinsky, Milliondollarman, Caporello.

AND to the outside — Blushing Groom, the Aga Khan's horse. Never beaten in its life. The favourite. The wonder horse.

And looking to the back markers it's Sultan's Ruby. Lordelaw. And in among the stragglers — Lester Piggott on The Minstrel.

3RD MAN. Where the hell is Lester?

4TH MAN. At the back. Like a monkey on your spine, waiting to pounce.

THE DERBY. And Night Before pulls up. Pat Eddery pulls up Night Before. A blood vessel burst.

THE DERBY *screams.* THE DERBY *actor arranges the* CROWD *into positions of the field.*

They race over the top of the hill. Baudelaire disputing it with Milliondollarman. Valinsky makes ground on the inside. Right up with them — Caporello and Lucky Sovereign and Noble Venture. Just in behind them, Willie Carson on Hot Grove. Behind Hot Grove, Henri Samani on Blushing Groom, well placed on the inside. Behind Blushing Groom, Lester Piggott on The Minstrel.

(Aside.) Lester — sneaking up from the back, to sniff the bollocks of the French favourite.

1ST JOCKEY. What the fuck is Lester doing?

2ND JOCKEY. Go down the hill you bugger.

3RD JOCKEY. What's that cunt trying to do to me?

4TH JOCKEY. Keep cool you beauty, you fucker.

5TH JOCKEY. For fucksake, someone bust that frog horse now.

6TH JOCKEY. Mille fois merdes.

7TH JOCKEY. Shit.

The CROWD *runs to another position as if on the inside of Tattenham Corner.* MR TILLOTSON *lets out a big breath and pants. The* CROWD *leaves litter behind.*

MR TILLOTSON. It's got to me again, every bit of my body. Gambling, I'm sorry I walked out on you.

THE DERBY. Milliondollarman from Baudelaire. Caporello. Lucky Sovereign.

In behind them – Be My Guest, Valinsky, Nebiollo, then Blushing Groom. Losing ground – Royal Plume. The backmarker is – Mr. Music Man.

AND at the front Milliondollarman takes over the lead!

THIRD CROWD.

1ST MAN. Milliondollarman! Sixty-six to one! I'm going to be rich!

1ST WOMAN. I want my kid to see The Derby!

2ND WOMAN. Hold her up then.

A CHILD, played by the 3RD WOMAN, burst into tears within the CROWD.

2ND MAN. Come on little girl. See The Derby. Tell your dollies all about it when you get back home.

THE DERBY. Hot Grove makes progress on the outside, Willie Carson like a pea on a drum.

AND they round Tattenham Corner. Where a jockey can utterly lose his bottle and the race. And a horse on the inside rail can have his hide peeled like a ripe tomato. Milliondollarman. Hot Grove. Caporello third. Baudelaire fourth. And fifth, the Minstrel coming strongly.

(Aside.) Lester's brain ticks – like an intercontinental ballistic missile, on trajectory.

The THIRD CROWD produces Union Jack flags in a tableau – the CHILD is held up above crying. At the back of the CROWD a STREAKER bares his behind.

THE DERBY. Milliondollarman from Hot Grove, to face the hill down to the finish.

The crucifixion of the horse that won't stay begins.

The CROWD runs to another position shedding litter to form the FOURTH CROWD around MR TILLOTSON.

GRANDPA *sits at the front of the* CROWD, *on his little canvas stool, impassive and silent.*

Three furlongs to run in The Derby. Milliondollarman is pressed by Hot Grove. The Minstrel in third place. Then Be My Guest.

AND Blushing Groom unleashes a run. Henri Samani asks the question.

(Aside.) Will the French favourite stay? Bred by Red God out of Runaway Bride. But Red God never did more than a mile. Genes in the animal's chromosomes grind and shudder.

Two furlongs to run in The Derby.

FOURTH CROWD.

THE DERBY. It is Hot Grove from The Minstrel. Then Blushing Groom still making progress. Monseigneur moves into fourth place. Hot Grove from The Minstrel from Blushing Groom.

The FOURTH CROWD *shouts the names of* HENRI, LESTER, WILLIE THE MINSTREL, HOT GROVE *and* BLUSHING GROOM, *as* THE DERBY *passes them.* GRANDPA *on his stool, silent.*

THE DERBY *is past the* FOURTH CROWD, *which strains to see the finish.*

The closing stages of the nineteen seventy-seven Epsom Derby Stakes.

Blushing Groom has nothing left.

Willie Carson on Hot Grove thinks the race is his.

Then Lester Piggott — lets the reins slip two inches through the palms of his hands.

The Minstrel responds. A bat out of hell, bullet out of a gun, the lash of a whip.

A hundred yards to run in The Derby. Lester Piggott and Willie Carson. The Minstrel on the near side, Hot Grove on the far side.

AND in the last second, like throwing a knife through a doorway as the door slams — The Minstrel wins.

THE DERBY *walks off.*

PUBLIC ADDRESS SYSTEM. Photofinish. There will be a photograph.

MR TILLOTSON. The Minstrel's Derby. I'ld tear my eyes out to bet on a race like that again.

MR TILLOTSON *studies his race-card feverishly. The crowd disperses, stunned, to become the* FIFTH CROWD, MARGARET, SANDY *and* GRANDPA *amongst them.*

FIFTH CROWD.

MARGARET. Sandy. We won.

SANDY. Maggy. Aluminium ladders.

1ST WOMAN. First I saw the race — just like a crowd of bees.

2ND WOMAN. What happened?

2ND MAN. They call for a photograph when it's under a length. But the word is definitely Lester.

The 3RD MAN *starts and runs off.*

SANDY. Take a picture of me.

MARGARET. We've not got a camera.

SANDY, *holding the winning ticket to his chest.*

SANDY. Someone take a picture of me. I won The Derby.

MARGARET. Someone take a picture of my husband.

SANDY. For crying out loud what am I doing? Let's get to that bookie.

SANDY *takes* MARGARET's *hand. They run off.*

1ST WOMAN. Like bees, on the horizon. Then they were dead in front of me. All whips and froth. Then just grass again.

A couple embrace.

PUBLIC ADDRESS SYSTEM. Here is the result of the third race, The Epsom Derby Stakes. First number twenty-three, The Minstrel. Second number six, Hot Grove. Third number three, Blushing Groom.

The couple lie on the grass, embracing.

MR TILLOTSON. The four twenty. Lester's on Golden Libra.

MR TILLOTSON *goes off*

GRANDPA. Lester Piggott? Win The Derby on The Minstrel? What good's that to the working man? Five to one, less tax? No good at all. Bloody conspiracy. That Lester Piggott. That trainer from Tipperary. Got together with that man on the telly with the hat. Done the working man in, yet again. The Minstrel? Drifts to the left. Oh well. Derby done. Heavy boozing starts.

GRANDPA packs up his stool and goes off. Necking couples on the grass. A cascade of litter falls from the roof of the theatre to the grass.

MR TILLOTSON and MISS MOTROM appear. She hits him over the shoulders with the 'NONE IN HELL' placard.

MISS MOTROM. Fallen.

MR TILLOTSON. I just had a little bet, Miss Motrom.

She hits him again, knocking him to the ground.

MISS MOTROM. Man fallen. Man turned against the light. Man in his own filth.

She hits him repeatedly on the behind.

MR TILLOTSON. But I backed The Minstrel.

MISS MOTROM. And on how many other horses did you squander God's given pennies?

MR TILLOTSON. The whole field. Ow.

MISS MOTROM. And what about the rent? And the collection at the Mission? And a cup of tea even?

MR TILLOTSON. All right, I did my money in.

MISS MOTROM. Did The Lord in.

MR TILLOTSON. Ow.

She is exhausted. She sags. She sits back down on the grass.

I sold the return half of my train ticket. To a wino for ten p. I had to make up a fifty p stake. To put on Milliondollarman. A horse with a name like that, could it fail?

MISS MOTROM. Could it?

MR TILLOTSON. Came eighth.

MISS MOTROM searches amongst the beer bottles.

What are you going?

MISS MOTROM. I want a drink.

MR TILLOTSON. No look, don't do that —

She scours the bottles on the stage, holding them up against the light to see if there is any drink in them.

Don't Jenny.

MISS MOTROM. I want a drink.

MR TILLOTSON. You'll end up hating yourself, and all that.

MISS MOTROM. I do hate myself, and all that.

MR TILLOTSON. We'll both go down then.

MISS MOTROM. We went down long ago.

MR TILLOTSON. Let's have a prayer.

MISS MOTROM. I want to have a prayer. No, stuff prayer.

She sucks at empty bottles.

MR TILLOTSON. Ooh. Eh, Jenny. You've given me religion, right at the base of me spine. Don't do that. For pity's sake.

He knocks a bottle out of her hand. She slaps him, he slaps her. They clutch each other's hand.

MISS MOTROM. What are we going to do, Jimmy?

MR TILLOTSON. Pub? On to an all night casino? Then dice with the winos on Waterloo Station, 'til the betting shops open, eleven o'clock in the morning?

MISS MOTROM. I want to kneel down and pray —

MR TILLOTSON. That's no good, religion? A hypodermic needle called God. I mean I tried to get it in me — the manger and the tomb. I've just ended up punctured all over, running sores of goodness up my arm —

MISS MOTROM. You've got to flood your life with Jesus. If you don't, you'll just flood it with beer.

MR TILLOTSON. We could just try — and get back home. And have a cup of tea. If you'ld, er, lend me the train-fare.

MISS MOTROM. Never lend to a gambler. Just give.

MR TILLOTSON. Tattenham Corner Station. Don't know if I'll make it. There'll be crap games spilling out from the Fair all over there.

MISS MOTROM. There are three public houses between here and Tattenham Corner.

They look at each other, holding hands loosely.

MR TILLOTSON. Give it a whirl, then.

MISS MOTROM. Go it alone.

MR TILLOTSON. Hack through the jungle.

They go off.

JOCKS *alone on the Downs, picking through the litter.*

JOCKS. Huh. Huh. Huh.

PRIMROSE *comes over the skyline.*

PRIMROSE. What you doing? Stable boy. Mister. Gorgio lover.

JOCKS *continues to pick through the litter.*

You gone daft or something?

JOCKS *straightens.*

JOCKS. I'm looking for a Tote ticket. Someone who got a winner. Or a double. Or a jackpot, who knows? Maybe they dropped their ticket. And I can find it. And have their winnings. For my train-fare. Off this place. Right?

He bends.

PRIMROSE. Got no money then.

He straightens quickly.

JOCKS. I was going to back The Minstrel. But I had a rush of the blood to the head and backed Royal Plume. Royal Plume came in last.

He bends.

PRIMROSE. Do you want a job?

He straightens slowly.

JOCKS. You what?

PRIMROSE. For ten pound.

JOCKS *stares.*

JOCKS. What job?

PRIMROSE. Not saying. You take the money. Then you do the job.

JOCKS. Work for some Gyppo? What do you want me to do? Shovel shit?

She looks at him.

No no, I. Bit low. Just working up to walk to London. They did it, the last century. Thousands out of the East End on foot. To see the race and back again. Christ are we soft!

He kicks at the litter.

PRIMROSE. Say yes. Get the money. Do the job.

She takes a ten pound note from her sleeve. He looks at the note, shrugs and takes it

JOCKS. What's the job?

PRIMROSE. Job's in two parts. First part — kiss me.

They kiss. They step back from one another.

JOCKS. Ah — what's the second part?

PRIMROSE. Go away.

She turns and goes off quickly, over the skyline.

JOCKS. Right.

JOCKS goes off.

LORD RACK *crawls over the skyline.*

RACK. Fell asleep! On the Downs! Oh. Have I been robbed?

He rolls on one side, then the other, patting his pockets.

Car keys. Notebook for me autobiography. Day's winnings — seventeen pence. Ey. To go through card on every race, and still end up even? That's maturity of judgement. Right.

He struggles to his feet.

Go and sleep it off in 'car. Perfect end to a perfect day. Hey, after a day's racing like that, even an old atheist, socialist life peer has to say — God's in his heaven and all's right with the world.

He falls over, back down the slope out of sight.

SUPERINTENDENT BLUE *and* CHARLES PEARCE *walk on over the skyline.*

BLUE. Evening stroll. Wind down. A civilised idea, Charles.

PEARCE. I do it every year, after The Derby. To lick my wounds.

BLUE. Poignant.

PEARCE. What?

BLUE. The litter.

PEARCE. Common ground. And look what they do to it.

BLUE. Be back to nature tomorrow morning, for another day's racing. The inmates of the local asylum will see to that.

PEARCE. Always found it in bad taste. Turning the loonies loose to clear up.

BLUE. A Derby Day tradition. They look forward to it. Bit of a bear with a sore head, aren't you Charles?

PEARCE. I made a foolish remark earlier in the day.

BLUE. What? Oh yes. If The Minstrel wins The Derby, you will eat the Pope.

PEARCE. Marry. Marry the Pope. I was going to eat the Pope if Blushing Groom won The Derby. Well, I've been tipped off. Somehow that remark has got into tomorrow's Daily Express.

BLUE. Don't let it get you down. I'm sure his Holiness is a very nice girl.

BLUE *shuffles a toe through the litter.*

PEARCE. I am a man at the top of my profession. Before I crawl to the Pearly Gates, dragging my ulcer behind me, I will win the Blue Ribbon of Racing. Even an MBE. Why, then, am I not calm? Why do I feel — abused?

BLUE. Relax, take up Sunday painting. I have. Scenes of trees.

BLUE *picks up a Tote ticket.*

Fifth race. Horse number four. Fifty p. stake.

PEARCE. Diomed Stakes. Won by Gunner B, twelve to one. Wait a moment. Gunner B was horse number four.

BLUE. Well.

PEARCE. Well.

PEARCE. That's six pounds fifty to you.

BLUE. Buy the Mrs. a Kermit Frog.

They go off.

MARGARET *and the* GHOST *of Emily Davison come on.* MARGARET *walks with her arms folded.*

GHOST. You dozy bitch.

MARGARET. We had a good day out.

GHOST. Family cow.

MARGARET. Bobby only hit Sharon a couple of times – Sharon only piddled her bed once in the night –

GHOST. And that is success?

MARGARET. That is success.

GHOST. Big deal.

MARGARET. And we backed the winner of The Derby.

GHOST. Stupid, crass dozy bitch of a family cow. Is it me who's dead or you?

MARGARET. What do you want me to do? Scream?

MARGARET *screams. A silence.*

I do see it. In between worrying that the kids' shoes are too small. That oranges are too dear. I do see it. As the Nappisan gurgles down the sink. A good life. Freedom. Being whole.

GHOST. I saw it too, for a second, before the man and the horse hit me.

The GHOST *and* MARGARET *embrace. Then the* GHOST *walks away. She remains on the Downs until the end of the play.*

MARGARET. When I'm tired out, sometimes I think – the real me – is sulking just behind my shoulder. I could turn, and look at her, and smile.

SANDY *comes on.*

SANDY. Maggy! Maggy!

MARGARET *and* SANDY *see each other.*

MARGARET. Thought you were with Grandpa. I don't like leaving him alone with the kids.

SANDY. They're all right. Bobby's fleecing the old man at snakes and ladders. One p. a snake.

MARGARET. Where did you put the money?

SANDY. In the dormobile. In the front seat. Where we put the hash once, going over the Turkistan border. Remember?

MARGARET. Before we had kids.

SANDY. Before we had kids.

MARGARET. I remember.

SANDY. Hey.

MARGARET. What?

SANDY *takes hold of her hands.*

One thousand nine hundred and twenty pounds.

SANDY. Lester Piggott, five to one. That little bookie from the sticks I put it on with. Writhe? I had to wait nearly an hour , while he called in all the money he'd laid off on me. God bless you, Lester! Wherever you are. Sipping your half glass of champagne, chewing your Ryvita biscuit.

MARGARET. It doesn't mean anything, Sandy. The money.

SANDY. Not as much as we'ld have got ante post —

MARGARET. It doesn't mean anything.

SANDY. Means a house. Just.

MARGARET. A house doesn't mean anything.

SANDY. What does then FOR FUCK'S SAKE?

For a time they do not look at each other.

MARGARET. It's all right.

SANDY. Yeah.

MARGARET. Everything is all right.

SANDY. Yeah. Here. We will tell our grandchildren — about the day we backed everything we had in our life — on the winner of The Derby.

MARGARET. Will we?

They go off. The GHOST *walks across the Downs.*
LUNATICS *appear with sacks, picking up the litter.*

1ST LUNATIC. They going to give us a cup of tea, when we've cleared this lot up?

2ND LUNATIC. It's a special treat.

1ST LUNATIC. Should bloody well hope they'ld give us a cup of tea.

3RD LUNATIC. Lester Piggott. Piggott.

2ND LUNATIC. It's a special treat, but your shoes get wet.

4TH LUNATIC. Grassy knoll. Loll on the grassy knoll.

3RD LUNATIC. Piggott.

1ST LUNATIC. In the sack, they said. Then they'd give us a cup of tea.

2ND LUNATIC. Terrible to tie up, wet laces.

1ST LUNATIC. Got to squeeze the tea-leaves, though.

4TH LUNATIC. On the knoll.

3RD LUNATIC. Piggott.

2ND LUNATIC. And wet socks, terrible.

3RD LUNATIC. Piggott.

4TH LUNATIC. Loll.

A sunset begins to flare. The lights go down.

SORE THROATS

An intimate play in two acts

SORE THROATS was first performed by the Royal Shakespeare Company at the Warehouse Theatre, London, on 8 August 1979, with the following cast:

Judy	Paola Dionisotti
Jack	Malcolm Storry
Sally	Ruby Wax

Directed by Barry Kyle
Designed by Kit Surrey
Lighting by Brian Wigney

I have heard that lovemaking can give you a swollen throat. I don't want one. But the swing-boats, I have heard, can give you a swollen throat too. So I shan't be able to avoid it.

Bertolt Brecht

Act One

A bare flat in South London.
    JUDY *is sitting on the floor. She is 39. A bottle of red wine, half drunk, is before her.*
    JACK *stands behind her. He is 45. He is dressed in the uniform of a Police Chief Inspector.*

JUDY. How's Celia?

Wait.

JACK. I —

JUDY. Do you masturbate on the side with her, too?

    (*Aside.*) Ha!

    Wait.

JACK. I —

JUDY. I thought you were asleep. You mumbled about the bathroom and got out of bed. You were gone a long time. I got out of bed. You weren't in the bathroom, you were lying on the sofa, having a good wank.

JACK (*aside*). Wouldn't shave your legs would you. Or would not, after the tenth year of our marriage. Not above the knees, oh no. And knew I hated the rasp where the smooth should be.

    Wait.

    (*To* JUDY.) I —

JUDY. What did you see in the dark? Dark living room. Of our house, of our happy marriage. Little Japanese girl? You had a thing about little Japanese girls. Yes, a little hara-kiri fifteen year-old. Flit, did she my dear? Adopt poses? In your mind? Rub the cleft of her little bum up the lamp standard? Hang in chains from that god-awful chandelier your mother gave us?

JACK (*aside*). Little monkey, crawling all over me. With her little thumb and finger.

    Wait.

(*To* JUDY.) I —

JUDY. Bugger off.

JACK. Oh dear.

JUDY. Yes I have become foul mouthed. It's an experiment in consciousness raising. Or lowering. So fuck yourself.

(*Aside.*) What do I mean by that? Anatomically? Pull his little willie back between his legs, jam it up his arsehole —

JACK. I —

JUDY (*aside*). So much of man remains a mystery to me and I married so long.

She giggles.

She stops giggling.

Wait.

(*To* JACK.) Does your solicitor know you're here?

Wait.

No.

Wait.

How did you find me?

JACK. Estate agent. He gave me the address of where — you are hiding away.

JUDY. Hideyhole.

JACK. Here.

Wait.

JUDY. Well.

JACK. Well.

JUDY (*aside*). Well! Well! Well!

Wait.

JACK. Damp in here.

JUDY. Then dry out.

JACK. Gas fire —

JUDY. Cut off.

JACK. Electric —

JUDY. The fuse is kerphut.

JACK. Mend it.

JUDY. Can't.

JACK. Don't be stupid.

JUDY. I cannot mend an electric fuse.

JACK. Course you can.

JUDY. Don't tell me what I can or cannot do. I know what I can or cannot do, surely to Christ!

Wait.

And little Jack always did fuses.

JACK (*aside*). Doing it deliberately! She is doing it deliberately!

(*To* JUDY.) Paraffin heater.

Wait.

Oh it's my fault then, that you're going to go down with rheumatism, in your sl — slum?

JUDY. No.

No.

JACK (*aside*). Breathe a bit.

JUDY (*aside*).

She giggles.

She stops giggling.

All right, what are you doing here? Revisiting the scene of the crime? Me?

JACK. I want —

JUDY. No, Jack —

JACK. See how —

JUDY. Go away —

JACK. See you.

(*Aside.*) I want! I want!

Wait.

(*To* JUDY.) See you. See how you are.

Wait.

How are you?

JUDY. I am about to be divorced from my husband. You. I am thirty-nine. I am selling the house of my broken marriage for thirty thousand pounds, thanks to my departing husband's dirty conscience. I am thinking of using this money to have an operation. I would like bits of ferocious animals grafted onto me. Adders' heads for breasts? Nipples that suck, rather than get sucked? And for a womb, what for a womb? Yes. A tiger's head for a womb. And I will roam the streets in a sort of wire, see-through blouse and leather zip, zip up the front skirt. Won't I be a nice surprise for middle aged men, cruising in cars? Or whatever your kind does, in the streets, out for a poke. Poke me, see what you get. Something really hot and surgical. Tiger snake woman. Remade. For a new life. Think I've got a chance?

JACK. ?

JUDY. For a new life.

JACK. Not really.

JUDY. Renaissance.

Wait.

JACK. But I did come to be friends. I mean why not? After —

JUDY. After the flood?

JACK. Yes.

JUDY. Flood of all the shit.

Wait.

JACK. Myself, I'm not so bad. Boil on the back of my neck's got a bit puffed up. What with the excitement of the divorce.

He gives a little laugh.

No, I'll nip into Kings's out-patients on the way back. Have it drained off.

Judy —

Wait.

Look I have a letter from Tommy.

JUDY. Oh.

JACK. Our son.

JUDY. I remember.

JACK (*aside*). Tell her what I want! Want! Have got to have! All of us have got to have, crawling on the face of this fucking planet!

He takes out a letter.

(*To* JUDY.) He's in Africa.

JUDY. Africa.

JACK. At least that is the address he gave. Africa, Sunday. No stamp. I had to pay two pounds surcharge.

JUDY. Africa, Sunday.

JACK. Do you want to read it? It must have been written months ago. Before we.

He puts the letter down on the floor.

JUDY. You know what I wanted when I was pregnant? With Tommy, all that summer? Back in the 1950s? A good shit.

JACK. For godsake.

JUDY. What?

JACK. No.

JUDY. What?

JACK. Don't turn on everything.

JUDY. But I want to.

JACK. Must dredge up some modicum —

JUDY (*aside*). Turn, turn around, turn on me —

JACK. Modicum of decency. You can't live on pain all the time. Sorry.

JUDY. Why are you sorry?

JACK. Priggish remark. Sorry.

JUDY. Not at all. The endless refinement of being really miserable — refreshes me. On the razor's edge. I cut myself with the facts of my broken marriage every morning. In the bathroom, slash slash. Nice and bloody for another awful day.

JACK. All right why — no.

JUDY. What?

JACK. No.

JUDY. What?

JACK. Why don't — no.

JUDY. What?

What? What?

JACK. No.

JUDY. Oh, that's the real you, that's the real heart of you. Your shying away. You look away. You never actually say what you want to say. Never actually put your hand in the fire. Always at the last second you shy away.

JACK. All —

I was going to say — why don't you, then — really go and do harm to yourself, eh?

Then, eh?

JUDY. Oh, I may.

JACK. Go on then.

JUDY. I may well.

JACK. Can I watch?

JUDY. I will. I can. I could. Don't think for a second I cannot — not.

Could not.

JACK. Want my penknife?

JUDY. Don't be petty.

JACK *takes out a penknife.*

JACK. A little boy's friend.

JACK *opens a blade.*

JUDY. Why did you never let me see your private parts?

JACK. Bit blunt.

JUDY. Always turning your fat behind.

JACK. Do though.

JACK *slides his penknife across the floor toward* JUDY.

JUDY. Babyish. Baby pink. Squidgy.

JACK. Chop away. Cut up Judy-wudy? Hurt me more than it hurts you? That the point, hurt me more?

JUDY. The spread of one's husband's arse. In marriage you feel your partner's physical peculiarities like an intimate growth. For example, that funny bit of skin on your right buttock, I feel as a bump on the bridge of my nose.

JACK. Go on.

JUDY (*sings*). 'No no, you can't take that away from me.'

She giggles.

JACK. A bit of danger? Go on then. Once in your light, feather-brained life. Vicious little negative life. Go on, you're free. There's no one to care. You don't do you. I don't, do I. The people the other side of that wall, don't care. This is Metropolitan London. The ambulance that comes to take you away will be of less interest than a minor traffic accident. Go on. Do it. A little real — private destruction.

No?

Wait.

Too English, my sweet. Are you not, are we both not.

Trouble with the English — we all go round with a Sunday-school teacher in our heads. Some all-seeing do-gooder in the English brain — stops us actually — breaking out. Going all the way.

God. Even a divorce, common enough thing, has almost destroyed me. The touch of illegality freezes my English blood.

Wait.

When I first saw her. Celia. You know — naked, I cried.

JUDY. Oh why don't you burn in hell.

JACK. I couldn't stop crying.

JUDY (*aside*). With a curling iron! Hot, old, electric curling iron! Burn them, right across the stomach, a hot red poker in a joint of lamb!

She laughs.

JACK (*looking at his hands*). I was helpless, my hands. I faltered. Felt ashamed. I. So real, she was the real world. The dignity, the — after so long. I'd forgotten, perhaps I'd never known.

How beautiful we are.

JUDY *laughs.*

How simple.

(*Aside.*) After all, we all want a good fuck! On the whole! In one hole or another!

He scoffs.

(*Aside.*) Human beings. Want to get up each other. Be got up by each other. That's life. Slosh about, have a heavy breathe. And burst, all over.

So why all the bitterness, why all the agony? When all you want is a bit of tenderness, a bit of tender — good time. Get warm, get inflamed. Stretched. So why this third world war, in your living room, in your bathroom in your bedroom, about who fucks who?

He scoffs.

(*Aside.*) And why, in marriage, when all you want is — comfort, just to get your cock and all the works behind, a bit comfortable — do you end up talking about the insulation in the loft all the time? The cost of sheets! Woodworm in the floorboards! The cost of kiddies' shoes! Domestic Savings Policy!

I mean not even a pig should be asked to fuck a Trustees Savings Bank Account!

In the last stages of my divorce, I had a bit of a fantasy. One night, driven mad by the mill of marriage and sex, I saw myself discovered by a fellow police-officer, outside a Trustees Savings Bank, my trousers and my Y-fronts down, my bum exposed to the night air and the fingers of passing drunks — with my cock jammed in a twenty-four-hour cash dispensing machine.

Trying to reconcile money and sex.

You've got to be free. Or you've got to feel free. That you do things freely. Or one thing, the best thing. Love.

Even if you're a policeman, you've got to feel that!

'Else, what is there?

JUDY. I found her knickers.

Wait.

In the trouser pocket of your second best uniform.

Wait.

Little shitty lacy things.

What did you do, sniff them on night duty?

JACK. Yes! All right! Yes!

JUDY. Yes all right yes what?

JACK. Yes all right! I'd have a good wank in them.

JUDY. Bully for you.

JACK. Her things — delight me.

JUDY. Ha.

JACK. Heated things. That have been warmed by her.

Made warm.

Tacky.

JUDY. There always was a strong whiff of old potatoes about you and sex.

JACK. You don't understand. I don't care how ridiculous a figure I cut.

I'll cut a hole in the crotch of my trousers and walk down the street, long as I can rub myself in her things, hard.

JUDY *shrugs.*

JUDY. What am I before such passion? A mere woman!

What do you talk about when you're together? You can't discuss the stains and smells of each other's clothing all the time. Or can you?

JACK. I just must have. Her.

JUDY (*low*). Herness.

JACK. Celia. Her.

JACK *takes out a pair of woman's pants.*

JUDY. Oh for godsake.

JACK. Sorry. I do pull myself up short sometimes.

JUDY. When you find yourself at the bottom of her laundry basket?

JACK. Times like that.

JUDY. What do you want Jack?

> (*Aside.*) Want! Want! Want! Want!
>
> *Wait.*
>
> What do you want?
>
> JACK *looks at the pants. He puts them away.*
>
> *Wait.*

JACK. The money.

> *Wait.*

JUDY. Oh.

> *Wait.*

JACK. The money —

JUDY. I said, oh.

JACK. Judy about the money.

JUDY. Blam splat.

JACK. What?

> *Wait.*

JUDY. I said — blam, splat.

JACK. It was our house.

JUDY. You gave me your share of our house. Take the house, you wrote.

> And I wrote back thank you very much.

JACK. The letter does not constitute a contract.

JUDY. It does constitute a contract.

JACK. My solicitor says no.

JUDY. My solicitor says yes.

JACK. I wrote that letter all night. The night I left you. Sat all night on Victoria Station, scribbling. Twenty pages. I poured myself out, that's all.

JUDY. Poured out fifteen thousand pounds.

JACK. They've made divorce liberal now!

(*Aside.*) Oh liberal with the tomato sauce —

(*To* JUDY.) We've got equal rights.

JUDY *laughs.*

It's immoral!

JUDY *laughs. Stops laughing.*

Wait.

Give me half.

JUDY. Ha.

JACK. What are Celia and I going to live off?

JUDY (*low*). What did you say?

JACK (*low*). You heard.

Wait.

JUDY. Live off each other.

Wait.

Each other? Yes. Eat each other. Lick each other. Suck each other. Get fat on each other.

I'll send you bits of me to eat. The wronged woman for breakfast. Ear? Finger? Nipple? 'Parcel for you darling' Celia will call. And bring a bit of me up to you in b — bed.

JUDY *weeps.*

JACK. No.

Look —

If —

No.

JUDY (*aside*). I'm not crying for him.

Not crying for our marriage.

I'm crying for me. Me! Me!

She stops crying.

Wait.

(*To* JACK.) What I want to know is, what no one will tell me is, how am I to think of myself?

Begin to think of myself?

I have never worked in my life. Even when I was a mother I took pills to dry up the milk. While a French or Swedish girl, here to learn the language, bottle-fed my baby. Washed the lumps of crap down the bathroom sink, well away from my eyes, let alone hands.

JACK. But you always wanted middle-classy things. And there was your mother to bump up things —

JUDY. Your fucking mother too —

JACK. My mum, both our mums, to bump up things. Au pair girls, cabinets with glasses in, sofas with skirts on.

Though your mum was the real Hoi-toi. My mum, poor old cow, was just trying to keep up. Witness that chandelier.

JUDY. In that house.

JACK. In that house.

(*Aside.*) The mums, all the mums — picking out your liver.

JUDY. You put me in that house. Or my mother put me in that house. Or I put me in that house. But put I was. Bored. My husband away hour after hour.

What was there for me? Charitable work? For the Police Fereration Widows and Orphans Fund? I am not a charitable person, why the hell should I be? Sexual dalliance, in my boredom? Why not, but what opportunity did I have? Stuff a breast through the letter box for the postman on his second delivery?

I sat alone in the living-room every morning, having my coffee Alone. Neat. Not even dunking my biscuit, for that would not be neat. Thinking — shall I wear sheer tights this afternoon? O is that a little too bold for a weekday?

Listening for something. But what? The sound of my own legs as I crossed them and crossed them again? Lightly. In light sheer. In a silent room. Alone, in silent — light.

There must be so many women in the city alone in rooms on afternoons. Listening, even beginning to count their own breaths.

Bleaching.

Bleached out.

I am bleached. Been bleached. Twenty years of married life and I am so very clean. What I could have been, the scientist, the doctor, the artist, the thinker, the lover, all the lovely dirt, s'washed away. Biodegradable. I'm blank. White. But for the faintest stains, like a sh — sheet on the line.

JACK. Look.

He swallows.

There's a job in Canada. The Royal Canadian Mounted Police.

JUDY. Ha.

JACK. A big country. A lot of light.

JUDY. There must be.

JACK. I want to live in a house with high windows, surrounded by water.

Wait.

JUDY. I see.

JACK. Do you Judy, do you?

Wait.

Celia and I will go. She won't marry me. It's difficult for me, there is — disapproval. But she says we should stay — lovers — and wait. She takes a very dark view of the world. You'd like her, you really would, it's a pity —

No.

Canada. That's why the money — but there we are.

Sorry.

He turns away. He argues with himself. He turns back and hits her in the mouth.

JUDY. Oh.

JACK. I hit you.

JUDY. I noticed.

JACK. Did I really catch you?

JUDY. I'm bleeding.

JACK. It is all right. Tissue. Be one in your bag.

He looks around. There is no bag.

Where's your bag?

JUDY. Don't know.

JACK. Got to be here —

JUDY. Not got one —

JACK. Don't be stupid every woman's got a bag —

JUDY. Not got one —

JACK. Where the fuck is it —

JUDY. Go away —

JACK. Don't worry.

Water.

JUDY. Water's not turned on. Go away.

JACK. Yeah?

What about washing?

JUDY. Baths. Public.

Baths at the Green.

JACK. God.

JUDY. Many bathe there. Mostly women. Go away.

JACK. I've got a hanky.

He takes out a handkerchief. He stares at it.

JUDY. Go.

(*Aside.*) He hates the idea of women bathing. It gives him a
picture in his mind he can't stand.

JACK (*aside*). Wash 'em —

JUDY (*aside*). Bodies not. Bodies not being what bodies should
be —

JACK (*aside*). Wash 'em —

JUDY (*aside*). God! I almost understand his mind. What he hates
about us. Us. Rows of women's behinds, nude, along the edge
of a swimming pool, spreading on the tiles.

JACK (*aside*). Wash the —

JUDY (*aside*). Swishing legs, running to fat, in the water.

JACK (*aside*). Blubber. Blubber.

Wait.

JUDY. Go.

JACK. No no. I'll dab it in the wine, yes?

He shouts.

Yes.

Reasonably.

Yes.

He tips the wine bottle's neck against the handkerchief. He goes to her. She snatches the handkerchief from him and dabs her mouth.

Why did you always let me hit you?

JUDY. I had the choice?

JACK. Course.

JUDY. My God.

JACK. Only little taps.

She lets him take the handkerchief from her hands. He kneels and dabs her mouth.

JUDY. The first time you hit me was in my mother's house, in Eastbourne, in the bathroom late at night in 1959.

JACK. Little flicks.

JUDY. Most blows were to the face. Though, three times in the sixties, you hit me in the breast.

JACK. Please.

JUDY. In a first class railway carriage in Italy. In a field beneath the walls of Avignon. In that Taverna in Yugoslavia when Tommy got lost.

And that disaster in Denmark on that beach with all the seaweed, when we wept and fought, then tried to make love in the pinewood, but beautiful young men kept running by in tracksuits.

JACK stops dabbing.

The worst, for bloodiness, was in a traffic jam on Westminster Bridge, behind a lorry that had shed its load. Tubular chairs all over the road. And you hit me in the ear.

The catalogue of blows ends with that time you hit me in the mouth, in a bare flat, the last time we set eyes on each other.

He lets her take the handkerchief back.

JACK (*aside*). You have the final row. Cataclysm. But you've still got to brush your teeth.

Under the blood on the wallpaper, sit down with a nice cup of cocoa, eh?

In married life, exhaustion and gentleness end up the same thing, eh?

Gentle Jesus.

(*To* JUDY.) Give me the money.

For Jesus' sake, for some fucking sake, I'm in hell. Give me the money.

B − B − I'll beat it out of you.

JACK *hits* JUDY *with a straight right to the head. She gasps. She steadies herself with the tips of her fingers on the floor. She goes slowly onto all fours.*

No, I was never really violent, was I? Not really, not really, I mean not really. Little taps. Always kept the floodgates shut.

He takes out a paper.

My solicitor drew up a paper. Now this is adult behaviour, this is reason. Don't crawl around. Please. Listen. Half the money of the sale of the house to you, half the money of the sale of the house to me. That's a pretty fair thing, that's a pretty rational thing.

Don't crawl Judy! I don't want you to crawl! I can't think if you crawl!

So don't!

He grabs her ankle.

You're doing it deliberately!

Holding her by the ankle he kicks her in the stomach.

(*Aside.*) Hunk off the turkey at Christmas!

He lets go her ankle as if throwing it.

What did you think? You'd get kicked and it wouldn't hurt?

He kicks her in the stomach again. She screams.

Don't! Don't! Don't! Don't! You'll get cut inside and bleed! I've seen that! I've seen that! You stupid fucking bitch, I beg you, I beg you, don't!

He takes out a fountain pen, unscrews the top and puts it on the end of his pen. In the last second of doing this his hands tremble.

Pen and paper.

JUDY. Ooh.

JACK. Sign.

JUDY. Ooh.

JACK. It's our only chance.

He steps on her head. She screams.

I'm choking. I'll be all right in a minute.

Ah. There we are.

So we've got the pen and we've got the paper.

JUDY. I can't see.

I can see.

His hand trembles. He drops the pen.

JACK. I've dropped the fucker.

JUDY. I can see a nail with a shiny head.

JACK. Don't roll over.

JUDY. Like a little metal worm.

JACK. Careful!

He kneels.

The nib's stuck in! It's fallen on the nib! Ooooh!

He pulls the pen out of the floor. He holds the nib close to his face, peering at it. He writes on the back of his hand.

It can still write. We're safe.

He smoothes the paper out on his leg.

Let's make it up and go out for a meal.

Oh this is the worst day in my life for a very long time —

He stamps on her arm. She yells then weeps. He argues silently with himself. He approaches her. She scuttles away. They stare at each other.

Do you know what makes the world go round, Judy?

JUDY. Uh.

JACK. Why the cogs turn?

JUDY. Uh.

JACK. Criminals and judges, husbands and wives?

JUDY. Huh.

JACK. The oil in our lives, keep us grinding on?

Torture, Judy.

He steps back. He weeps.

Sign the thing or I'll break your hands.

Please. Please.

He lowers his head. He stops weeping. He argues with himself. He picks up the pen and paper. He goes to JUDY, *putting the paper near her hand. He is about to give her buttocks a little slap, but stops.*

Judy's bot bot.

He turns away. She looks at the pen in her hand. She signs.

I'm sorry.

He shrugs.

But it's out there, somewhere, over the forests, lakes.

My freedom.

He picks the paper up. She turns over and lies loosely on her side, her head on an extended arm.

There's got to be something getting at me! Making me do —

JUDY (*low*). Do things to your wife?

JACK (*aside*). Is it money? Can't be money. Money can't make me boot in a woman lying on the floor, pissing in my pants the while, hating myself. Not the filthy lucre.

If I could catch myself at it. Cold. And look and see. I would be clear.

Looking through a clear and clean window.

In peace.

Say it's the money. Got to pay Air Canada somehow. Buy half-a-dozen VAT 69 miniatures and ginger ales on the flight, for fucksake! Get me on the island. A bit of barbed wire, a bit of a private army, with big dogs, 12 millimetre machine guns — around me to keep you, all of you away from me!

Keep me my bit of peace!

Does cost a bit.

He gives a little laugh.

I mean anything you think, anything you do, must be good. You can't live with yourself all the time, thinking you're a shit. I am human! What I think what I do, s'got to be good!

No.

I know I am a shit.

(*To* JUDY.) Sorry love. But —

JUDY. I want you to die.

A pain touches her in her stomach.

JACK. Are you hurt?

Come to the hospital, it —

Wait, be looking down and she lying still.

Gently?

JUDY (*aside*). Don't bring that into the house! Years of thinking that.

Don't bring that — disease. Dirt. Debt. Violence. That thought.

Into my house, into me! That vile thing. Sh, listen. It's crawling around out there, trying to get in. Stick up the cracks! It's getting under the door! Get a knife from the kitchen drawer, cut it to pieces! Ha!

The years of terror for a woman of my class. The creepies, the ghouls, men in macks with bags of sweets, something pink and wriggly like a pound of sausages hanging between their knees, dragging themselves in the gutter, deformed, loathesome, around the wheels of parked cars — on dark Saturday nights — leering up at you, wanting to show you, do you.

And all the time. All the years, sticking up the cracks — it's been inside. Got into you. Day after day, night after night, you have licked it and are covered in its slime.

JACK. Gentle?

He reaches out a hand slowly, squatting. He touches her ankle. She recoils.

No.

He takes two steps forward on his knees. She scrambles away on her behind. They do not look at each other.

No.

She scrambles on her behind to a corner.

No.

He stands. He feels his boil. He straightens his jacket.

Didn't shy away that time. I did it, didn't I, really did it to you, I really did.

Woopee.

He goes, weeping.

Wait.

She sits up suddenly. She catches her breath. She goes onto her knees. She breathes out carefully. She leans forward and picks up the wine bottle and the letter.

She reads the letter aloud.

JUDY. Africa, Sunday. This part of the country is Muslim. The Koran gives the law that a convicted thief accept the punishment of being stoned, in public. Should the thief refuse the stoning his right hand is cut off, in public. With the twentieth century the stoning has become ritualised. The thief is not hit by stones but stands to be jeered at while pebbles are rolled towards his feet. After this humiliation he is fined or goes to gaol.

But the other week a thief refused the stoning. Police, the Iman from his mosque, his family, all pleaded with him, but he would not change his mind. The authorities were embarrassed, no one wanted it to come to the axe. But it did.

I stood in the crowd. A doctor advised where the blow should fall. An ambulance stood by, engine running. The hand was struck off and the thief was rushed to the American Hospital.

She puts the letter down. She takes a swig of the wine. She is sick. She puts a hand to her forehead. She stands. She shivers. She goes off.

The doorbell rings.

She comes back with a rag. The doorbell rings again. She ignores it and wipes up the mess. She goes off.

SALLY *comes on. She is 23.*

JUDY *comes back.*

SALLY. Hello.

   JUDY *stares at her.*

   You the landlady?

   For the flat?

   Wait.

JUDY. I've been sick.

SALLY. Yeah?

   Are you all right —

JUDY. The advert —

   Wait.

   I mean the advert's not in the Standard 'til tomorrow.

SALLY. I work there. On the 'phones.

   Are you sure you're all right?

JUDY. As rain. I'm a bright penny.

SALLY (*aside*). Is the smell the place or her?

   (*To* JUDY.) Can I see it?

JUDY. What?

SALLY. The flat.

JUDY. This is the flat. Yes. It's got a kitchen, it's got a bathroom. There are two rooms, this is one of them.

   My husband was here.

SALLY. ?

   Oh, the copper on the stair.

JUDY. We were celebrating our divorce.

SALLY. Yeah, he looked pissed off.

JUDY. Oh no!

> JUDY *sinks to the floor.*

SALLY. You —

JUDY. His little friend!

SALLY. What?

JUDY. He left his penknife behind!

SALLY. Yeah?

JUDY. He'll be back for it won't he!

SALLY. Will he?

JUDY. Course he will! He's had it since he was a boy! He slept with it under his pillow when he was nine years old! He cut up frogs with it!

SALLY (*aside*). You open a door, any door. And you find yourself in an abattoir.

> (*To* JUDY.) Look Lady, all I want to know is am I going to live here —

JUDY. What do they call that little bit of skin, on the top of chickens' heads?

SALLY. ?

> Comb?

JUDY. The little thing on his bottom, it's like that, hanging upside down. I think about it, for hours. Well, not hours, in between hours.

> I take money out of my purse, and I'm thinking about it.

> With all my hate, fixed on it.

SALLY. Look it's nothing to do with me, but —

> Look —

> You been beaten up?

> *Wait.*

JUDY. No.

> Hit a bit.

SALLY. There's a lot of it about. Cuts —

JUDY. No.

SALLY. Bones —

JUDY. No!

SALLY. That's all right then. Or not.

JUDY. Have you — been — anywhen?

SALLY. What's that to you?

JUDY. Sorry. I'm sorry.

SALLY. I knew a man who wanted to put a ring in my cunt, so he could fix a dog lead to the ring and lead me about.

JUDY. Did —

SALLY. What do you think?

I settled for having a butterfly tattooed on my arse instead.

Which seemed a good idea at the time.

'Til I took against it, got the needle off him and jabbed him in the eye.

It stinks in here, I don't think I'll take it. Bye bye.

She turns to go. She stops.

(*Aside.*) Oh no. I can hear him coming up the stairs. Oh fuck. Just go round and see a flat these days, what have you got to wear? Thick rubber gloves, wellies and a gas-mask?

Get out, Sally.

JACK *comes on.* JACK *and* SALLY *stare at each other.*

Wait.

JACK. What are you?

SALLY. What are you?

Wait.

JACK (*to* JUDY). My —

He looks around the floor.

SALLY (*to herself*). Don't Sally —

JACK. My —

SALLY. Your little friend.

JACK. I beg your pardon?

SALLY. You are looking for your penknife. Are you highly
    sexed?

*JACK stares. He sees the penknife near SALLY's foot. He
stoops for it. She pushes it away with her toe. He reaches for
it, she pushes it away again.*

You've got a funny little bit of skin on your arse.

JACK freezes.

Red.

JACK frozen.

Like a chicken comb, hanging upside down.

*Again JACK reaches for the penknife, again SALLY pushes it
away with her toe. He straightens.*

JACK. Old friend of the family, are you?

SALLY. Known you what, a minute? Don't need any longer to
    know anyone, do you?

(*To herself.*) Get out!

(*To* JACK.) Just don't bop her one again, all right?

All right?

Mister?

Just don't hit her again.

JACK. What do you know of my life?

SALLY (*aside*). Oh no.

JACK. You're not — intimate to my life.

SALLY. Look, all I know is you'd better walk down the stairs in
    front of me. All right?

JACK. My dreams!

JUDY (*to* SALLY). Don't go.

JACK. Ideals! What I have got to have!

He scoffs.

Why should I get carried away with you, some skirt off —

Cunt off —

The street, the filthy street!

No no.

Tenderness, you see.

In my hands, and —

He looks at his hands and splays them open.

SALLY. Holy mother.

SALLY swings her bag. It strikes JACK on the back on his neck. He clutches his neck. Blood runs down his wrists. He kneels.

JACK. My boil!

Someone get someone quick!

The stuff's come all it's coming out!

He looks at his hand. Quickly he puts it back.

Can't be all that blood in that! Mind you, I knew it was really puffing up —

He looks from SALLY to JUDY and back to SALLY.

Come on!

Girls?

He walks on his knees a little way, to go out. He blacks out and keels over. JUDY and SALLY look at him.

Wait.

JUDY. He's —

SALLY. Blacked out.

JUDY. Yes.

SALLY. Pain.

JUDY. He's been run-down, in himself.

They look at each other. They giggle, laugh, then stop laughing.

I better —

A helpless gesture.

Him. Or something.

SALLY. That's up to you. Ta ta.

JUDY. Don't leave me alone with him —

SALLY. Look this kind of thing happens to me. I walk into rooms and find people writing about on the floor. Then I get involved and end up fucked. Something wrong with me. Brain, personality or something.

So I think I'll get back on a 68 bus.

JUDY. Please.

SALLY. Look —

JACK groans. He turns a little. His arm arcs through the air and bumps down. Then JUDY goes to him and scrabbles through JACK's pockets as she speaks.

JUDY. I'll do the flat up. Nice things. Shower in the bathroom. Proper cooker.

JUDY finds the woman's pants in JACK's pocket.

The other woman's knickers.

SALLY. Oh dear.

JUDY stuffs the pants back in JACK's pocket and continues to search his pockets.

JUDY. You can have your own room.

SALLY. Really.

JUDY, a hand in one of JACK's pockets, stops searching and looks at SALLY.

JUDY. I want a good time.

Wait.

I want to change myself.

Wait.

Inside out.

Wait.

Skin inside?

Eh?

Hanging down me, on their little tubes, all the bags and things, kidneys, liver. Precious things, heart. The real me, exposed.

Eh?

SALLY. I don't know, lady —

JUDY. Well if I can't do that the least I want is a good fuck.

SALLY. Don't we all.

They laugh.

JUDY continues to search JACK's clothing.

(*Aside.*) Well.

She shrugs.

While we're waiting for the bastards who run our lives to die out. Or give up. Or the Russians to come. Or the Cubans to land in Kent.

Or more than the odd nutter in this fucking country to up and say 'no' — a measly million or so to up and say 'Enough is enough!' Of sitting in this tatty public lavatory on the edge of the continental shelf, constipated right up under the rib cage, bursting for something to happen. Peace to break out, truth to break out, something to break out. The end of the world as we know it, eh?

She shrugs.

While waiting for that — what does it matter who is sliding their finger up and down you?

In one movement JACK comes round and goes on all fours as JUDY removes the solicitor's paper from the pocket. JUDY looks at the folded paper not attempting to hide it. In a dog like position, JACK blinks. He stands unsteadily. He goes to the penknife and picks it up. He holds it out in front of him. He raises it to his lips and kisses it. He lurches away one hand on his neck, hesitating to say —

JACK. Cunts.

He goes off, JUDY tearing the paper up.

Wait.

SALLY *sighs.*

SALLY. A shower?

Act Two

The flat. Darkness.

JUDY. We're coming. Little boy.

> SALLY *giggles.*

> Don't giggle.

SALLY. Sorry.

JUDY. We know you're there.

> *Wait.*

> Not in the kitchen. Not in the bathroom. Not in the bedroom. So there you are.

> You little bastard.

> *Wait.*

> Got a reputation, in the area, have we? Among your little friends?

> *Wait.*

> Cocky little friends.

> *Wait.*

> Sneering, fat-lipped fourteen-year-olds.

> *Wait.*

> In your snazzy pullies, over the nipples on your boy pigeon chests. In your terylene trousers. Two-tone plims. Marks and Sparks boy briefs underneath —

SALLY. Oh dear. It'll be stains all over the carpet again.

JUDY. We know you talk about us! The two old slags, the older and the younger one, up in that flat? Knock on their door, an' Saturday night. See what you get. A five pound note. A free bath. Your first fuck —

SALLY. Judy, love —

JUDY. Shut up.

SALLY. Sooner or later, old lady, you are going to bite off more than you can chew.

JUDY. It's all right I know his kind.

I know your kind, little boy. Hiding there.

I see you. By parked motorbikes. Before record shop windows. Herds of you. Thousands and thousands. Hands in your pockets, stroking your balls. Boasting of school girls' tits and holes. And I ask, what are you for? What needs you?

England?

She scoffs.

England has abandoned you. The big city's just a tank, rusty old sludge tank, storing you for nothing. All your lovely green spit and spunk, cock and pride, swishing about the streets.

Well, I'll show you what you're for.

SALLY. He's gone home Judy.

JUDY. Please!

SALLY. Your little furry animal. Little hot-arsed child of the streets —

SALLY scoffs.

JUDY. We're playing sardines.

SALLY. You don't play sardines in the dark anyway.

JUDY. You do.

I did when I was a child.

SALLY. But now you're a dirty old slut.

Sardines? Who's going to crawl into your tin? Ugh, squeeze up to you in rancid oil.

JUDY. You're no teeny-bopper tiddler.

SALLY. I know I know, when you're twenty-four — you start to give off that fishy smell of the older woman —

JUDY. We going to do this or aren't we?

SALLY. So difficult, sexual pleasure at an advanced age. So po-faced.

JUDY. Just try.

SALLY. Like the Spanish Inquisition.

JUDY. Please.

SALLY. Oh all right.

Wait.

He's very quiet.

Wait.

Didn't hit him, did you?

JUDY. Sh!

The sound of breaking glass.

SALLY. My foot!

JUDY. Oh put the lights on!

SALLY. I cut my foot!

JUDY. The plug's near you.

SALLY. There's blood all over the place!

Crockery being kicked.

JUDY. The mess in here —

SALLY. Who made the mess?

JUDY. Can't you wash up?

SALLY. We. We wash up.

This is an experiment in living, remember? Blood is pouring out! It's sticky!

JUDY. Get out the way —

SALLY. You trod on my foot!

The lights go on — two table lamps on the floor.

SALLY and JUDY are tangled up. SALLY is wearing a large, floppy towelling bathrobe. JUDY is also barefoot, wearing an evening dress.

All the furnishings of the flat are rugs and cushions. No chairs. It is a mess, records out of sleeves, unwashed crockery, a coffee percolator, books and the bric-a-brac of indiscriminate buying for pleasure. There is a mound of cushions.

No blood. There ought to be blood. I feel cheated that there's no blood.

She tastes her foot.

The stickiness was olive oil.

JUDY. Is it on the hairy rug?

I hate domesticity. I wanted to get away from domesticity.

SALLY. We have. We don't wash up.

Spill olive oil on hairy rugs hey — your rough trade.

SALLY *indicates the pile of cushions. They look at the pile.*

Wait.

SALLY *lifts the cushions one by one, carefully. No one is beneath. She sighs and sits back then looks about the floor.*

Judy, where's the digital clock?

JUDY. What would I be doing with the digital clock?

SALLY *shrugs.*

SALLY. Wiring your nipples up to it in the bathroom, I don't know.

JUDY. The digital clock is gone.

SALLY. With your under-aged fuck.

JUDY. Looks like it.

SALLY. Well, if you set out to seduce the entire local school population, there will be risks.

We'll end up like old-aged P's, tied up by children. Stripped naked. Hair set alight.

JUDY. I'll warm the coffee up.

SALLY. You'd like that wouldn't you.

Wait.

JUDY. The coffee.

JUDY *picks up the percolator.*

SALLY *gestures at the space where the young man should be.*

SALLY. Look.

A body of a young man.

Chest, stuck up, like a cheap chicken, waiting to be cooked. A bit bluey. Goose bumps. For he's naked, look. Your forty-year-old roué's hands, Judy, have fiddled all his clothes away.

See how he's cut his finger-nails? He's got a little manicure set, in a little plastic case. This one fancies he's sharp.

But oh dear, look at his toe-nails. Look. Split. And his little toe's made a sore on the toe next door. And — little sausages of dirt, in the clefts between his toes too, tut tut.

Lovely arms. Lovely legs. Elasticky. Bendy. Very very smooth.

Faint lines, quartering his tummy, button in the middle. Faint ridges round his groin. Very faint — the statues of boys, in great museums, in the colour pics of travel brochures?

But not perfect. Bit skinny that rib cage, bit swollen that tummy. What with a childhood eating baked beans and crisps. And now take-away chop sueys and Bounty Bars.

Balls — a yoyo, in a little bag of old man's skin. Cock, not circumcised, bit red on the tip — doesn't roll it back and clean himself. All the self-love of this one goes on his finger nails.

A sharp breath.

Oh! He's scratching an ankle. With his heel, in his sleep.

A sharp breath.

Oh! He's moving his arm back, under his head.

A sharp breath.

Oh! His foot's resting now. On his other ankle. His knee, look — slightly bent.

A sharp breath.

Oh! His cock's moving. The centipede. Wriggle and ripple. Maybe he's dreaming of women, eh Judy?

Wait.

Or freedom, Judy?

The animal, Judy? The natural animal in his natural state, Judy? Free?

Eh Judy?

Or is he just scared in his sleep. In his ugly little soul. Ugly little worm, coiled up in him, in fear.

Still. Stifle all pity. This is a man who wants to do us harm. So get in quick, love. Do what you want with him — what is it you want to do with him?

Wait.

What exactly is it that you have in mind — my love?

Wait.

JUDY. Sally, if —

SALLY. I know! Poke something up his arse. Give him a big hard-on. Now what —

SALLY scrambles about the mess on the floor.

JUDY. Please —

SALLY. Four inches we need. Can he take four inches? Given that he's not got an arseful of piles — a lot of 'em have I am told, the youth of today. City life is so unhealthy, street corners, the wind and the rain. And even if he is clear —

JUDY. Please!

SALLY stops scrambling about.

SALLY. Clear? Up the base? Up his hole? Open?

Nothing from JUDY.

SALLY scrambles about again.

Funny skin up an arse. Like a long balloon. Ah! 'Course!

She picks up a dinner knife with a smooth, stainless steel blade, holding it by the blade.

That four inches?

She measures it between index thumb and forefinger.

Make it warm with me phlegm.

She puts the knife handle into her mouth.

JUDY. I beg you —

SALLY. Warm and slippery.

JUDY. All right! All right!

Wait.

SALLY. Oh no, old lady.

You're the deep sea diver. Trying to grow gills, live at the bottom of the ocean, eh? So come on, get him up! I'll fuck him, you sit on his face, get him gobbling as he wriggles down below while we, why while we kiss fondly — all come together

— and sink in a great big sea of shit —

JUDY *lifts the coffee percolator above her head and smashes it down on the floor.*

Wait.

SALLY *sticks the knife handle in her mouth and looks up and away.*

Wait.

SALLY *takes the knife handle out of her mouth.*

Drink a bottle of vodka? You fall asleep halfway through.

Whip yourself? You get septicaemia.

Pick up a man in a pub? You end up in St. Thomas's hospital, your legs up in the air, doctors poking around in you for gonorrhoea.

Yes, it's very very dodgy, the search for ecstasy.

No wonder millions settle for a nice cup of tea.

Wait.

JUDY. I did actually, an afternoon last week, take a fourteen-year-old boy to bed.

Gently.

And lay there with him, listening to the traffic across the city. Pigeons on the roof of the flats.

SALLY. Then he got up, pulled on his pants and nicked the bathroom scales.

We need the bathroom scales. We are eating very fancy food.

JUDY. Yes. All right. All right. Yes.

Wait.

I want to show you something.

SALLY. Not your body. I didn't mind that on holiday. But not in everyday life.

A gesture at the floor.

Given that we call this everyday life.

JUDY. Stay there.

JUDY *goes off.*

SALLY. Stay there.

Wait.

A kid's game.

Go there.

Wait.

Right.

She shuffles on her knees. Stops.

Are you there?

No I'm here.

Come here!

Right.

She shuffles on her knees. She stops.

There you are.

No I'm here.

No you're there.

Wait.

I think I've got that wrong.

Counting on her fingers.

I can't be there, because I'm here.

If I go there, there will be here.

Here will be over there. Over here.

I think I'm going to be sick.

JUDY comes back on carrying a Fortnum and Mason plastic carrier bag. She up-ends it. Ten-pound notes fall onto the floor.

JUDY. I got the money out.

Wait.

The money from the house.

Wait.

What's left of it.

SALLY. It looks a lot.

JUDY. It's not.

SALLY *picks up a handful of the money and lets it fall.*

SALLY. Love and money running out, are they dear?

JUDY. Love and money are running out.

Wait.

SALLY. So?

JUDY. So?

SALLY *sighs.*

SALLY. Where are my fags is there a fag in here?

She scrambles about.

JUDY. Listen to me.

SALLY. There's got to be a fag in this dump!

JUDY. You know where your fucking cigarettes are, stop it!

SALLY. Fag. Fag. Fag. Fag.

JUDY. We've got to talk about it.

SALLY. All right!

She stops scrambling about.

All right.

She takes a packet of cigarettes out of the pocket of her bathrobe, lights one and blows smoke.

What do you want? Us to be good little housewives? Economise? Little lists, little budgets? Save the silver off the tops of milk bottles? Cook bread puddings?

I thought the idea was to say goodbye to that.

Just 'Live'.

Scavenge off the leftovers of your marriage. The meatscraps o what you and your husband did to each other?

All right.

That's what's left of the rotting pile. Let's get on with it.

JUDY. We could burn the money. Now.

Wait.

SALLY. And?

JUDY. Improvise.

SALLY. On what?

JUDY. Bank robberies?

No, muggings. Two strong, healthy girls like us — knock over old ladies and old men very, very easily. Tape our tits down. Zip-up plastic jackets, pom-poms. The police will go hunting for black kids, not we English roses. We could get away with it for years.

SALLY. Oh well.

Back on the phones at the Evening Standard.

JUDY. We've got to — go further —

SALLY. To where?

JUDY. With ourselves.

SALLY. Doing what?

JUDY. I don't know!

SALLY. We have already been through this and that. Could have gone further with drugs I s'pose, if you'd not kept on throwing up.

And we fucked and got fucked here and there.

Talked.

Ate a lot.

Exotic holidays. America? The fuck bars of New York? Bottoms up in the back room?

JUDY. It was a nice break, America.

Cept for American men.

SALLY. There are a lot of 'em in America.

They glance at each other and giggle.

Not a bad blow-out, Judy. Not a bad use of your ill-gotten gains. Your windfall. Fall-out from your little mushroom cloud. In the married suburbs.

Not bad.

Points at the money.

With that, let's buy — a professional footballer. For one night. And fuck him so dry he can never kick a ball again.

Then, come the dawn, go our separate ways.

No?

No.

Ring ring. Advert for a 1969 Morris-Austin, Sir? With a fur-lined steering wheel?

Ring ring. Three single girls, share a villa in Tuscany in July, Sir?

Ring ring. No gay adverts in the Standard, Sir.

Fucking Editorial Policy to you, too.

With a flick of a finger.

Click.

Click.

JUDY. Burn what's left of the money.

Wait.

Burn what's left of the money, and steal if we have to. Nail the door up if we have to. Block the windows with bricks. Move. Sleep in the open. Sell ourselves. Get guns. Kill, if we have to.

I'll not go back in that front room.

In the back of my mind, like a ghost, I am still there. Drinking coffee, listening to the rain drip in the hedge.

I don't know where, but I saw a picture. People, leaning out of windows, of English houses. Their souls floating away out of their mouths. Their real selves, flying away.

SALLY reaches out her arms. JUDY kneels in front of her. They rest, arms loosely about each other's shoulders.

SALLY, gently.

SALLY. What is it?

You poor, raddled old cow?

I've started to stay awake 'til you're asleep. Frightened of what you're going to do yourself.

JUDY. I do think, sometimes, of violent things. Cutting myself.

Little cuts, all over.

SALLY. Well. There you are. What? Think you'd grow feathers, out of the little cuts eh? Grow into a bird?

SALLY *scoffs. Still gentle.*

You'll end up drinking blood. Yours or someone else's.

JUDY. Think so?

SALLY. I do.

Wait.

You trying to give me a funny look?

JUDY. No.

SALLY. Don't then.

They laugh a little.

JUDY. You really think I'm raddled?

SALLY. Deeply.

JUDY. I think you're — no.

SALLY. What?

JUDY. No.

SALLY. What?

Wait.

JUDY. Sorry.

SALLY. For what!

JUDY. For thinking you're beautiful.

SALLY *giggles.*

So beautiful, I do want to hurt you.

SALLY. What, clothes-peg on my nipples?

JUDY. You know.

SALLY. I don't.

Wait.

I don't.

They laugh.

They stop laughing.

(*Aside.*) You slum. You slink around. Don't go out for weeks. Don't get dressed. Don't even stand up much, just lie on the floor. When you want a drink, walk to the fridge on your knees.

JUDY (*aside*). You want 'An experience'. The moment, once and for all, when everything — burns.

SALLY (*aside*). You watch the tomato sauce on the old dinner plate. First it goes hard, then greeny. One of the reasons you get up around midday is to see — what's happening to that bit of tomato sauce.

JUDY (*aside*). Sometimes you see it. Sometimes you don't.

SALLY (*aside*). Yeah, there's a lot to do when you personally disintegrate. Counting the bits of you as they fall off.

JUDY (*aside*). See a country, the other side of the wall. Sweet fields, rivers, forests. All you have to do is knock a few bricks out, wriggle through a hole onto the grass.

SALLY (*aside*). Still, it's warm. For a while.

JUDY (*aside*). You think — when the sunlight falls on the floorboards, along that edge of the rug, it'll begin.

'The new life?' The walk in the Paradise Gardens?

But the sun goes in.

Or you weren't actually looking for that split second.

Or fall asleep and wake up when it's raining.

She scoffs.

What am I trying to do, make magic?

She scoffs.

SALLY (*to* JUDY). What?

JUDY (*to* SALLY). Do you believe in magic?

SALLY. What you got in mind? Take the leg of a frog and the liver of a schoolboy?

JUDY. Something like that.

They laugh.

The doorbell rings.

Wait, SALLY *and* JUDY, *their arms still loosely about each other's shoulders.*

SALLY. Hordes of children?

JUDY. Think so?

SALLY. Could well be the local youth, inflamed.

JUDY. Witch-hunting?

SALLY. Daring 'emselves. Counting their pennies, to buy a couple o' beer bottles, to shove up us.

JUDY. Or ring the bell and run away.

The doorbell rings.

(*Low.*) The door's on the latch.

SALLY (*low*). Told you not to do that.

JUDY (*low*). See what you can get.

SALLY (*low*). Into your fly trap?

They giggle.

JACK *comes on. He wears a shabby coat and scarf over a shabby, charcoal suit. In one hand he carries a carrycot, the hood up and rain cover on, cot toys dangling. In the other hand he carries a large, black umbrella, extended. The umbrella and he are very wet. On his back he carries a large rucksack.*

JUDY *and* SALLY *are dead still.*

JACK. Er, the door was open.

So I came in.

He looks at the carrycot, he looks at the umbrella.

He puts the carrycot down.

It's all right she's asleep.

Now.

Had to change her twice, on the train. From Southampton.

Wait.

Boat.

Wait.

Didn't want to fly. She's got an ear. Ear infection.

Worried about the popping. So came by sea. She loved it. I was sick as a dog.

Wait.

No, she'll sleep. Gave her her bottle in the Horse and Shoe Bar on Victoria Station. Had a Guinness myself.

He tries a laugh, fails.

Usually have to change her after a bottle, but with that on the train —

Got the nappies, screwed up in a plastic bag. If you've got a bucket I could dunk 'em.

SALLY. Fucking Jesus Christ.

Wait.

Then JACK *looks at the umbrella in his hand.*

JACK. And maybe stand this in your bath?

Wait.

Anyway, look, just let me —

He puts the umbrella down and shifts the rucksack from his back onto the floor.

Ooh that's good.

He turns a shoulder.

Wait.

He licks a hand, then stoops and feels around the carrycot.

Sorry. Draughts. With that ear.

He straightens, clumsily.

Well.

Bit —

In here.

Had a party?

He claps his hands together loudly. He rubs them.

JUDY *and* SALLY *still silent, not looking at him.*

He stops rubbing his hands. He still holds them together.

Celia and I were driving from the East to the West. The Trans-Canadian Highway.

Things hadn't gone that well, in the East. I didn't join the Mounties.

I wanted to be a timber merchant. A country of trees, Canada. But I ended up a salesman for lavatory brushes.

Yup!

He claps his hands.

Yup.

Wait.

Could do me the grace, at least to giggle, eh?

He tries a laugh. Fails. He sniffs back a cold, twice.

She was very pregnant. Auditing at Central Office had shown up a little thing, just a little thing — I'd been up to. And, wildly, we thought — the West. British Columbia. Where the trees are. And the lakes.

Wait.

We were going through Saskatchewan. 'Indians live here' she said and not discussing it, we turned off the Highway — right.

Turn right, going West in Canada, where are you heading?

Toward nothing. Bang in the middle of nowhere.

Wait.

Drove for four hours, saying nothing. Then I said 'This is stupid'.

And rowed.

And I turned the car round. And crashed it.

Wait.

When I came to I heard dripping and smelt petrol. The car was on its side. I was in the car. A balmy day, I thought. Not barmy, stupid though it was, a fucking stupid thing to do — balmy in the sense of cool — air on my cheek.

Wait.

Then, oh terrible — the fear for her, flooding everything. But she wasn't in the car. I got the glass out the windscreen.

A little jerk of his elbow.

Crawled out. All the while, calling to her but not really making a sound. Like in a nightmare, you scream — but when you wake up you known — you've not made a sound.

She was a way off.

Crawling over the ground, carefully.

Her back, hollow. Her backside, looking big. Clothes round her tummy, loose. Lumpy — she seemed. Though, of course, she's only a bird of a thing.

Then she rolled on one side. And had a birth pain.

Stuff this for a load of hot bricks I thought.

He tries a laugh. He fails.

Someone bound to come along, we said. Someone must know, we said. Telephones, telexes, cities, all around the earth, fucking satellites photographing every inch of the planet. Yeah! Any moment, ambulances'd come over the horizon, on caterpillar tracks. Helicopters, parachuting commandos down. A whole town of rescue vehicles, lights flashing, men and nurses in white masks, 'd come up any moment out of the ground.

They didn't.

No one knew of Cei'l and Jack, by that road. Not in all the world.

Wait.

Made one trip to the car. Got hold of what I could think of. Suitcase out the boot. Wanted to get the back seat out as a bed but couldn't. Torch. Road map, what did I want a road map for, I mean? Bottle of brandy. But the smell of petrol got me scared and I ran with what I'd got. And up it went. Electrics sparking somewhere I don't know. A 'Pop' rather than a bang. Nothing to echo the explosion, just — wide, wideness.

'Pop!' And of course at once I knew — I'd forgotten the baby book! With the pictures of heads coming out and all that!

Wait.

Two days and the night in between, it took. Dear oh dear.

In that flat, what? Wilderness? We felt bloated. Great lumps. As the hours went by, as her pains went by, we got bigger and bigger, 'til our hands, our feet, calves, backs were huge. Could've just kicked the car wreck away, like a dinky toy.

Wait.

Gave her the brandy. Heard somewhere, alcohol can hold back labour. Pain killer. Nelson on the deck having his arm off.

A little laugh.

Poor cow, poor cow. Poor, poor little mother, eh? And poor father, his knees damp in the scrub beside her, wondering how — to be delicate and clean. Great hands, great knuckles like boulders, covered with dirt, terrified of infection.

It wouldn't stop.

It went on.

Wave after wave, rushing her down the tunnel.

Crawl away and do it in the bushes, don't they? Parts of the globe? Nothing more than a piss in the grass? I don't believe it. I believe women crawl away in the grass and suffer, suffer their children to be born.

Washed my fingers in brandy. Tried to feel the neck of her womb, but didn't know what I was meant to feel, what was the opened neck of a womb, what was not.

So ignorant! I mean Judy, when Tommy was born, you in the white nursing home, me round the corner in the pub, drinking white gin. And then, you look through the glass, at a white room, the kid bundled up in white.

White's not the colour of birth. It's livid black.

Tried to see the baby's hair, between her legs. But it was that livid black. Not a slit at all. And wet, black, all matter down there, I s'pose from the broken waters.

'Go on, go on, feel it' she said, holding my wrist, tight. Making a wrench of her finger and thumb, trying to guide me.

Delicately, eh?

Wait.

If it had been winter, not midsummer, we'd have been found like that. Frozen, the man bent over the woman, she guiding his hand. And in her tum, dry and curled up in a complicated way, a little nut in a walnut shell, the babe. Eh?

Wait.

What frightened us was she'd tear. And we knew that when you want to push, at first, you must not. Known that since the cave, Book of Genesis, since the slime — a woman must not push at first, in childbirth. How do we know it? When her body screams, along with all of nature, to push that knot — that hard, bloody knotted ball out of her works, eh?

What comes naturally, eh?

Nothing does. You just got to get your hands in it, right up the arms in the stuff and —

He grips his hands tightly, looking at them. They shake. He relaxes.

Wait.

Top of the head. A dirty tennis ball, covered in grease.

When it slid I shouted 'Push'. When it stuck I shouted 'Don't push'. Knowing from some old TV movie, that's what midwives do.

Mid-husbands, ha!

And there was the head. Perfect, eyes, lips. Mouth open. A little carving in pinky stone. Tiny gums and tongue. But not breathing and I thought it was dead.

Cei'l, her face black. Cheeks swollen up. Bulging to burst the bundle, all of it, out of her.

Then a kind of squelch. And with a flobble it all came. Into the wodge of clothes, towels, a new cotton shirt I'd torn up. The cord, a long, bluey sausage of white meat. Blood running in thin streams over the child, over the insides of her mother's legs and her father's hands.

It didn't breathe. A plug of greasy stuff in its mouth, I smeared away. Still it didn't breathe.

The cord. Didn't think, I just bit it. The gristle. Tied a big knot. Still not a breath!

The whole earth was a clock. That barren place, turning under the sky, tick-tock. Then it — sucked a breath. Cried. Moved. Before my eyes, the crease of the little body softening, filling out with flesh and blood.

And then my daughter got her eyes open and looked. Over my shoulder. Sort of wise.

Matter of fact.

For the first time, I was filled with terror.

Wait.

Cei'l got rid of the afterbirth with a little cough. I held it, a parcel of blood in a skin of water.

And three hours on, a beat-up Camero drove up. A French speaker. Qui fucking passe ici and all that.

We'd survived it.

Between the three of us, not a runny nose.

Tore me to bits though.

I'm singing for my supper.

Nothing from JUDY *and* SALLY.

Girls, ladies?

He gives a little laugh.

A thing like that, got to mean something han't it? Worth something, in human terms.

Least a fag or a cup of tea.

SALLY (*to* JUDY). What do you think happened to Wonder Woman?

JACK. She went off with a lumberjack.

JUDY and SALLY look at each other then laugh. They lie back on the cushions, helpless with laughter and giggles.

Yeah.

Between us, it was like we were still stuck out there. All the hot soup in all the ambulances 'd not get the cold out.

Our deep cold.

I don't blame her for taking against the kid. What's blame got to do with it?

No. Spent all my pennies on the boat fare and getting here. To you.

JUDY and SALLY are still helpless with laughter.

JUDY. Can't you — go to your mother?

JACK. She died, didn't you know?

Nothing from JUDY.

Her little bit kept me going.

He scoffs.

Didn't take a bean from you did I? In the end.

Let you in peace. But now —

Wait.

Stop laughing at me you fucking bitches!

Wait.

Please?

He unclasps his hands.

Wait.

Then he takes a step forward, stumbles and sits down suddenly.

I am on my uppers.

JUDY. The ugly, ludicrous brute I really do believe, loves the baby.

SALLY. Oh we all love the baby.

Wobbles toward you from all sides, the baby. From billboards.

You want to sell soap? Off goes the baby, a bar of it stuck in its nappies.

You want to see the filthy world? Off goes the baby, flies in its eyes, crawling in the mud in black and white.

The radiation burns of the unborn generations?

JUDY. But can you have sex with a baby?

JACK. You asking me?

SALLY. You can have sex with anything, from Charlton Heston to the door-knob.

JUDY. I bet she's got a sweet, pinky little pocket.

JACK. I —

JUDY. For a cunt?

Wait.

JACK. Look —

JUDY. In your big hairy father's hands. Lying on her bouncy bum, on her soft nappies.

Don't tell me you've never had a lick.

JACK. C'up —

JUDY. Poke?

JACK. C'up —

JUDY. Big Daddy?

JACK. Couple o' — what are you?

SALLY. We don't know but we're working on it.

> JUDY *laughs.*

JACK. All right!

> Tell you what I'll do. Give me what's left of my bit of the money. And me and the girl — we'll go.

> Never bother you again.

> *Wait.*

SALLY (*low*). Sweet. Sweet.

JACK. Just go back in the night.

> *He nods at the money.*

> That some of it?

> Ha! Get it out of an evening do you? Give it a bit of a caress?

> *He reaches out a hand to the money.* JUDY *slaps his hand, hard. He withdraws it.*

> I warn you bitches, I will fight for me and mine.

JUDY (*crawling toward the carrycot*). Let's see the brat.

JACK. No.

JUDY. Oogy boogy.

JACK. No.

JIDY. What's the matter with it? Got flippers?

> JACK *grabs* JUDY's *waist.*

JACK. Hands off.

JUDY. Give her a tickle.

> JUDY *gets hold of the carrycot.*

JACK. You'll wake her up! She'll want a bottle! She'll get burpy!

> JACK *wrenches* JUDY *away, half-throwing her.* JUDY *bangs on to the carrycot, taking it with her. It flies through the air and ends upside down.*

> *The three of them stare at the carrycot.*

> *Wait.*

SALLY *goes to the carrycot. She turns it over, carefully. She takes out two house bricks, wrapped in baby blankets.*

SALLY. No baby.

JACK. I can explain that.

SALLY. A con man.

She laughs.

JACK. The birth was real.

That did happen.

That can't be taken away.

That's memory.

JUDY (*low*). Jack, what are you doing, stumbling round the London streets, with a carrycot full of bricks?

JACK. It's my little girl's.

They wouldn't let me have her.

So I nicked a few of her things.

To — to kiss.

SALLY. Oh my God.

JACK. Why can't men have wombs, breasts, the works?

SALLY. Want the whole world do you, mister?

JUDY (*aside*). Just three people in a room.

JACK. Judy.

JUDY. What?

JACK. Could I —

JUDY. What? What?

JACK. Don't like to say.

He nods at SALLY.

SALLY. Oh don't mind me.

JUDY. You can say it in front of Sally.

JACK *mumbles indistinctly.*

I'm sorry?

She leans her ear to JACK's *mouth.*

He mumbles again.

She is still.

(*To* SALLY.) He says he wants to come between my breasts.

SALLY. Ah.

Married life crawls back into the pond.

JUDY. Shall I —

Wait.

Shall I put the kettle on for a cup of tea?

The three of them look at each other then laugh, helplessly.

JUDY *comes out of it, picks up a handful of notes and tears them up.*

JACK *and* SALLY *stop laughing and look.*

JUDY *continues to tear money up.*

JACK. Just a couple o' hundred.

Twenty. A fiver —

JUDY. The quick fuck. The words. The fights. The hot bath. The bodies. The late nights. The drinking. The kisses. The caresses. The secrets. The confessions. The lips on you, the fingers in you. The hard things in bed, the soft things in bed.

And always the money. Always the money.

JACK (*to* SALLY). You can stick 'em together with Sellotape. Still legal tender.

SALLY. Wow — ee.

JUDY. Tear it up. Cut it. Burn it. Not go back.

SALLY. Maybe I need a holiday. After this holiday.

JACK. Look — I'll be quiet. Never put my hands on anyone again. Live like a monk. Get a job as a night security guard.

Just give me a couple o' quid!

Tube fare!

SALLY *crouches.*

SALLY. What are you going to do? Work?

SALLY *laughs.*

JUDY *strikes a match.*

JUDY. I am going to be fucked, happy and free.

She looks from the match to the torn money.

Blackout.

For a Complete Catalogue of Methuen Drama titles
write to:

Methuen Drama
215 Vauxhall Bridge Road
London SW1V 1EJ

or you can visit our website at:

www.methuen.co.uk

Methuen Classical Greek Dramatists

Aeschylus Plays: One
(Persians, Seven Against Thebes, Suppliants,
Prometheus Bound)

Aeschylus Plays: Two
(Oresteia: Agamemnon, Libation-Bearers, Eumenides)

Aristophanes Plays: One
(Acharnians, Knights, Peace, Lysistrata)

Aristophanes Plays: Two
(Wasps, Clouds, Birds, Festival Time, Frogs)

Aristophanes & Menander: New Comedy
(Women in Power, Wealth, The Malcontent,
The Woman from Samos)

Euripides Plays: One
(Medea, The Phoenician Women, Bacchae)

Euripides Plays: Two
(Hecuba, The Women of Troy, Iphigeneia at Aulis,
Cyclops)

Euripides Plays: Three
(Alkestis, Helen, Ion)

Euripides Plays: Four
(Elektra, Orestes, Iphigeneia in Tauris)

Euripides Plays: Five
(Andromache, Herakles' Children, Herakles)

Euripides Plays: Six
(Hippolytos, Suppliants, Rhesos)

Sophocles Plays: One
(Oedipus the King, Oedipus at Colonus, Antigone)

Sophocles Plays: Two
(Ajax, Women of Trachis, Electra, Philoctetes)

Methuen World Classics
include

Jean Anouilh (two volumes)
John Arden (two volumes)
Arden & D'Arcy
Brendan Behan
Aphra Behn
Bertolt Brecht (six volumes)
Büchner
Bulgakov
Calderón
Anton Chekhov
Noël Coward (five volumes)
Eduardo De Filippo
Max Frisch
Gorky
Harley Granville Barker
   (two volumes)
Henrik Ibsen (six volumes)
Lorca (three volumes)
Marivaux
Mustapha Matura

David Mercer (two volumes)
Arthur Miller (five volumes)
Molière
Musset
Peter Nichols (two volumes)
Clifford Odets
Joe Orton
A. W. Pinero
Luigi Pirandello
Terence Rattigan
W. Somerset Maugham
   (two volumes)
Wole Soyinka
August Strindberg
   (three volumes)
J. M. Synge
Ramón del Valle-Inclán
Frank Wedekind
Oscar Wilde

Methuen Modern Plays
include work by

Jean Anouilh
John Arden
Margaretta D'Arcy
Peter Barnes
Sebastian Barry
Brendan Behan
Edward Bond
Bertolt Brecht
Howard Brenton
Simon Burke
Jim Cartwright
Caryl Churchill
Noël Coward
Sarah Daniels
Nick Dear
Shelagh Delaney
David Edgar
Dario Fo
Michael Frayn
John Godber
Paul Godfrey
David Greig
John Guare
Peter Handke
Jonathan Harvey
Iain Heggie
Declan Hughes
Terry Johnson
Sarah Kane
Charlotte Keatley
Barrie Keeffe
Robert Lepage
Stephen Lowe

Doug Lucie
Martin McDonagh
John McGrath
David Mamet
Patrick Marber
Arthur Miller
Mtwa, Ngema & Simon
Tom Murphy
Phyllis Nagy
Peter Nichols
Joseph O'Connor
Joe Orton
Louise Page
Joe Penhall
Luigi Pirandello
Stephen Poliakoff
Franca Rame
Mark Ravenhill
Philip Ridley
Reginald Rose
David Rudkin
Willy Russell
Jean-Paul Sartre
Sam Shepard
Wole Soyinka
C. P. Taylor
Theatre de Complicite
Theatre Workshop
Sue Townsend
Judy Upton
Timberlake Wertenbaker
Victoria Wood